TRANSPARENT
GOVERNMENT

WHAT IT MEANS AND HOW YOU CAN MAKE IT HAPPEN

DONALD GORDON

FOREWORD BY
JOSEPH FERGUSON

℗Ⓑ Prometheus Books
59 John Glenn Drive
Amherst, New York 14228

Published 2014 by Prometheus Books

Cover image © Media Bakery
Cover design by Grace M. Conti-Zilsberger

Inquiries should be addressed to
Prometheus Books
59 John Glenn Drive
Amherst, New York 14228
VOICE: 716–691–0133
FAX: 716–691–0137
WWW.PROMETHEUSBOOKS.COM

18 17 16 15 14   5 4 3 2 1

Library of Congress Cataloging-in-Publication Data

Gordon, Donald, 1949-
    Transparent government : what it means and how you can make it happen / Donald Gordon.
        pages cm
    Includes bibliographical references and index.
    ISBN 978-1-61614-919-2 (pbk.)
    ISBN 978-1-61614-920-8 (ebook)
    1. Transparency in government—United States. 2. Government information—Access control—United States. 3. Public administration—United States. 4. United States—Politics and government. I. Title.

JK468.S4G67 2014
352.8'80973—dc23

2013043637

Printed in the United States of America

To Bonnie—my wife, life partner, and soul mate—
and our beautiful daughters, Meghan and Shanna,
without whose patient encouragement
and tolerance for the irascible behavior of a writer
this book would never have been written.

Contents

Foreword

"A democracy requires accountability, and accountability requires transparency."
— President Barack Obama,
memorandum for the heads of
executive departments and agencies,
January 2009

The endorsement of the most powerful leader of the democratic world renders complete the manifestation of transparency as a bedrock value of contemporary democratic culture. But while invoked by every stripe of candidate and elected official hoping to burnish a "reformer" narrative, this critically important value functionally remains undefined. Thus, it is at grave risk of being reduced to just another hackneyed political and rhetorical term. We simply cannot allow that to happen. And to prevent it from happening will require a great deal of work in a short amount of time. Indeed, we are at the end of a small and rapidly closing window of opportunity for establishing the meaning of *transparency*. Defining transparency's elemental components will ensure and safeguard its place as a bedrock institutional value and feature in government for the next generation.

That window of opportunity is the product of the confluence in the troughs of two cycles of American history. One is the bubble-crash economic cycle, which in recent years brought public and private finance systems to the brink of collapse. The second is the pendulum swing of corporate corruption, and the government neglect and systemic oversight failures that enabled it. Those failures took multiple forms here. They included failures in financial-market oversight that are traceable to the wholesale deregulation of the finance industry in the 1990s and a paralleling run of willfully neglectful, if not knowingly irresponsible, fiscal practices at all levels of government.

We tend not to seek or embrace meaningful change except in response to a manifest crisis that carries immediate and direct adverse consequences. The geneses of our latest cyclical crises prove that tendency. The distorted incentives of our financial industry, the latest generation of market bubbles, and our collective fiscal irresponsibility in the public sector each constitutes an example of the boiling-frog phenomenon—a metaphorical reference to the asserted fact that a frog dropped into a pot of boiling water will immediately leap from it, but that that same frog, dropped into a pot of temperate water that is then gradually heated may perceive the mounting heat but will fail to respond to the magnitude of the mounting danger and ultimately will suffocate and will be boiled to death. The frog is us. Indeed, our very cleverness at rationalizing the irrational and denying manifest risks in our midst arguably make this the age of the boiling frog.

The ongoing fiscal crises at all levels of government were eminently predictable but developed in incremental, nondramatic fashion. They were not the product of unforeseen events but rather were a collective disaster we all but courted, slowly, gradually, perceptibly, over the course of many years. In the '90s and '00s, we responded to the bursting of market bubbles with short-term firewall correctives and continued blithely on an uninterrupted path of expanding government obligations and financial commitments that we simply did not pay for. "Progress" was built on debt, and our public accounts told us of a slowly growing chasm between obligations and resources; but like proverbial boiling frogs, we blinked at the looming crisis and sat in fiscal water that grew to a boil.

True transparency would give us a real-time read that would shatter our predisposition to myopia and permit us to drive our governments to higher accountability. Because we are boiling frogs, it is all but inevitable that once the immediacy of the present fiscal crises passes, the public's recently found sense of urgency about the need for higher orders of accountability and, therefore, transparency, will recede from its current high-water mark, leaving both in the control of those in power.

To Lord Acton's 1887 maxim that "power tends to corrupt, and absolute power corrupts absolutely"[1] we should add that *"the less transparent the actions of those in positions of authority, the more absolute their power."* Transparency matters, but its very intuitive importance is what is rapidly driving the term, the concept, and its value, to its hackneyed state in our civic discourse. It is an easy precept to invoke and support because it at once communicates something aspirational and oriented to our better angels while being seemingly mindful of darker, less noble impulses.

One of the most insidious of mythological civic narratives is that our leaders are selfless public servants serving a higher call and order. In a lesser quoted part of Lord Acton's power/corruption axiom, he offers the chilling statement: "There is no worse heresy than that the office sanctifies the holder of it."[2] Generally, people employed in the public sector are not selfless public servants. They are simple people whose *job* it is to serve the public. They work for the public, but does that really ennoble them? By the evidence of corruption and venality arrayed about us, the answer must be emphatically, "No." Yet we still fall prey to the mythology.

Most hold high public office not because they are noble, selfless beings, but because it makes them feel good. This takes various forms, some more admirable than others. It makes many feel important; it feeds the ego; it engenders public attention and acclaim; it allows some to convince themselves and project to the world that they are all that! No one is all that—and most everyone, including most everyone in public life, is a whole lot less than all that. And that is okay. But it is also why transparency is so very important.

Yet transparency, remaining largely undefined, is susceptible to cooptation and conceptual exploitation by the very people who should be subject to it. And when a term is bandied about in political speech in as commonplace a manner as *transparency* is today, we should be wary. What George Orwell noted in his 1946 essay "Politics and the English Language" is very much in operation today. Paraphrasing Orwell, political speech is more often employed to conceal than to inform and, at its worst, used to justify the unjustifiable.

So when political actors line up to speak of transparency, we have to resist the reflexive impulses to tune them out or dismiss them as insincere. Doing so gives those in power ownership of the meaning of this important term that is the public's to determine. Instead, we must know what it is they are referring to, what we understand it to mean, and what we understand it to require; and we must hold those in power accountable based on those answers.

Transparency has long been appreciated as a critical public good necessary to an effectively functioning democratic society. The push now is for online access to data and for uniform data standards that allow for a comparative analysis of the information at government departmental, program, and unit levels, from both funding and expenditure perspectives. Only from there can meaningfully informed public assessment and discussion begin. Political leaders seeking to burnish reformer credentials have responded to these imperatives through more programmatic, proactive publication of datasets online in user-friendly formats and called it transparency. But while the forward progress is an accomplishment worthy of note, it is simply a starting point that should rouse all of us to ask a number of questions:

- How were the datasets selected?
- What fields of information have been included or excluded, and why?
- Who selected the datasets?
- What form of constituent or community inputs are received for that process?
- Even if not yet available in suitable digital format, what other data or datasets exist?
- When will ledgers or logs of datasets be posted to facilitate inquiry by interested citizens?

- Is there legislation *requiring* the updating, refreshing, and enhancing of datasets once posted?

These and similar questions take me to a broader observation. I seriously question whether we are actually at the leading edge of a new paradigm in which government will obligate itself to post in user-friendly format all data and records for which there is no compelling reason for nondisclosure. In the meantime, we are left with the Freedom of Information Act, or FOIA. It is something elected officials invoke as demonstrative of their commitment to transparency. FOIA has itself become a term of political speech and thus should prompt us to invoke Orwell again—as often as not, the tendency of political speech is as much to conceal as it is to enlighten.

There are countless public examples of FOIA often operating quite at odds with the title. The reason is this: in the name of public access, FOIA actually channels and filters access to public records. It is a process that permits those who control that information to slow its production, creating time to fashion rationales triggering one of a host of exemptions from public disclosure of government records and information. Twenty years as a lawyer has accustomed me to a default culture of nondisclosure and privileges respecting public disclosure. In fact, there are truly compelling policy reasons for nondisclosure of certain types of records and information, even if they are government records relating to government business.

While we reflexively decry secrecy, it would be hard to take issue with safeguarding personal identifiers, financial information, tax information, health and medical information. Similarly, grand-jury secrecy is fundamental to a fair and equitable justice system. Disclosure of criminal investigations and investigation materials would tarnish the reputations of thousands who are investigated and found not culpable—who are merely subjects of an investigation, rather than targets. And the imperatives of national security in the face of asymmetrical dangers in the age of terrorism bring their own compelling reasons for secrecy in the intelligence and national-security realms.

But in each of the foregoing respects, we must be fully conscious of the fact that we are talking about information that is gathered, generated, and used by government in the service of activities taken ostensibly on the public's behalf and funded by taxpayers. In short, it is the public's information. Yet, in most respects, there is broad unexamined and unquestioned acceptance of nondisclosure. I stress this because of another human tendency: the internalization of the commonplace. Each pillar of exemption from accessing information desensitizes us to the maintenance of secrecy or nondisclosure relating to government action in the execution of the people's business. We subconsciously internalize some realms of secrecy as acceptable, even as we generally decry it. We must therefore be mindful that unexamined acceptance of nondisclosure is corrosive to and is always at risk of encroaching on what should be public without having to ask for it.

Among the most commonplace exemptions that threaten to swamp the purposes and the values of FOIA is the deliberative-process exemption, under which opinions or recommendations that apply to official government functions can be exempt from public-records disclosure. The general notion is that by not disclosing such deliberative information, we encourage candid and frank discussion and advice from government employees and prevent them from being second-guessed by outside parties. We of course want government employees to give candid assessments of the merits of final government action. But what does it say about us, our government, and our public officials if we accept that a competent, diligent government employee or an elected official would or should ever be embarrassed that their work or opinion was disclosed publicly?

The information and opinions gathered by, and provided to, public officials to inform their decisions is the very essence of the day-to-day workings of government. Yet, far from transparent, this most critical element of the public's business is rendered opaque and is often walled off from public scrutiny. Indeed, the deliberative-process exemption is thrown up in almost knee-jerk reaction, for usually self-serving purposes, and has itself become corrosive to the public trust. However, even without these exemptions, can we rely on government to adequately inform the public? In an April 1903 speech before the Boston Unitarian Club, US Supreme Court Justice Louis Brandeis declared that the public actions of the government, no matter how dedicated to openness, would never be enough to keep the public sufficiently informed. Said Brandeis: "The individual citizen must in some way collect and spread the information." This meant not so much individuals acting alone but organizations such as civic groups and, even more important, the press. Speaking at a time when the only way to reach large audiences on a regular basis was through print, Brandeis saw the press as potentially "the greatest agency of good government"—but only "if the people are sufficiently interested to desire it."

This raises a number of questions critical to Brandeis's time and ours, foremost of which may be, how do the people become "sufficiently interested"? Again, we are back to the boiling-frog phenomenon. We may take notice but not speak up or act unless things reach crisis stage in a way that puts us in *immediate* fear for our well-being. In Brandeis's estimation, the public was "ignorant of the facts—ignorant of the specific acts of misgovernment—ignorant of the low character or quality of many of the men by whom in public life they are misrepresented." Yet he believed that no one could possibly "look into the details of [government] administration and be indifferent." Such information would naturally lead to indignation, and out of that indignation would come a movement for "remedial action." He believed that public disclosure might overcome apathy.

The print media continue to play an important role in generating interest in government and misgovernment. But print media is under enormous financial pressure today. The decimated ranks of regular news staffers that must feed a daily newspaper have reduced much of our political and governmental reporting to an activity that contemporary media and social critics refer to as "churnalism"—the publication as news of an article that is a cut-and-paste of a press release. Journalists, especially beat reporters, operating under enormous competitive deadline pressures, are no longer gathering news but are reduced instead to uncritical processors of whatever material comes their way. Print media must sell newspapers. To do so, they must present news that is timely and relevant, placing a premium on scooping competitors: "Get it right, but get it first."

The media offices of major government agencies satisfy both of those otherwise-incommensurable requirements by serving up "news" in ready-to-publish form, favoring those reporters who they know will publish it largely unfiltered in order to get it out first. They time their press releases—the midnight press release is in present vogue—to bury bad news or to assure that first accounts are published without vetting or opposing view. This backdrop results in media that are at times a pass-through for untruths that in politics we refer to as "spin" or "political rhetoric," but in most every other endeavor would be called lies.

So Brandeis's notion of the media—print or otherwise—as an effective check functions nowhere near as effectively as the times require. The verdict is still out on whether the Internet fills the void left by crimped traditional mainstream media reporting. The Internet as a medium for news and information about the function of government principally does three things:

1. It amplifies what already exists: most blogs are simply aggregators of mainstream media, functioning as echo chambers for the compromised work of mainstream media.
2. It provides in these blogs, in a more impactful way, a critical framing lens that supplies a perspective on what is generated by mainstream media. But those of us inclined to engage generally gravitate to websites that confirm our existing views.
3. It provides new avenues for people in different places with shared interests to discuss, and potentially organize, coordinated action in the service of important public issues.

Human nature and history counsel that we cannot rely on those in power to always be honest, unselfish in motive and deed, infallible, and self-regulating. Free-market imperatives and values suggest that the media—the nongovernmental body upon which we have long relied for information—are not as reliable a source or as effective a check as once assumed and hoped. With no one to do our work for us, we are left with the irreducible bottom line that we truly have met the enemy, and it is us. We must recover ownership of our government and generate a new template for engaged citizenship. But to do so requires that we the people wrest from our leaders ownership and control of the definition of transparency in government, require our governments to adhere to it, and drive it to forms of accountability equal to the worst impulses in our leaders. This book steps into this civic void and provides the foundation for enabling those actions and helping us frogs out of that boiling pot.

—Joseph Ferguson

Joseph Ferguson is a member of the board of directors of the Association of Inspectors General. Since 2009 he has been the inspector general for the City of Chicago. From 1994 to 2009, he worked for the United States Attorney Office in Chicago, where he was chief of the money-laundering section. This foreword is adapted from the annual Ruth Winter Lecture, delivered at Lake Forest College in April 2012.

Acknowledgments

First I want to extend my deepest thanks to my agent, Nancy Rosenfeld, who believed in my work, appreciated my passion, and was so dedicated in finding just the right publisher for my book. I reserve a heartfelt gratitude to Steven L. Mitchell, who saw in me and my devotion to our democratic principles a kindred spirit whose ideas needed to be promoted and promulgated to as wide an audience as possible. And a special thanks to Jade Zora Scibilia, whose expert eye for editing and many weeks of patient advice made this work comprehensible and easy to read.

Finally, I would be remiss in not mentioning that much of the inspiration for my writing came from my students at Northwestern University, who often challenged me as much as I did them. Through my courses on transparency in government, they were a constant source of ideas. In particular, I would like to thank the following students whose research greatly contributed to this book: Karen Badawi, Phil Boardman, Nicole Bronnimann, Peter Contos, Brandon DeLallo, Elizabeth Franz, George Geiger, Matt Marcus, Shireen Ali Mirza, Jessi Reber, and Bryan Weber.

I truly believe that this generation of young people are up to the task of creating a more open and responsive government, espousing the new politics of civic engagement, embracing the ideals of our founders, and thus securing our democracy for the twenty-first century—or I never would have written this book.

Introduction

The word *transparency* can conjure up all sorts of meanings and cover a wide swath of social interactions. This book, however, is specifically about full transparency in American government and how it can enable a more open and effective democracy.

Chapter 1 gets right to the task of defining what we mean by transparency in government. By its nature, government is a public sphere, and the notion of privacy in that sphere is not only an unattainable expectation but borders on cover-up and corruption. Chapter 1 also discusses why transparency in government matters—that is, why you should give a damn.

Chapter 2 is a complement to the first chapter, exploring the history of transparency in government. There are three reasons to do this: (1) to provide a foundation of thought on the subject from a long line of influential Americans, (2) to establish a consensus regarding the necessity for transparency in government from a wide range of noteworthy thinkers, and (3) to build a case for the notion that as a constitutional republic, we are the government that we are governed by, and thus we own the information that makes our government function. The intent is to show that as owners, and not just clients, of our government, we are entitled to know everything about our government as well as the activities of those we elect to represent us—however unpleasant, vulgar, and repulsive that information may be.

This ownership doesn't come without responsibility, and that is what chapter 3 delves into by exploring the inseparable relationship between transparency in government and civic engagement. It's a symbiotic relationship in that one can't flourish or even exist without the other. Transparency in government both engenders and is imbued by civic engagement. Both are integral components of a thriving and effective democracy—something we have yet to achieve.

The first three chapters—part 1 of the book—place transparency in government within the context of the fabric of American democracy. Part 2—chapters 4, 5, and 6—moves on to the methodologies of measuring that transparency and devising ways to foster its expansion. Chapter 4 examines the best practices in transparency efforts and how implementation of sunshine laws in these states has promoted transparency and, in turn, civic engagement. The point of this chapter is to highlight those states where aspects of transparency are successfully implemented and serve as examples for other states to emulate.

Chapter 5 identifies the factors critical for measuring transparency, with the intent of building a useful set of criteria that can be applied to create a transparency index. The purpose of such an index is to be able to compare states' efforts to create more transparency in government. An index distills those efforts into a recognizable number that citizens can reference in determining how open their state government is to providing ever-increasing transparency. Think of it as a "civic hammer" to drive nails into the "coffin" of obfuscation and obtuseness in government.

Chapter 6 presents a final version of the transparency index. Individual evaluations are based on the criteria established in chapter 5 to measure transparency. You'll probably want to jump right to this chapter, but trust me, the index makes more sense if you read chapters 1 through 5 first.

Part 1

Making the Case for Transparency in Government

Chapter 1

What Transparency Is and Why It Matters

"The liberties of a people never were, nor ever will be, secure, when the transactions of their rulers may be concealed from them."
—Patrick Henry, June 9, 1788,
Virginia Constitutional Convention

What is this thing we call transparency in government? And why has the word *transparency* become so ubiquitous that it has replaced the word *reform* as the new mantra of any politician who wants to get elected or stay in office? In fact, the word *transparency* has been used so often that it has become virtually meaningless.

How are we to know when the actions of our elected representatives or civil servants contribute to more transparency in government or are simply so much political spin? Does it really matter if we know the difference? Is more transparency in government a good thing and something we should strive for, or can it be a detriment to good governance?

These are important questions that must be answered if we're to survive as a democracy, and, as one of America's founders, Patrick Henry, so aptly put it, if we're to retain our liberties as a free people. Yes, it's *that* important!

WHAT IT IS

Let's be clear, right from the beginning, that you and I—and every American citizen—have a right to full transparency regarding any facet of our government. It's not a question of what but when. Almost all information about our government should be made accessible as it becomes available—we have the tools to do that. What remains, information that would be classified as sensitive, should be made accessible when it becomes prudent to do so within a reasonable period of time.

There is *no* information about our government that should be sequestered for an indeterminate period of time or withheld simply to appease the desires of those in government. This isn't just a personal opinion, which you will see as this book unfolds. It is the opinion of many great thinkers who have preceded us throughout our history, so you and I stand on very firm ground—or should I say shoulders? Yet after more than two hundred years, transparency in government continues to elude us. If we are to propose and defend the notion of full transparency in government, we first must come up with an acceptable definition of transparency in government. We all have to be using the same language, so to speak, when talking about transparency. Ask citizens if they are for transparency in government, and they will say yes. Then ask them what it means, and you will get a different, if nuanced, answer every time.

More important, without a definition that can be commonly agreed upon, many in government will spin their own ideas of what transparency means. Experience has shown that their definition will often pale in comparison to the more rigorous interpretation we are about to produce—sometimes so they can avoid the work of providing true transparency, sometimes so they can avoid the awkward and embarrassing exposure that comes with opening government to public scrutiny.

If It Looks Like a Duck . . .

If we're to discuss transparency, we must objectively come up with a comprehensive definition that will be immediately recognizable and widely accepted. You know, like distinguishing a duck from, say, a kangaroo. We need the quack, the waddle, and the webbed feet, or we don't have a duck. We need obvious characteristics and discernible boundaries.

So let's start where most definitions start: with a dictionary. I used the Oxford online dictionary, and as you might suspect, its primary definition of *transparency* is "the condition of being transparent."[1] Well that's not very helpful! Let's move on, then, to its definition of *transparent*. Several definitions are given, but the meaning that's relevant for us is:

Easy to perceive or detect:

- having thoughts or feelings that are easily perceived; open: *you'd be no good at poker—you're too transparent*
- (of an organization or its activities) open to public scrutiny: *if you had transparent government procurement, corruption would go away*[2]

In particular, note the references to "easily perceived" and "open to public scrutiny." To easily perceive something you need a clear understanding of what it is you're looking at. In other words, it must be comprehensible. When we open government to public scrutiny, the implication is that whatever you're looking at is easily accessible. Keep both of these concepts in mind—comprehensibility and accessibility. We'll need them later.

By the way, the word *transparency* comes from Medieval Latin (Latin as written and spoken ca.700–ca.1500) meaning "to shine a light through." It was first used in the sense of "easily seen through" in the 1590s. Now, when was the last time you envisioned government of any kind being "easily seen through"? When was the last time you imagined that you, the average citizen, could "shine a light through" the morass of policies and laws that we've come to know as government?

Consider some synonyms for *transparent: clear, plain, lucid*. Be honest. Are those words that come to mind when you think of government? Now consider some antonyms for *transparent: cloudy, dark, opaque*. Now we're getting somewhere!

So far we have explored definitions for *transparent*, and a few synonyms and antonyms to boot. Let's build on all that and apply it toward a practical, empirical definition of transparency in government, one that we can use every day and that we can hold our elected officials and government employees to.

Pick a Card, Any Card

Any magician worth his or her salt is good at the arts of deception and diversion, and a politician is like a magician in a business suit. Often what is sold as transparency is simply the deceptive or diversionary tactic of making disclosure appear to be transparency. But wait—aren't they the same, disclosure and transparency? On the contrary, they are quite distinctive. So, back to the dictionary, which defines *disclosure* as:

1. The action of making new or secret information known
2. A fact, especially a secret, that is made known[3]

What's important to point out here is that disclosure, by definition, is simply making information known—be it new, secret, interesting, boring, extensive, trite, whatever. It is the simple act of disclosing. Note that there is no requirement that the information be comprehensible or easily accessible. So remember those two words—*comprehensible* and *accessible*. Disclosure could mean making information public that requires a citizen to file a Freedom of Information request (no easy task), appear at a designated location to view the information (not always possible), and do all of this within a very strict time frame (highly unlikely)—with no guarantee the person would understand what he was looking at.

Prior to the advent of the Internet, very little data was digitized, and for the most part the process laid out in the previous paragraph is how you typically got your information, if you could get to it at all. Given the existence of the Internet, you would think it would be easier. On the contrary, information can be even more confusing and even more difficult to obtain. We'll talk about that a little later. What's important to understand now is that the conditions to satisfy full disclosure pale in comparison to those for full transparency, which is why we're sold so much disclosure as if it were transparency. Many in government are happy to provide disclosure so long as they don't have to provide transparency.

So no, disclosure is not transparency, but it is a starting point. You need information to be disclosed in order to achieve full transparency. Disclosure is the foundation upon which transparency is built. You wouldn't live in the foundation of a house, would you? Of course not! You'd expect a structure to be built on that foundation. Think of it this way: Transparency is to disclosure as a house is to a foundation.

Now we could start from scratch to craft our common and comprehensive definition of transparency. But why should we? So many good organizations out there have been working at achieving transparency in government for years and have at least attempted to define transparency within certain constructs. I've looked around at a number of these organizations, and one in particular stood out: Transparency International. The name just about says it all, and it's been around for a while. For over twenty years, this nongovernmental organization has tracked political corruption worldwide, and it has a pretty good track record for understanding the need for political transparency. It currently defines *transparency* as follows: "Transparency is about shedding light on rules, plans, processes and actions. It is knowing why, how, what, and how much. Transparency ensures that public officials, civil servants, managers, board members and businessmen act visibly and understandably, and report on their activities. And it means that the general public can hold them to account."[4] However, at one time it defined *transparency* as "a principle that allows those affected by administrative decisions, business transitions or charitable work to know not only the basic facts and figures but also the mechanisms and processes. It is the duty of civil servants, managers and trustees to act visibly, predictably and understandably in such a way as to enable this transparency." It is this older, but no longer expressed version that I prefer as a basis for creating our definition specific to transparency in government.

The key takeaway here is presenting to those affected "the basic facts and figures" *as well as* "the mechanisms and processes" behind those facts. You can't begin to have real transparency if any of these elements of *disclosure* are missing. However, what often passes for transparency, what government officials would like you to *think* is transparency, is merely a bunch of facts and figures—and sometimes not very good facts and figures. And seldom do we get the mechanisms and processes that drive those facts and figures or show us how they were arrived at: the meeting minutes, the decision trees, the e-mails, the phone calls, the memos, and so on. And here's the real kicker: when all is said and done, even *if* we get the facts, figures, mechanisms, and processes, what we have been given is still only disclosure.

In its definition, Transparency International also presents us with two other important points as we gravitate toward a common and comprehensive definition of *transparency*. The first is to characterize the audience for transparency in government: "those affected by administrative decisions, business transitions or charitable work." Transparency International does not concentrate only on government but targets a broader range of entities. Because our focus is strictly on government, we are concerned with "those affected by administrative decisions" and legislation.

The second point that Transparency International makes is to characterize who is responsible for transparency and to define their tasks: "civil servants, managers and trustees to act visibly, predictably and understandably in such a way as to enable this transparency." Again, in limiting the scope to government, we would characterize those responsible and their tasks as "civil servants and elected officials to act visibly, predictably and understandably in such a way as to enable this transparency."

In the end, however, the best one can say is that Transparency International gives us a good definition of *disclosure*, but as we have seen, disclosure isn't transparency. So all we have is a good definition of *disclosure* and an abbreviated, dictionary definition of *transparency*. It's time we bring this discussion, and our building of a definition of *transparency*, to a conclusion. We're ready to put up that house of transparency on our foundation of disclosure.

Ace in the "Whole"

Earlier we distilled two key concepts from the dictionary definition of *transparency*: comprehensibility and accessibility. Now we're going to use them. Those facts, figures, mechanisms, and processes (disclosure) have to be presented in a way that is accessible and comprehensible. In other words, those who are affected by governmental decisions—in particular, citizens—must be able to get to the information easily (accessibility) and understand what they're looking at (comprehensibility). That might seem obvious to you and me, but it seems to be rocket science to those in government charged with the responsibility to provide transparency.

Accessibility should be effortless given the Internet. Every piece of knowledge seems to make it there, and most of it is free. And getting to information is as easy as opening a laptop, a tablet, or a smart phone and doing a search in any number of easy-to-use browser tools. It's getting to the point that if information *isn't* digitized, it doesn't exist! When was the last time you went to a library, and how often have you done that recently? And when was the last time you went on the Internet, and how often have you done *that* recently?

Yet in the dark and cloistered world of government, that message seems to have fallen on deaf ears. Sure, records are being digitized, but for the most part you and I can't get to them. Why is that? After all, it's *our* information. Yet we have to present a note—a Freedom of Information request—in many situations to get to it. And then we have to make a case for why we want the information. Here's a thought: let's turn Freedom of Information Acts on their Luddite heads and require government agencies to provide a reason why they *don't* make information available. It does us no good if information, disclosed by various government departments, is available only to intellectuals and scholars who know what to ask for and how to get it. Disclosure without accessibility, or even limited accessibility, is a nonstarter. It's a foundation buried in the rubble of obscurity, with no hope of our being able to construct that house of transparency.

But let's assume that our governmental agency has figured it out, overcome the barriers to access, and in the spirit of best practices made all its information easily accessible. Now what? It's one thing to put a 150-page city budget on the Internet, a mere click away from accessibility, in a portable document format (pdf) that makes it easy to read or print out. It's another thing entirely to present that information in a way that is comprehensible. Sure there are accountants and experts in public policy who could analyze such a document expeditiously, but all the rest of us would muddle through a few pages and give up. Just making information accessible doesn't make it useful. Information has to be presented in a way that the average citizen can digest.

There's one more criterion that we haven't mentioned yet, and it is critical to achieving full transparency from disclosure. The information must be presented in such a way that citizens actually *want* to examine it. In other words, it must be enticing. In drawing on our analogy, we laid the foundation and built the house using the best materials and going beyond any of the building codes for safety and functionality. But the house is ugly. The contractors did their job, but the architect had no sense of allure or symmetry. So there it stands, but no one wants to live in it! So, too, it is with information. It has to be presented in a way that's interesting, intriguing, and relevant. In other words, it must pass the enticement test: people must want to buy it, or in our case of transparency, buy *into* it.

What good is it to make information accessible and comprehensible if no one cares to examine it and find it beneficial? The information must motivate individuals to engage in dialogue directed toward improving the efficiencies of their government and mitigating corruption. This is why enticement is so critical to achieving full disclosure from transparency. It is the raison d'être of transparency. It is why we go through the trouble of bringing about transparency out of the morass of disclosure in the first place. Think of it this way: we must ACE disclosure (make it **A**ccessible, **C**omprehensible, and **E**nticing) in order to get transparency. So now we have a common and comprehensive definition of *transparency*:

The principle by which those affected by administrative decisions and legislation are made aware of the basic facts and figures as well as the mechanisms and processes of their government. This information must be presented in a way that is accessible, comprehensible, and enticing, thus motivating citizens to engage in the dialogue necessary to improve the efficiencies of government and mitigate corruption. It is the duty of our elected representatives and of civil servants to act in such ways as to enable this transparency.

Now What?

We now appear to have a practical and empirical definition for transparency in government, one that we can hold elected representatives and government employees to. With this definition as a baseline, we could work to legislate a standard level of transparency across all government entities, create a transparency index to measure performance, periodically review transparency efforts based on that index, and make that data publicly available. In the second half of this book, we examine all of those options.

But what good would it do to have the power to accomplish these things if no one cared to use that power? And how important is it, really, that as citizens we know how our government is being run? We vote in order to elect people to represent us and in turn expect that they'll do a reasonably good job running our government. Do we really need to get involved beyond that? After all, we have lots of other things going on in our lives and probably have little time to keep an eye on our government and elected officials. In other words, does this transparency stuff really matter? Let's consider that next before moving on. ·

WHY IT MATTERS

Three Little Words

We the People—possibly the three most significant words in the history of the United States. The first three words of the Preamble to our Constitution.[5] We the People "establish Justice." We the People "insure domestic Tranquility." We the People "provide for the common defence." We the People "promote the general Welfare." We the People "secure the Blessings of Liberty to ourselves and our Posterity." We the People "do ordain and establish this Constitution for the United States of America." As so eloquently and succinctly put in a single, short paragraph, We the People establish the government by which we are then governed. In a somewhat Zen-like logic, we are at once the government and the governed.

As most political scientists will tell you, ours is not a democracy, but rather a constitutional republic. But we certainly practice democracy—from the people in tiny New England towns who follow the traditional, direct style of ancient Greece,[6] to the rest of us, who choose representatives rather than make decisions directly. Thus, it might be more accurate to say we are a representative democracy.

Leave it to James Madison to make it about as clear as can be. In the Federalist Papers, Number 10, he wrote, "The two great points of difference between a democracy and a republic are: first, the delegation of the government, in the latter, to a small number of citizens elected by the rest; secondly, the greater number of citizens, and greater sphere of country, over which the latter may be extended."[7] So we are a republic of citizens practicing democratic principles. But let there be no doubt that We the People are responsible for creating the government to which we submit as the governed. "We the People . . . do ordain and establish this Constitution for the United States of America." Our founders, reeling from the aristocracies and monarchies they left behind, wanted to be absolutely clear as to who was in charge. We the People are in charge, and no one, including the president, stands above We the People. But because we do such an awful job of educating our children in the duties of citizenship—if we educate them at all—we have lost sight of the meaning behind "We the People."

Why bring all of this up? Because it's critical to understanding why transparency matters. To practice democracy in a republic requires that we not abdicate our role as citizens. And that role is not passive but rather requires that as citizens we have access to information on how our government is run. Again, citing the wisdom and expectations of our founders, I believe Thomas Jefferson laid out for all generations the role of the engaged citizen, within the context of full transparency. In a letter to his friend Edward Carrington, he alluded to transparency in government and the duties of citizenship. The following excerpt is packed with meaning: "Cherish therefore the spirit of our people, and keep alive their attention. Do not be too severe upon their errors, but reclaim them by enlightening them. If once they become inattentive to the public affairs, you and I, and Congress, and Assemblies, judges and governors shall all become wolves."[8]

First, there is the recognition of what I like to call the sanctity of citizenship. In the first sentence, Jefferson recognized its importance and went so far as to tell his friend to "cherish" this spirit. But it's not enough to simply revere the spirit; we must also "keep alive their attention." This is critical. More than a century later, American philosopher John Dewey, in his book *The Public and Its Problems*, lamented the difficulty of holding citizens' attention: "The increase in the number, variety and cheapness of amusements represents a powerful diversion from political concern. The members of an inchoate public have too many ways of enjoyment, as well as of work, to give much thought to organization into an effective public."[9]

That was in 1927. Can you imagine what Dewey would have thought about the "number, variety and cheapness of amusements" today? What good is providing transparency in government if no one is paying attention? Achieving transparency in government is a fool's errand if we don't have an active and engaged citizenry. They go hand in hand. There's no sense doing all the hard work of ensuring that government is open and accessible if we don't simultaneously work toward ensuring that we educate citizens about their responsibilities. This brings us to the second sentence in the excerpt above.

Jefferson understood that educating citizens about their responsibilities can be difficult, which is why he cautioned "not [to] be too severe upon their errors," while embracing the notion that we must "reclaim them by enlightening them." Earlier in this same letter, he told Carrington, "The people are the only censors of their governors: and even their errors will tend to keep these to the true principles of their institution. To punish these errors too severely would be to suppress the only safeguard of the public liberty." A nod toward the need for transparency in government if I've ever heard one, since it must be assumed that people can act as censors only if they have the information to do so. Couple this with the good sense of knowing that transparency requires an educated citizenry.

Finally, in the third sentence, Jefferson explains what will happen if we allow government to run rampant without the oversight of an engaged citizenry. He warns that elected officials "shall all become wolves." How prescient Jefferson was is evidenced in our infamous history of political corruption. If we had heeded his wise advice, we might not have had such a sullied past. But it's not too late to do so, and that's why full transparency in government, joined with an enlightened citizenry, is so important in mitigating the corruption that Jefferson warned about.

By the way, this is the same letter in which he wrote the famous phrase "were it left to me to decide whether we should have a government without newspapers, or newspapers without a government, I should not hesitate a moment to prefer the latter." Jefferson wrote thousands of letters, but this one stands out, and it's worth the short read to see what led to that famous quote. There is no doubt that he laid down the gauntlet for all generations of citizens to strive for more transparency in government.

So we see that recognition of the need for transparency in government is not a recent phenomenon. In fact, one could find numerous instances in American history of calls being made for opening up government to the governed. Besides the one in Jefferson's letter to Edward Carrington, and others that we'll explore in the next chapter, I'll bring up one more instance here.

Another of our founders, Patrick Henry, an avid anti-Federalist who was wary of any strong central government, was an early proponent of transparency in government. During the Virginia Constitutional Ratifying Convention in June 1788 in Richmond, Henry spoke frequently. However, on one particular day, June 9, he spoke quite eloquently and directly of the need for transparency in government. Here is an excerpt from that speech:

> Give us at least a plausible apology why Congress should keep their proceedings in secret. They have the power of keeping them secret as long as they please, for the provision for a periodical publication is too inexplicit and ambiguous to avail anything. The expression "from time to time," as I have more than once observed, admits of any extension. They may carry on the most wicked and pernicious of schemes under the dark veil of secrecy. *The liberties of a people never were, nor ever will be, secure, when the transactions of their rulers may be concealed from them.* The most iniquitous plots may be carried on against their liberty and happiness. I am not an advocate for divulging indiscriminately all

the operations of government, though the practice of our ancestors, in some degree, justifies it. Such transactions as relate to military operations or affairs of great consequence, the immediate
promulgation of which might defeat the interests of the community, I would not wish to be published, till the end which required
their secrecy should have been effected. But to cover with the veil
of secrecy the common routine of business, is an abomination in
the eyes of every intelligent man, and every friend to his country.[10]

This speech was given before our constitutional republic even
had a ratified constitution! That wouldn't happen until nearly a
year later. Transparency and an open government were considered
necessary for liberty to thrive. These were people who had just won
a revolution and their freedom from a monarch who didn't put much
value on an enlightened citizenry. Rather, King George III found it
to be an annoying hindrance to his absolute power. Our founders
wanted to ensure that this wouldn't happen here, and transparency
in government would go a long way toward ensuring that. We'll see
more of this in the next chapter, but it wouldn't be a stretch to call
Patrick Henry "the father of transparency in government" because of
this speech.

Take a Stand!

Some of my favorite movie dialogue is from *A Few Good Men*, in
which Tom Cruise plays the tough US Navy lawyer Lieutenant Daniel
Kaffee and Jack Nicholson plays the defiant Colonel Nathan Jessup.
Kaffee has been grilling Jessup incessantly on the witness stand, and
then in the classic exchange toward the end, he asks the colonel for
answers. Jessup echoes Kaffee's demand, shouting the question back
at him. In response, Kaffee firmly tells the Colonel that he wants the
truth. Jessup then utters one of the classic lines of the cinema when
he tells Kaffee, "You can't handle the truth!"[11]

Allow me to paraphrase this exchange: "Transparency? You
want transparency? You can't handle transparency!" Maybe Colonel

Jessup is right. Maybe we aren't prepared to take on the responsibility that comes with full transparency, preferring instead to simply let those we elect get things done regardless of how they do it. In the movie, the colonel goes on to chastise the lieutenant by telling him that we live in a world with walls that need to be guarded, and he challenges him to take a stand and protect those behind the walls—otherwise, shut the hell up and let him do his job, but in either case he could care less what the lieutenant thinks he's entitled to.

And so, too, with government? When it comes to being an engaged citizen, have you ever felt like a Lieutenant Kaffee being lectured by a Colonel Jessup? Years of community activism have taught me not to be intimidated by the people we elect to run *our* government. Yet I'm also a realist. I understand that for many citizens, the relationship with their elected representatives is often one of awe driven by a sense of cowering capitulation under a misguided perception that politicians have, if not all the answers, certainly better answers than you, the uninformed citizen, have. In the movie, Jessup derives his sense of authority and power from the fact that those around him succumb to his degrading treatment of anyone who would challenge him. Our history is rife with examples of politicians who see themselves in the same light—especially those incumbents who have been in office for so long that, like Colonel Jessup, they become imbued with an arrogance that defies the notion that they should be first and foremost public servants.

But before we fix all the blame on those in government, let's be candid about the fact that we, too, share some responsibility. We encourage our elected representatives to embrace authoritarian attitudes and actions by capitulating to their authority, and that's because we neglect our role as citizens and have a woefully inadequate understanding of our government. Jefferson admonished Carrington that "Congress, and Assemblies, judges and governors shall all become wolves"—and so they have, as we have relinquished more and more of our responsibilities of citizenship. It's not good enough that we just want transparency—"the truth." We have to be able to handle it. We have to be able to accept the challenge and take a stand by becoming civically engaged. In chapter 3, we'll delve into how intrinsically linked are transparency and that civic engagement, but it's worth noting here that transparency also serves to keep a short leash on those we elect.

In his 1788 speech quoted earlier, Patrick Henry says, "I am not an advocate for divulging indiscriminately all the operations of government, though the practice of our ancestors, in some degree, justifies it." Here he is saying that while there are operations of government that need to be kept back from public scrutiny, experience dictates that it is wise to err on the side of divulgence. Why? Because from time to time elected officials and other government workers trend toward abusing power.

Again, Henry: "They may carry on the most wicked and pernicious of schemes under the dark veil of secrecy." In recent American history, you need to look no further than the Watergate scandal. Our founders were quite sensitive to this type of abuse; we should remain so vigilant. Transparency in the affairs of government serves to rein in these abuses and keeps those we elect under the watchful eye of the public that elected them.

Jefferson believed in the superiority of newspapers over government. He would have been proud of the work of Bob Woodward and Carl Bernstein, reporters for the *Washington Post*, in uncovering the cover-up of the Watergate scandal. But Jefferson also understood that "the people are the only censors of their governors." The media certainly play a major role in keeping government honest, but in the end it is We the People who are inevitably responsible for keeping our democracy. It is better to have a thousand eyes than just a few focused on the workings of our government. Given the tools of communication available today, true transparency empowers everyone. Blogs, Facebook posts, tweets, and all avenues of social media empower the citizen journalist. Yes, mistakes are made, but Jefferson understood that "even their errors will tend to keep these [governors] to the true principles of their institution."

Henry recognized, however, that at times it is necessary to withhold information until it is prudent to release it: "Such transactions as relate to military operations or affairs of great consequence, the immediate promulgation of which might defeat the interests of the community, I would not wish to be published, till the end which required their secrecy should have been effected." In 1971, Daniel Ellsberg, a military analyst, released the Pentagon Papers—a disclosure of government decision making during the Vietnam War era.[12] And in 2010, Private Bradley Manning, an army intelligence analyst, turned over to WikiLeaks thousands of diplomatic cables that offered insight into international relations, as well as intelligence reports on the war in Afghanistan, which, like the Vietnam War at the time of Ellsberg's release, was still in progress.[13]

Both examples show that when government fails to set the parameters for the timely release of sensitive information, citizens will fill the void by making that decision *for* government. Whether "mistakes were made" by either Ellsberg or Manning in their decisions to release information is so much water under the bridge. Once the information is released, no punishment can put it back in the box. It's done. So it behooves government to provide the transparency that as citizens we must demand. Even information on "military operations or affairs of great consequence" has an expiration date on concealment. The requirement for transparency in government eventually trumps any furtive interests of government. However, we can take comfort in the notion that few activities of government require such secrecy. Let's look at a more typical example.

One area of less consequence than national security is the day-to-day operation of government—the mechanisms and processes. In 2011, *Chicago Tribune* investigative journalist David Kidwell interviewed the city's then newly elected mayor, Rahm Emanuel, who had campaigned vigorously on the notion of transparency in government. After being elected, Emanuel used the term repeatedly to convince voters that the decision to install cameras around the city to catch traffic speeders was fully transparent. The transcript of the interview, nearly an hour's worth of conversation, was made available to the public by the *Chicago Tribune*. It shines a light on the mayor's attitude toward what he believes is and isn't the proper boundary for transparency.

Given Emanuel's rhetoric about transparency in government, the interview consisted of numerous attempts to get the mayor to talk about releasing information on decisions that were made regarding the placement of speed cameras and the release of various conversations among staff and contractors. Near the end of the interview, the mayor was candid about where he believes the line should be drawn regarding transparency in his administration. In the following excerpts from that interview, Emanuel responds to questions asking for more information on how he conducts business with his staff:

David Kidwell: Let me explain to you what it's about, again. The emails are an avenue to get there, but it's about how you govern. Not how you say you govern. But how you govern, and in order to do that we took your transparency pledge on its face and we asked for not only emails but interoffice correspondence, we asked for cellphone bills. (Mayor talking over question.) Can I ask the question?

Rahm Emanuel: You're not asking a question, you're making a statement. I've done exactly what I pledged to do, which is why I said to you when I try [sic] to go back three questions. The assumptions are behind what I said. I am making . . . I have been in an executive position, and I mean this [sic] insulting so get it right, you haven't. You have not been in the White House. You have not been in the mayor's office. And the ability to govern allows you the ability to have honest conversations about the process and we have that, OK, and you have the right to get information and I am making that information available and that's why you can't—

DK: Are you saying that these conversations can't be honest if they're done in the open?

RE: No, and you have this on tape and I am not going to let you twist it. I am not going to let you twist it, and you're going to have to do something that is very . . . and I am going to say it right . . . you're going to have to actually do it right and honest. I have to have the ability to have people tell me their opinions and that is what every chief executive relies on whether you are in the private or public sector, including your own newspaper. I made a pledge to make information public and I am doing that, then you say, Well, that's not what you pledged. That is what I pledged. I pledged to make sure city government and the information it has is public.

RE: I also have the responsibility to govern. If in fact every communication cannot be done, some communication and you guys will have to respect that because FOIA doesn't allow for everything, that's why [Corporation Counsel] Patton is important. Other than that everybody will just say things are great, there's a white picket fence. The ability to have a meeting, to have an honest discussion requires certain information, consistent with the law, will be made available. Certain information, when my staff has given me unfiltered opinion, I need that as a chief executive and that doesn't mean you get to sit at the table.

DK: Let me ask the question please. Is it of any concern to you, that the fact that we can't see 90 percent of the correspondence that led to this [decision on speed cameras] would feed into the theory . . .

RE: I'll ask my staff about what we can make available, but I don't want to get into a position where I can't get honest opinions. So, between what you want and what I've got to do to be able to govern, we will find where we can find a happy middle ground. OK, but I have to be able to govern and that means people giving me unfettered and open opinion. Other than that, you know. And that's not unique to me being mayor. This is a public policy for every mayor, every chief executive, every governor, every president and every press corps. So it's not unique to me and I am not going to let you play that game. And it's not like I am unique in the sense of opinion. I need to get opinions, advice from my staff and I am going to continue to do that. I will never allow that to get hampered. They have provided you information, and as I continue to say, there is nothing of these subjects that hasn't been out in the public.[14]

Let's be clear that this example is not meant as an overall indictment of the mayor's performance in office. On the contrary, it was quite refreshing to see that an elected official of his stature would actually permit such an open interview with a journalist who had been less than kind in his previous articles about the mayor. This interview was also one of those rare occasions when an entire, unedited transcript was immediately made available for public consumption, and it provides a window into how this mayor frames the concept of transparency. We can be only moderately critical of our elected representatives if we don't set the level of expectations by defining exactly what is meant by transparency in government.

Also, to be fair, the mayor's opinion is probably similar to the opinion of other elected officials—that transparency ends at the door of a mayor, governor, president, and any other chief executive. It is the belief that an "unfettered and open opinion" cannot be obtained if those in public service feel their opinions will be made public. As jaded as I've become about politics and those whom we elect, even I was taken aback at first by the mayor's candor and then by his seemingly unmitigated arrogance.

I believe his candor was a result of his truly believing that citizens feel the same way he does. Whether or not that's true is debatable, but it shouldn't be acceptable. Personally, I don't believe that most people think it's necessary that in order to get unfettered and open opinion from someone, you to have to have complete secrecy and confidentiality in the public sphere. In the private domain, corporations are sensitive to competition, so it is sometimes necessary to keep secret what is discussed behind closed doors, not because someone fears personal reprisal for their opinions, but rather to protect corporate strategy.

Such conditions rarely exist in the public domain. One example might be the need for confidentiality during an open bidding process. But that's a temporary situation, and information can be released immediately after the bidding process is complete. The implication here, as stated by the mayor, is that staff—government employees—would fear their opinions being disclosed to the public. Really? What's going on behind closed doors that people would feel that way?

As for the mayor's arrogance, if he is correct in his assessment, and I have no doubt he is, then many others in government believe that honest and forthright opinions cannot be given if those opinions might see the light of day, for fear of retribution. If the character and temperament of those we elect and in turn those they appoint to government is such that transparency must end where government decision making begins, then we're putting the wrong people in government to represent us, and they're appointing and hiring the wrong people to serve them.

The mayor and others of similar ethos are like our Colonel Jessup. They believe you and I simply can't handle the truths of transparency. It's time we set them straight. It's time we pick up the weapon of transparency, take up civic engagement, and purge this attitude about the need for clandestine behavior from our government.

What we've covered so far—defining transparency in government and making the case for why it matters—has simply laid the groundwork for what is to come. In chapter 2, we'll review the history of transparency in government so that we're "fully armed" with a proper sense of entitlement to full transparency. We'll examine what others have thought and said about it—and not just anybody, but a well-respected and successful army of journalists, authors, historians, philosophers, statesmen, and politicians. In chapter 3 we'll dig deep into the relationship between transparency and civic engagement. As we connect the dots, we'll see that transparency in government leads to civic engagement and in turn is sustained by that engagement. Let there be no doubt that, as Patrick Henry said over two hundred years ago, "The liberties of a people never were, nor ever will be, secure, when the transactions of their rulers may be concealed from them."

THINK ABOUT IT

The Tyranny of Transparency

Could transparency in government be detrimental? In October 2009, Lawrence Lessig, professor of law and director of the Edmond J. Safra Center for Ethics at Harvard Law School, wrote an article for the *New Republic* titled "Against Transparency: The Perils of Openness in Government."[15] In it he makes a number of cogent and at times salient points about the dangers of what he terms "naked transparency," which he defines as a "movement [that] marries the power of network technology to the radical decline in the cost of collecting, storing, and distributing data. Its aim is to liberate that data, especially government data, so as to enable the public to process it and understand it better, or at least differently."

After referencing the famous line by Supreme Court Justice Louis Brandeis that, "Sunlight is said to be the best of disinfectants," he poses a rhetorical question: "How could anyone be against transparency? Its virtues and its utilities seem so crushingly obvious." In answering his own question, he expresses his fears that "the inevitable success of this movement [naked transparency]—if pursued alone, without any sensitivity to the full complexity of the idea of perfect openness—will inspire not reform, but disgust."

Lessig continues to lament naked transparency by quoting from and crediting the book *Full Disclosure: The Perils and Promise of Transparency*.[16] As authors Archon Fung, Mary Graham, and David Weil define it, targeted transparency "represents a distinctive category of public policies that, at their most basic level, mandate disclosure . . . of standardized, comparable, and disaggregated information regarding specific products or practices to a broad audience in order to achieve a public policy purpose." As Lessig points out, they borrow from Brandeis's school of regulatory theory of giving the market sufficient information and then letting the market sort it out.

This can be a problem, as Lessig tells us, in that Brandeis didn't necessarily have it right. After further quoting from *Full Disclosure*, Lessig reminds us that "responses to information are inseparable from their interests, desires, resources, cognitive capacities, and social contexts. Owing to these and other factors, people may ignore information, or misunderstand it, or misuse it. Whether and how new information is used to further public objectives depends upon its incorporation into complex chains of comprehension, action, and response."

I present all of this to alert the reader to the fact that transparency, especially what Lessig terms naked transparency, doesn't necessarily improve things and can, in fact, make things worse, or at least more confusing. I'll talk more about this in chapter 3 as we look at the relationship between transparency and civic engagement, but for now it's worth noting that transparency in government can sometimes lead to obfuscation rather than clarity if these issues aren't addressed.

This naked transparency, weaved into the deficiencies of targeted transparency, is only one of the shortcomings that he points out. As he goes on, Lessig cites an example of full transparency in political contributions that involved then First Lady Hillary Clinton and carried over to when she became Senator Clinton. He writes about the challenge of associating political contributions with the behavior of elected officials and subsequent legislation passed:

All the data in the world will not tell us whether a particular contribution bent a result by securing a vote or an act that otherwise would not have occurred. The most we could say—though this is still a very significant thing to say—is that the contributions are corrupting the reputation of Congress, because they raise the question of whether the member acted to track good sense or campaign dollars. Where a member of Congress acts in a way inconsistent with his principles or his constituents, but consistent with a significant contribution, that act at least raises a question about the integrity of the decision. But beyond a question, the data says little else. But then, so what? If the data does not tell us anything, what is the harm in producing it? Even if it does not prove, it suggests. And if it suggests something false, then let the offended legislator rebut it. The public will weigh the truth against the charge. Enter another Brandeisean cliché: "If there be time to expose through discussion the falsehood and fallacies . . . the remedy to be applied is more speech, not enforced silence." This sounds right.

However, Lessig argues that Brandeis's approach is once again flawed and that more "speech," in the example of Clinton's campaign contributions, would have cleared up nothing. Beyond 140-character tweets, he adds, we Americans have little time to focus on the correlations exposed in the disclosure of campaign contributions. And therein lies another powerful argument against more transparency in government: the short attention span attributed to the average citizen. Lessig tells us:

> To understand something—an essay, an argument, a proof of innocence—requires a certain amount of attention. But on many issues, the average, or even rational, amount of attention given to understand many of these correlations, and their defamatory implications, is almost always less than the amount of time required. The result is a systemic misunderstanding—at least if the story is reported in a context, or in a manner, that does not neutralize such misunderstanding. The listing and correlating of data hardly qualifies as such a context. Understanding how and why some stories will be understood, or not understood, provides the key to grasping what is wrong with the tyranny of transparency.

Well, damn, that's pretty powerful stuff. The "tyranny of transparency" it is, indeed, if we don't take the time to fully comprehend these issues. The three years since Lessig wrote his article have only further confirmed his concerns. We continue to feed from a deeper and deeper trough of wild accusations and irrelevant correlations mixed in a stew of opinionated drivel. Remember one of our conditions of transparency in extracting it from simple disclosure: comprehensibility? Yet to make all those facts and figures, mechanisms and processes, comprehensible requires that someone interpret the data. When Lessig talks about reporting in a context that doesn't neutralize misunderstanding, we're getting right to the heart of the challenge of making all of this information coherent in a way that is stripped of biases and ambiguity.

Lessig closes his article with optimism wrapped in benign admonishment:

> There is no questioning the good that transparency creates in a wide range of contexts, government especially. But we should also recognize that the collateral consequence of that good need not itself be good. And if that collateral bad is busy certifying to the American public what it thinks it already knows, we should think carefully about how to avoid it.

We've pried open the doors of transparency, and there's no going back. But if we're to employ transparency for the practical ends of arousing civic engagement and in turn mitigating corruption while vastly improving the efficiencies and responsiveness of government, then we have our work cut out for us. More on that in chapter 3, but first let's hear what others throughout our history have said about transparency in government.

Chapter 2

A History of Transparency in American Politics

"Cherish therefore the spirit of our people, and keep alive their attention. Do not be too severe upon their errors, but reclaim them by enlightening them. If once they become inattentive to the public affairs, you and I, and Congress, and Assemblies, judges and governors shall all become wolves."

—Thomas Jefferson,
letter to Edward Carrington,
January 16, 1787

"Cherish" indeed! Unfortunately, being "inattentive to public affairs" has been a hallmark of our citizenry. But let's not be too quick to judge because we've had a truly tumultuous history, filled with every sordid political character and failed efforts of reform. For goodness' sake, it took over a hundred years before we gave the *other half* of our population the right to vote, and only if the color of their skin was like the first fallen snow—and governments at all levels are still bereft of any serious percentage of women representing their constituencies. Thirteenth and Fourteenth Amendments aside, we really didn't get around all those Jim Crow laws, poll taxes, and other sorts of devious methods to deny blacks the right to vote until well into the later part of the twentieth century—and we're still wrestling with attempts to deny suffrage! So let us not be *too severe upon our errors*. After all, democracy, if anything, is a work in progress.

That *work in progress*, however, is also replete with dialogue supporting the principles of transparency in government, going as far back as revolutionary times and the founding of our country. To understand this legacy is to find comfort today in the fact that we stand on the shoulders of intellectual giants in our quest to finally open up government to its citizens, who *are* the government. It is within these echoes of reason from our past that we should be emboldened further, securing us in the knowledge that we pursue a lofty and righteous goal. Let there be no doubt, though, that we face a herculean challenge in wresting information from those in government—elected representatives and bureaucrats alike—who prefer maintaining their control over the reins of government by keeping that information to themselves. They are further enabled only by the fact that over the past two-hundred-plus years we citizens, willingly and unwillingly, have relinquished that control to them.

Today, we are now heartened by the confluence of greater communication, expanded citizenship (read: suffrage), and over two hundred years of working on this experiment of self-governance. This has brought on the perfect conditions for a storm of transparency here in the early twenty-first century. Make no mistake, mind you: there was never a "golden age" of democracy in this country to which we could return, so our quest is not to *take back* our government because we never *had* our government. Rather, our quest is to finally seize the power that our founders expected *for* us, our constitution granted *to* us, and this *perfect storm* enabled *in* us. Yet we cannot do that without full knowledge of how our governments operate and why our governments—federal, state, and local—do what they do. As you learned in the first chapter, it is only through full transparency that we can indeed assume that control. As you will learn in the next chapter, it is only through full transparency that we can become the engaged citizenry that our American democracy, expressed in the form of a republic, demands of us. And as you will learn in this chapter, full transparency in government is both our birthright and our entitlement as citizens. So say many learned Americans. So too should say you!

Therefore, in examining this history, I've presented the ideas and observations of some credible voices from the earliest revolutionary period of American history through to the present. This is not to say that others haven't spoken well for the cause of transparency, it's just that I had to limit my list to fit into a chapter. Another book could expand on this theme, but for now I've taken from those whom I consider the most recognizable among American pundits, scholars, and philosophers throughout our history and presented them here. Most of this chapter is devoted to the words of those individuals rather than to my rhetoric on the topic. Consider me simply as your guide leading you to the words of those who spoke so eloquently on transparency in government. And in the end, when you finish this chapter, there should be no doubt in your mind that transparency in government is not a group of "apps" concocted by twenty-first-century geeks but rather an integral part of the fabric of our democracy coveted throughout our history. It is only recently that it has gained the traction necessary to actually be expressed—though somewhat modestly. We still have much road to cover to achieve the transparency in government that will make this democracy of ours fully participatory.

In that letter to Edward Carrington quoted above, Jefferson wrote another line for which he is often quoted: "The way to prevent these irregular interpositions of the people is to give them full information of their affairs thro' the channel of the public papers, and to contrive that those papers should penetrate the whole mass of the people. The basis of our governments being the opinion of the people, the very first object should be to keep that right; and *were it left to me to decide whether we should have a government without newspapers, or newspapers without a government, I should not hesitate a moment to prefer the latter.* But I should mean that every man should receive those papers and be capable of reading them." The problem with quotes is that we are left without the benefit of context. The newspaper quote is often used to support the notion of a free press, and justifiably so. However, the true meaning of the quote was to support

Jefferson's notion of a well-informed public through "full information"—that is, transparency.

We ignore history at our peril, whether by not learning from our past or by not building on the deliberations of so many learned men and women. So come with me on a whirlwind examination of American ideation regarding the necessity for transparency in government. Then embolden yourself with the notion that no elected politician, no government bureaucrat, no paranoid citizenry is going to stand between you and the information that we as citizens rightfully own. The time has long passed for us to assume the prostrated roll of obedient subjects to the aristocracies of phony populist power. The time instead is for us now to open up government—even if we have to break it open! Our partners in this endeavor are a Who's Who of American history. Embrace their passion for transparency, secure in the comfort of knowing that they echo a long and glorious legacy.

Patrick Henry (May 29, 1736–June 6, 1799)

American liberty is a tenuous state, always challenged by those who would steal it from us in degrees and thus secured only through a constant state of vigilance, dependent upon a transparency in governments that fuels the civic engagement necessary for that vigilance to persist. And when we speak of those who have stood for and defended our American liberties, we need look no further than the colonists who struck a blow against the bow of British repression and gave birth to a nation based on "liberty and justice for all"—many who made the ultimate sacrifice for our country. Of the colonists who wore the mantel of Founding Fathers, one in particular stands out for his stridency and oratory in defense of liberty, both before and after our revolution—Patrick Henry.

Henry was most notable for his "Give Me Liberty, or Give Me Death" exhortation during the onset of our Revolutionary War. That quote is from a rousing speech he gave at the Virginia Convention in Richmond at St. John's Church on March 23, 1775, which has become known as the St. John's Church speech. There has been considerable controversy surrounding the actual wording of the speech because it was transcribed years later by Henry biographer William Wirt, who reconstructed the speech from numerous interviews with people who were at the convention. Controversy aside, though, the speech has become a cornerstone of American revolutionary rhetoric, but more so a glowing example of Henry's oratorical and intellectual prowess.

It was well known at the time that Henry, like many other colonists, was ready for war with England. Yet there was still a reticence at the convention to pass a resolution that would authorize Virginia to arm itself and establish a militia. Henry had no reservations and introduced an amendment to a motion that had already passed. Here is an excerpt of that amendment, dated March 23, 1775.

> Resolved, That a well regulated militia, composed of gentlemen and yeomen, is the natural strength and only security of a free government; that such a militia in this colony would forever render it unnecessary for the mother country to keep among us, for the purpose of our defence, any standing army of mercenary soldiers, always subversive of the quiet, and dangerous to the liberties of the people . . .[1]

The resolution aroused a great deal of angst among the delegates, who were concerned that it might call attention to the colony from King George and who believed that it was premature to act so aggressively. Not so, Patrick Henry.

Heated debate ensued, and in the end Henry, calm and collected, rose to speak at the end of the day. The speech, reconstructed as it was, reflected Henry's intense commitment to liberty and the liberation of the American colonies from the shackles of British rule. It lays the groundwork for the numerous speeches he would give more than a decade later at the Virginia Constitutional Convention, and one in particular on transparency in government. But for now, on this day, he would make his case for American freedom from England and utter the words that would forever resonate throughout our history. Here is that excerpt in context, as written by William Wirt:

> "It is in vain, sir, to extenuate the matter. Gentlemen may cry, peace, peace—but there is no peace. The war is actually begun! The next gale that sweeps from the north will bring to our ears the clash of resounding arms! Our brethren are already in the field! Why stand we here idle? What is it that gentlemen wish? What would they have? Is life so dear, or peace so sweet, as to be purchased at the price of chains and slavery? Forbid it, Almighty God! I know not what course others may take; but as for me," cried he, with both his arms extended aloft, his brows knit, every feature marked with resolute purpose of his soul, and his voice swelled to its boldest note of exclamation—"give me liberty or give me death!"[2]

To understand Henry's healthy paranoia of government that he would exhibit later and his unabashed support for full transparency in governments, one must understand what led to that temperament and the justification for it. Here, in this most famous of his speeches, one can appreciate the circumstances that shaped the mind of this exceptional patriot.

Years later, Patrick Henry would address that support for full transparency when he spoke at the Virginia Constitutional Convention of 1788. In fact, he would speak more than anyone else at that convention, giving numerous speeches on any particular day. In one speech alone he held the floor for seven hours! Altogether, over six hundred pages of printed debates were transcribed at the convention, and of that nearly a fifth were Henry's speeches. He was firmly in the anti-Federalist camp at first, suspect as he was of a strong and overbearing centralized government. Yet he would eventually be swayed to approve the new constitution, but never to give in to his principle of liberty first, union second.

However, the full impact of Henry's speeches can't be determined simply by reading them. Rather, the comments of those such as St. George Tucker, a Virginia lawyer and professor of law at the College of William and Mary, and who was present when Henry spoke at the Virginia Convention of 1775, may have expressed Henry's impact most succinctly when Tucker was quoted as saying to William Wirt: "At that time it appeared to me that Mr. Henry was sometimes as great" as at the Convention of 1775. "I recollect the fine image he gave of Virginia seated on an eminence and holding in her hand the balance in which the fate of America was weighing. . . . The variety of arguments which Mr. Henry generally presented in his speeches, addressed to the capacities, prejudices, and individual interests of his hearers, made his speeches unequal."[3] And Tucker was no unabashed admirer of Henry!

Tucker, of course, was speaking of when Henry once again made the kind of impact he did when he aroused Virginia to take up arms back in 1775. The Virginia Constitutional Convention in June 1788 would be a watershed time for American democracy. Eight states had already approved of the new constitution, but acceptance by the State of Virginia was crucial if the rest were to follow—and Virginians weren't all that enthralled, Henry in particular. Tucker, again weighing in on the impact of Henry's oratory, said: "If he soared at times like the eagle, and seemed, like the bird of Jove, to be armed with his thunder, he did not disdain to stoop like the hawk to seize his prey, but the instant he had done it, rose in pursuit of another quarry."[4]

It is Henry's speech at the convention given on June 9 that is of specific importance, as it relates to his commitment to transparency in government. In speaking to the issue of states' rights and the need for amendments to the new constitution that address that issue among other individual rights—the eventual first ten amendments to the Constitution—he was an early and vociferous proponent of inclusion of those amendments being enacted immediately after ratification. It is here that Henry ties the knot of liberty to transparency and from which his quote, used at the beginning of the last chapter, is derived. But it is in context that the words carry even more meaning:

Congress, by the power of taxation, by that of raising an army, and by their control over the militia, have the sword in one hand, and the purse in the other. Shall we be safe without either? Congress have an unlimited power over both: they are entirely given up by us. Let him candidly tell me, where and when did freedom exist, when the sword and purse were given up from the people? Unless a miracle in human affairs interposed, no nation ever retained its liberty after the loss of the sword and purse. Can you prove, by any argumentative deduction, that it is possible to be safe without retaining one of these? If you give them up, you are gone.

Give us at least a plausible apology why Congress should keep their proceedings in secret. They have the power of keeping them secret as long as they please; for the provision for a periodical publication is too inexplicit and ambiguous to avail anything. The expression *from time to time*, as I have more than once observed, admits of any extension. They may carry on the most wicked and pernicious of schemes under the dark veil of secrecy. *The liberties of a people never were, nor ever will be, secure, when the transactions of their rulers may be concealed from them.* The most iniquitous plots may be carried on against their liberty and happiness. I am not an advocate for divulging indiscriminately all the operations of government, though the practice of our ancestors, in some degree, justifies it. Such transactions as relate to military operations or affairs of great consequence, the immediate promulgation of which might defeat the interests of the community, I would not wish to be published, till the end which required their secrecy should have been effected. But to cover with the veil of secrecy the common routine of business, is an abomination in the eyes of every intelligent man, and every friend to his country.

[The reporter here states that Mr. Henry then, in a very animated manner, expatiated on the evil and pernicious tendency of keeping secret the common proceedings of government, and said that it was contrary to the practice of other free nations. The people of England, he asserted, had gained immortal honor by the manly boldness wherewith they divulged to all the world their political disquisitions and operations; and that such a conduct inspired other nations with respect. He illustrated his arguments by several quotations. He then continued as follows.]

I appeal to this Convention if it would not be better for America to take off the veil of secrecy. *Look at us—hear our transactions.*[5]

Thomas Jefferson (April 13, 1743–July 4, 1826)

As the principal author of the Declaration of Independence, Jefferson certainly needs no introduction when it comes to his commitment to liberty; for it is evidenced in the very first words of our declaration:

When in the Course of human events, it becomes necessary for one people to dissolve the political bands which have connected them with another, and to assume among the powers of the earth, the separate and equal station to which the Laws of Nature and of Nature's God entitle them, a decent respect to the opinions of mankind requires that they should declare the causes which impel them to the separation.[6]

Surprisingly, however, few realize that Jefferson was a prolific writer of letters. Estimates are that he wrote nearly nineteen thousand letters during his lifetime.[7] Begun in 1943 as the first modern historical documentary edition, the Jefferson Papers project includes not only the letters Jefferson wrote but also those he received. Julian P. Boyd, librarian, scholar of the Declaration of Independence, and first editor, designed an edition that would provide accurate texts with accompanying historical context. Poised to complete the written legacy of the Jefferson corpus by the bicentennial of Jefferson's death in 2026, these volumes provide the foundation of the Jefferson electronic edition, now sponsored by the University of Virginia Press and appearing through Founders Online.[8]

Between June 1780 and April 1791, Jefferson exchanged twenty-seven letters with Edward Carrington. Some, of course, stand out from the rest, such as the letter to Carrington written on January 16, 1787, while Jefferson was in Europe serving as the first minister to France. Carrington, a lieutenant colonel in the Continental Army during the American Revolution, was a Virginia delegate to the Continental Congress at the time of this letter—January 16, 1787. A number of notable quotes have been extracted, such as the one at the beginning of this chapter, and the context surrounding it, which was integral to Jefferson's position on transparency in government. So it's interesting to note why Jefferson wrote this letter to Carrington to put all of the quotes into context. The letter was meant to give Carrington an update on the state of affairs in France and the rest of Europe, as well as their opinions of our fledgling nation, and thus it provided Jefferson an opportunity to expound on his faith in the citizens to do what is right to preserve our liberties.

> The tumults in America, I expected would have produced in Europe an unfavorable opinion of our political state. But it has not. On the contrary, the small effect of those tumults seems to have given more confidence in the firmness of our governments. The interposition of the people themselves on the side of government has had a great effect on the opinion here. I am persuaded myself that the good sense of the people will always be found to be the best army.[9]

Following this is the first of many quotes popularized over the years and centered on Jefferson's commitment to trusting in the people to keep their government in check:

> They may be led astray for a moment, but will soon correct themselves. The people are the only censors of their governors: and even their errors will tend to keep these to the true principles of their institution. To punish these errors too severely would be to suppress the only safeguard of the public liberty.[10]

He continues by making a clear and unequivocal call for transparency in government to inform and embolden citizens in their quest for knowledge to safeguard their liberties:

> The way to prevent these irregular interpositions of the people is to give them full information of their affairs thro' the channel of the public papers, and to contrive that those papers should penetrate the whole mass of the people.[11]

And what means are available to provide that information? As he goes on in the next sentence, he makes his case for the Fourth Estate. Today, of course, we have the Internet, but that only further makes for Jefferson's case:

> The basis of our governments being the opinion of the people, the very first object should be to keep that right; and were it left to me to decide whether we should have a government without newspapers, or newspapers without a government, I should not hesitate a moment to prefer the latter.[12]

Finally, he admonishes all citizens should they not pay attention and take advantage of the "full information" provided them, by making a most prescient remark that would prove to be our bane throughout our history. If there is any better reason than this for full transparency in government, it has yet to be made:

> If once they become inattentive to the public affairs, you and I, and Congress, and Assemblies, judges and governors shall all become wolves.[13]

James Madison (March 16, 1751–June 28, 1836)

I could probably just stay with our Founding Fathers and have plenty of material justifying transparency in government, but I won't. However, I can't fail to bring up James Madison before moving on. The "Father of the Constitution" and one of the authors of the Federalist Papers, Madison had a thing or two to say on transparency in government as well. And like Jefferson, Madison corresponded prolifically, such as in the Federalist Papers, which were really letters written to the people of New York by James Madison and Alexander Hamilton (and a few of them were by John Jay).

The most quoted of Madison's letters regarding transparency in government is the one written to William Taylor Barry from August 4, 1822. Barry served in numerous political offices during his life, including senator from the state of Kentucky. At the time of the communication, Barry was lieutenant governor of Kentucky. Madison's correspondence was specifically directed to the subject of education in Barry's state. In writing to him, Madison expresses his strong support of higher education and access to that education for everyone, regardless of their ability to pay:

> No error is more certain than the one proceeding from a hasty & superficial view of the subject: that the people at large have no interest in the establishment of Academies, Colleges, and Universities, where a few only, and those not of the poorer classes can obtain for their sons the advantages of superior education . . . that wherever a youth was ascertained to possess talents meriting an education which his parents could not afford, he should be carried forward at the public expence, from seminary to seminary, to the completion of his studies at the highest.[14]

Madison goes on to write about the advantages of a well-educated populace and its relationship to a strong democracy and the liberties that ensue:

> The American people owe it to themselves, and to the cause of free Government, to prove by their establishments for the advancement and diffusion of Knowledge, that their political Institutions, which are attracting observation from every quarter, and are respected as Models, by the new-born States in our own Hemisphere, are

as favorable to the intellectual and moral improvement of Man as they are conformable to his individual & social Rights. What spectacle can be more edifying or more seasonable, than that of Liberty & Learning, each leaning on the other for their mutual & surest support?[15]

All of that said, and armed with the context of what Madison wanted to convey to the lieutenant governor, it was the very first paragraph of his letter that set the stage for the rest of what he was to write and from which he is often quoted regarding transparency in government:

A popular Government, without popular information, or the means of acquiring it, is but a Prologue to a Farce or a Tragedy; or, perhaps both. Knowledge will forever govern ignorance: And a people who mean to be their own Governors, must arm themselves with the power which knowledge gives.[16]

Now you might say that this isn't about transparency in government at all and it's been misrepresented as such. In the regard that the letter was pointedly about the value of education, you might be right. However, you would also be missing the point that it is *exactly* why, in the end, his words are all about transparency.

Without a properly educated populace, all the government transparency in the world will be worth little more than the paper and digital bits that it's delivered upon. If citizens don't have the education to deliberate and analyze what is being given to them, then not only will it be impossible to provide the comprehensibility necessary for true transparency, but it can very well have the unintended consequences of creating knee-jerk democracy. By that I mean if citizens are not capable of the intellectual rigors when it comes to reflecting upon the information given to them, then they will act from and be influenced by an appeal to emotions rather than intellect—thus diminishing the very democracy that transparency should be enhancing!

Yet there is another quote of Madison's that brings closure to the necessity of transparency in government, expressed by him in the Federalist Papers, Number 49, and pointing to the fact that as citizens we must be constantly vigilant and aware of what our government does because in the end it is we who give legitimacy to that government:

> The people are the only legitimate fountain of power, and it is from them that the constitutional charter, under which the several branches of government hold their power, is derived.[17]

He was speaking in a series of papers—Number 49 through Number 58—on the issue of separation of powers, and it is this series, when he speaks about checks and balances, that gives us another famous Madison quote:

> But what is government itself, but the greatest of all reflections on human nature? If men were angels, no government would be necessary. If angels were to govern men, neither external nor internal controls on government would be necessary.

And so too with transparency in government. There would be no need for us to keep watch if "men were angels"! We are not, and thus we must keep watch; and to keep watch, we must have access.

Woodrow Wilson (December 28, 1856– February 3, 1924)

The only American president to have earned a doctorate, Wilson's contribution to the cause of transparency in government came years before he served as this country's twenty-eighth president— and contribution it certainly was! Beginning in 1884, the young Dr. Wilson first wrote an article for the *Overland Monthly* titled "Committee or Cabinet Government." The article was an analysis of committee government (congressional) versus cabinet government (parliamentary), which Wilson favored:

None can doubt, therefore, that we are fallen upon times of grave crisis in our national affairs, and none can wonder that disgust for our present system speaks from the lips of citizens respectable both for numbers and for talents. Every day we hear men speak with bitter despondency of the decadence of our institutions, of the incompetence of our legislators, of the corruption of our public officials, even of the insecurity of our liberties.[18]

The more things change, the more they seem to stay the same. Wilson could have written those words today without a change of a single word! He goes on to speak of the "decay and rottenness" of political parties and how to reform the system. It is here that he waxes favorably on parliamentary (cabinet) government as a solution to the decay and rottenness of political parties, recommending amendments to the Constitution that would lengthen both the president's term as well as that of congresspeople. In addressing the positive elements of cabinet government, he says this:

> For it would secure open-doored government. It could not suffer legislation to skulk in committee closets and caucus conferences. *Light is the only thing that can sweeten our political atmosphere—* light thrown upon every detail of administration in the departments; light diffused through every passage of policy; light blazed full upon every feature of legislation; light that can penetrate every recess or corner in which any intrigue might hide; light that will open to view the innermost chambers of government, drive away all darkness from the treasury vaults, illuminate foreign correspondence, explore national dockyards, search out the obscurities of Indian affairs, display the workings of justice, exhibit the management of the army, play upon the sails of the navy, and follow the distribution of the mails—and of such light Cabinet government would be a constant and plentiful source.[19]

And to that he adds this admonition regarding the necessity for publicity:

It becomes every citizen to bethink himself how essential a thing to the preservation of liberty in the republic is free and unrestricted debate in the representative body. . . . The press is irresponsible, and often—too often—venally partisan. But representatives must criticize legislation in their own proper persons, and in the presence of the knowledge that constituencies have ears, and that by any blunder of judgment, or meanness of sentiment, the fairest reputation may be stained and the safest prospects blasted. *It is good for these things to be done in the glare of publicity. When legislation consists in the giving of a silent judgment upon the suggestion of committees, or of caucuses which meet and conclude in privacy, lawmaking may easily become a fraud.*

Whew! Now *that* is quite an endorsement for a more transparent government—parliamentary or otherwise. Interestingly, Brandeis, about whom I write next, wouldn't pen his famous line "sunshine is the best disinfectant" until almost ten years *after* Wilson published this article! One wonders if Brandeis subscribed to the *Overland Monthly*? Or possibly the *Atlantic Monthly*, in which, two years later, Wilson would write an article titled "Responsible Government under the Constitution," supporting his argument regarding parliamentary-type government and full transparency.[20]

And again, a year after that, Wilson wrote an article for the *Atlantic Monthly* titled "The Character of Democracy in the United States," in which he speaks to the evolution of our government and our democracy over the preceding hundred years since the adoption of our Constitution. In it he writes about how democracy has spread around the world and makes the strongest argument to date for transparency in government and the flowering of democracy and from which the following quotes are derived:[21]

First, then, for the forces which are bringing in democratic temper and method the world over. It is matter of familiar knowledge what these forces are, but it will be profitable to our thought to pass them once more in review. They are freedom of thought and the diffusion of enlightenment among the people . . . the progress of popular education and the progress of democracy have been inseparable. . . . Yet organized popular education is only one of the quickening influences that have been producing the general enlightenment which is everywhere becoming the promise of general liberty. . . . But through the mighty influences of commerce and the press the world itself has become a school. *The air is alive with the multitudinous voices of information.* Steady trade-winds of intercommunication have sprung up which carry the seeds of education and enlightenment, wheresoever planted, to every quarter of the globe . . . for the small price of learning to read and keeping its ears open. All the world, so far as its news and its stronger thought are concerned, is fast being made every man's neighbor.

And he wrote this over a hundred years before the existence of the Internet and at a time when the transatlantic cable was just beginning to be laid. What prescience to foresee the notion that education of the masses would not only occur in the classroom but also "through the mighty influences of commerce and the press." We take that mass education for granted today with the rise of the citizen journalist and the variety of news platforms on the Internet and social media. Wilson could not have been more accurate as to the opportunities that would inform an ever-growing educated world populace:

These are the forces which have established the drift towards democracy. When all sources of information are accessible to all men alike, when the world's thought and the world's news are scattered broadcast where the poorest may find them . . . the many will no longer receive submissively the thought of a ruling few, but insist upon having opinions of their own. The reaches of public opinion have been infinitely extended; the number of voices that must be heeded in legislation and in executive policy has been infinitely multiplied . . . and *by rising the multitude to take knowledge of the affairs of government directly, prepare the time when the multitude will, so far as possible, take charge of the affairs of government.*

Yes! Transparency, properly executed, engenders civic engagement, such that citizens can indeed "take charge of the affairs of government," which rightfully is the duty and responsibility of citizenship. And the very nature of our democracy dictates its dependency on full transparency and civic engagement, as Wilson further explains:

> Liberty is not something that can be created by a document; neither is it something which, when created, can be laid away in a document, a completed work. It is an organic principle,—a principle of life, renewing and being renewed. Democratic institutions are never done. . . . Such government as ours is a form of conduct, and its only stable foundation is character. . . . Governments such as ours are founded upon discussion, and government by discussion comes as late in political as scientific thought in intellectual development. . . . When practiced, not by small communities, but by wide nations, democracy, far from being a crude form of government, is possible only amongst peoples of the highest and steadiest political habit.

Louis Brandeis (November 13, 1856–October 5, 1941)

Of all our great American thinkers, when it comes to transparency in government, Brandeis is without a doubt the most often quoted, and I include him in my short list first and foremost for that reason. Being a brilliant jurist and writer, and the first Jewish justice of the Supreme Court, only adds to his reputation. However, we have had many great thinkers in our history who never spoke on the topic of transparency in government. What is curious about Brandeis is how *little* he said directly regarding the necessity for transparency. What he did say was almost all related to the need for more transparency in the private sector, from which we derive his famous quote—though one time in particular he addressed the Boston Unitarian Club regarding corruption in city affairs. The meeting and his speech were covered the next day in the *Boston Herald*: "USE SEARCHLIGHT ON THE CITY HALL: Brandeis Says It Is High Time to Delve into Corruption in City Affairs."

For this research I must defer to an intern for the Sunlight Foundation, Andy Berger, because neither the speech nor the *Boston Herald* article is available online or in local research libraries. In Berger's research, he discovered that Brandeis spoke to a few issues related to transparency in government. One area in particular intrigued me, and that was Brandeis's recognition that government alone cannot do it all: "The individual citizen must in some way collect and spread the information."[22] This was meant to be an endorsement of civic groups and third parties or the press becoming involved in the dissemination of information. The press is potentially "the greatest agency of good government"—but only "if the people are sufficiently interested to desire it.[23]

This gets to the heart of what I called the enticement aspect of transparency in my definition. You can have government put all the information in the world out there, but if it's not sufficiently interesting enough for citizens to pay attention, then it's all for naught. As Berger points out and further quotes Brandeis from that speech: "No one, [Brandeis] said, could 'look into the details of our city's administration and be indifferent.' Such information would naturally lead to indignation, and out of that indignation would come a movement for 'remedial action.' Publicity would overcome apathy."[24] To that I would add, no one could possibly look into the details of any city or state administration, much less the federal government, and be indifferent.

This speech came in between the letter that Brandeis wrote to his then fiancée, Alice Goldmark, on February 26, 1891, and the series of articles he wrote for the *Harper's Weekly*, which were to be gathered into book form and published in 1914 under the title *Other People's*

Money and How Bankers Use It. An excerpt from the letter provides us the source from which Brandeis would later utter his famous quote in one of those *Harper's Weekly* articles. In the letter Brandeis is considering a follow-up piece to his famous 1890 article "The Right to Privacy,"[25] for which he collaborated with his law partner and Harvard University friend, Samuel Warren. He laments to his fiancée that he has been putting off writing about his concerns of the "wickedness of people shielding wrongdoers" in this excerpt:

> Lots of things which are worth doing have occurred to me as I sit calmly here. And among others to write an article on "The Duty of Publicity"—a sort of companion piece to the last one that would really interest me more. You know I have talked to you about the wickedness of people shielding wrongdoers & passing them off (or at least allowing them to pass themselves off) as honest men. Some instances of that have presented themselves within a few days which have fired my imagination.
>
> *If the broad light of day could be let in upon men's actions, it would purify them as the sun disinfects.*
>
> You see my idea; I leave you to straighten out and complete that sentence.[26]

Publicity is just another term for transparency that was used instead in nineteenth and earlier twentieth century. In this case, though, he was not thinking about corrupt politicians, but rather those in private industry. Don't forget that this was a time of the burgeoning growth of the robber barons and a long, protracted global depression that lasted through most of the 1880s and early 1890s. However, that doesn't detract from the wider applicability of his famous quote. Certainly this was not a time of honest government, and if any institution should be exposed to the "broad light of day," it was late nineteenth-century governments. But it would be over twenty years before Brandeis would get around to writing about "the wickedness of people."

He did so in 1913 in a series of articles for *Harper's Weekly*, of the one that is of particular interest here is titled "What Publicity Can Do," published on December 20, 1913, and found in the book *Other People's Money and How the Bankers Use It*. It begins quite matter-of-factly, stating the quote derived from that earlier letter to Ms. Goldmark: "Publicity is justly commended as a remedy for social and industrial diseases. Sunlight is said to be the best of disinfectants; electric light the most efficient policeman."[27] Speaking to the findings of the Pujo Committee[28]—a congressional committee appointed in 1912 to investigate the undue influence of Wall Street bankers over the nation's finances—Brandeis held this out as proof that publicity (transparency) does work to expose wrongdoings and corruption:

> The Pujo Committee has, in the disclosure of the facts concerning financial concentration, made a most important contribution toward attainment of the New Freedom. The hostile forces have been located, counted and appraised. That was a necessary first step—and a long one—toward relief.[29]

The findings of the committee led to the creation of the Federal Reserve later that year. However, it also inspired Brandeis to see publicity as a remedy; as he further goes on to say in his article:

> Compel bankers when issuing securities to make public the commissions or profits they are receiving. Let every circular letter, prospectus or advertisement of a bond or stock show clearly what the banker received for his middleman services, and what the bonds and stocks net the issuing corporation. That is knowledge to which both the existing security holder and the prospective purchaser is fairly entitled.[30]

From this quote, though specifically directed at the financial industry, we begin to see the foundation laid for the concept of "the right to know" in the sphere of government, which will unfold a half century later with the passage of a federal Freedom of Information Act.

John Dewey (October 20, 1859–June 1, 1952)

As a well-known American philosopher and educational reformer, Dewey had much to say on the state of our democracy as well as on the value of publicity (transparency) and its handmaiden, communication, in a healthy democracy. One book in particular stands out as it relates to our topic at hand: *The Public and Its Problems*, published in 1927. In a chapter titled "Search for the Great Community," he expounds on the role that publicity and communication play in the attainment of knowledge, which, of course, is a crucial element of civic engagement:

> It has been implied throughout that knowledge is communication as well as understanding. I well remember the saying of a man, uneducated from the standpoint of the schools, in speaking of certain matters: "Sometime they will be found out and not only found out, but they will be known." The schools may suppose that a thing is known when it is found out. My old friend was aware that a thing is fully known only when it is published, shared, socially accessible. Record and communication are indispensable to knowledge. Knowledge cooped up in a private consciousness is a myth, and knowledge of social phenomena is peculiarly dependent upon dissemination, for only by distribution can such knowledge be either obtained or tested.[31]

What is transparency if not "fully known only when it is published, shared, socially accessible"? And doesn't the Internet, and the vast stores of public data being made available online, disseminate knowledge to anyone for the taking, "to be obtained or tested"? Dewey couldn't foresee the technological breakthroughs of the twenty-first century, but he did understand the importance of communication's role in transparency, regardless of the form of that communication:

> Opinions and beliefs concerning the public presuppose effective and organized inquiry. Unless there are methods for detecting the

energies which are at work and tracing them through an intricate network of interactions to their consequences, what passes as public opinion will be 'opinion' in its derogatory sense rather than truly public, no matter how widespread the opinion is. . . . But genuinely public policy cannot be generated unless it be informed by knowledge, and this knowledge does not exist except when there is systematic, thorough, and well-equipped search and record.[32]

As Dewey further elaborates, regarding the equalizing effect of knowledge disseminated, transparency is innately a tool for the masses to achieve parity with those whom we elect to govern us:

Why should the public and its officers, even if the latter are termed statesmen, be wiser and more effective? The prime condition of a democratically organized public is a kind of knowledge and insight which does not yet exist. . . . But some of the conditions which must be fulfilled if it is to exist can be indicated. . . . An obvious requirement is freedom of social inquiry and of distribution of its conclusions. . . . There can be no public without full publicity in respect to all consequences which concern it. Whatever obstructs and restricts publicity, limits and distorts public opinion and checks and distorts thinking on social affairs.[33]

This is an essential inference for Dewey in constructing his profile of what is meant by "the public"—that "without full publicity [transparency] there can be no public." It's also an important premise in that he surmises that without transparency, or if transparency is severely limited, "thinking on social affairs" is distorted. Well, of course! We wouldn't want the facts to get in the way as we shape our opinions, would we? In conclusion to this chapter he comes full circle to what makes for a "Great Community":

We have but touched lightly and in passing upon the conditions which must be fulfilled if the Great Society is to become a Great

Community; a society in which the ever-expanding and intricately ramifying consequences of associated activities shall be known in the full sense of that word, so that an organized, articulate Public comes into being . . . democracy will come into its own, for democracy is a name for a life of free and enriching communion. . . . It will have its consummation when free social inquiry is indissolubly wedded to the art of full and moving communication.[34]

Theodore Roosevelt (October 27, 1858– January 6, 1919)

At about the same time that a young doctoral graduate by the name of Woodrow Wilson was writing essays on transparency for the *Overland Monthly* and the *Atlantic Monthly*, an even younger Theodore Roosevelt was elected to the New York State Assembly (1882). Not long after, the twenty-four-year-old Roosevelt gave a speech to the Liberal Club of Buffalo, New York, on January 26, 1883. In this rather-lengthy address, he spoke on the duties of American citizenship and, even at this early stage of his life, showed the sometimes-brusque and always-candid rhetoric that would come to define him as he immediately cut to the chase at the beginning of his "sermon" on citizenship—paraphrasing to some extent what Pericles had to say about the political life of Athenians in his famous funeral oration, and from which the following quotes are derived:

The people who say that they have not time to attend to politics are simply saying that they are unfit to live in a free community. Their place is under a despotism; or if they are content to do nothing but vote, you can take despotism tempered by an occasional plebiscite.[35]

Civic engagement of course is the result of successfully implementing transparency initiatives in government, motivating citizens to be more than just the suffragist disparaged by Roosevelt in that quote. One cannot speak of transparency in government without speaking to the duties of citizenship, and though Roosevelt didn't speak of transparency in government directly, I include excerpts of his speech here because he makes such a compelling case for the civic engagement so intrinsically dependent upon a more open and transparent government. He makes it very clear that being a good citizen does not often entail—in fact seldom does entail—running for political office, but rather toiling in the good fight to make our communities a better place to live:

> I do wish that more of our good citizens would go into politics, and would do it in the same spirit with which their fathers went into the Federal armies. Begin with the little thing, and do not expect to accomplish anything without an effort. . . . Let him make up his mind to do his duty in politics without regard to holding office at all, and let him know that often the men in this country who have done the best work for our public life have not been the men in office.

That quote is the strongest ever endorsement for transparency in government because in saying this Roosevelt validates the role of the individual citizen in our democracy and it is only through a more open and transparent government, informing such citizens upon whom Roosevelt heaps so much praise, that these citizens can be successful. He then goes on to chastise those who would encourage the type of indifference that is perpetuated by those who would rather complain and belittle rather than take the time to understand the issues and constructively work to make things better:

> It may be taken for granted that the man who is always sneering at our public life and our public men is a thoroughly bad citizen, and that what little influence he wields in the community is wielded for evil. The public speaker or the editorial writer who teaches men of education that their proper attitude toward American politics should be one of dislike or indifference is doing all he can to perpetuate and aggravate the very evils of which he is ostensibly complaining.

Throughout the speech, Roosevelt is speaking on the periphery of transparency, because it is transparency that enables the type of civic action he calls for throughout. And at one point he even points out the dangers of false information being spread and the truth sequestered. It speaks volumes to the point that if we are to promote and implement a more transparent government at all levels, then we must be very diligent in making sure that we get it right—that the information being disseminated is not inaccurate or unreliable in any way and that it is never employed in the service of doing harm, when doing so is a miscarriage of justice:

> But exactly as the public man who commits a crime against the public is one of the worst of criminals, so, close on his heels in the race for iniquitous distinction, comes the man who falsely charges the public servant with outrageous wrongdoing; whether it is done with foul-mouthed and foolish directness in the vulgar and violent party organ, or with sarcasm, innuendo, and the half-truths that are worse than lies, in some professed organ of independence. . . . Criticism should be fearless, but I again reiterate that it should be honest and should be discriminating. When it is sweeping and unintelligent, and directed against good and bad alike, or against the good and bad qualities of any man alike, it is very harmful.

Near the end of the speech he waxes on about what the good citizen must be imbued with, and in doing so, he makes an excellent case for access to the information necessary to inform the good citizen about the workings of government:

> Above all things he must not, merely because he is intelligent, or a college professor well read in political literature, try to discuss our institutions when he has had no practical knowledge of how they are worked. . . . No spirit can be more thoroughly alien to American institutions, than the spirit of the Know-Nothings. In facing the future and in striving, each according to the measure of his individual capacity, to work out the salvation of our land, we should be neither timid pessimists nor foolish optimists.

Transparency in government is simply a very expensive exercise in futility if not a harbinger for driving civic engagement, and Roosevelt certainly makes a case for both. Years later, the work of an American political theorist and author would expound on that relationship of transparency and civic engagement.

Benjamin Barber (August 2, 1939–)

Not everything that has been said about transparency in government is from our past. There are many alive today who are strong and vocal proponents for more transparency. One of those is Benjamin Barber, a renowned American political theorist and author of numerous books, of which one is *Strong Democracy: Participatory Politics for a New Age*.[36] In the second half of this book, Barber makes his case for a democracy that engenders a strong commitment to the responsibilities of citizenship. Throughout he supports his arguments for a more direct democracy and makes his case repeatedly that a representative government such as we have restricts our freedoms. He contests those who say that more public participation in politics produces no greater results in governing by making a solid Jeffersonian argument for better informing the public:

It has in fact become a habit of the shredder defenders of representative democracy to chide participationists and communitarians with the argument that enlarged public participation in politics produces no great results. Once empowered, the masses do little more than push private interests, pursue selfish ambitions, and bargain for personal gain, the liberal critics assert. Such participation is the work of prudent beasts and is often less efficient than the ministrations of representatives who have a better sense of the public's appetites than does the public itself. But such a course in truth merely gives the people all the insignia and none of the tools of citizenship and then convicts them of incompetence. Social scientists and political elites have all too often indulged themselves in this form of hypocrisy. They throw referenda at the people without providing adequate information, full debate, or prudent insulation from money and media pressures and then pillory them for their lack of judgment.[37]

Whether you and I agree with Barber's notion of a strong democracy through more direct participation in governance is not material to the argument he makes for more transparency, which is relevant regardless of the form of democracy we might subscribe to. When we "throw referenda at the people without providing adequate information," we're doing no justice to any form of democratic rule. In further making his case for transparency, Barber clarifies his definition of participation in that it is not "to be understood as random activity by maverick cattle caught up in the same stampede."[38] It is with this interpretation that he marries the definition of transparency found in chapter 1 with the basis for participation—that is the idea that true transparency is effective only when it engenders civic engagement, and from which the following quotes are derived:

> As with so many central political terms, the idea of participation has an intrinsically normative dimension—a dimension that is circumscribed by citizenship. Masses make noise, citizens deliberate; masses behave, citizens act; masses collide and intersect, citizens engage, share and contribute. At the moment when masses start deliberating, acting, sharing, and contributing, they cease to be masses and become citizens. Only then do they "participate."[39]

Transparency is simply an academic exercise if it does not create the action of civic participation, and as defined here by Barber, that participation is intrinsically intertwined with government that is fully transparent such that citizens are informed sufficiently to be able to deliberate and subsequently act upon their deliberations. Finally, in tying together citizenship, participation, and community, Barber comes back to John Dewey and the belief that democracy is the idea of community life itself:

To be a citizen *is* to participate in a certain conscious fashion that presumes awareness of and engagement in activity with others. This consciousness alters attitudes and lends to participation that sense of the *we* I have associated with community. To participate *is* to create a community that governs itself, and to create a self-governing community *is* to participate. Indeed, from the perspective of strong democracy, the two terms *participation* and *community* are aspects of one single mode of social being: citizenship.

It is here that we come full circle with the underlying necessity for transparency in government when we consider that the ability for citizens to participate is dependent upon access to the information that will allow for the kind of deliberation that is requisite in creating a community reflective of democratic principles. The dependencies—transparency, deliberation, participation, citizenship, community—are all far too apparent. The very notion of democracy depends on it.

Beth Simone Noveck (1971–)

Let me first state that I didn't throw in Beth Simone Noveck as a token female among the males listed here. Noveck comes with some extremely high credentials, having led President Barack Obama's Open Government Initiative,[40] whose prime directive is:

> *Publish Government Information Online:* To increase account-ability, promote informed participation by the public, and create economic opportunity, each agency shall take prompt steps to expand access to information by making it available online in open formats. With respect to information, the presumption shall be in favor of openness (to the extent permitted by law and subject to valid privacy, confidentiality, security, or other restrictions).[41]

Noveck's credentials include being a magna cum laude graduate from Harvard and obtaining a PhD from the University of Innsbruck and a JD from Yale. *Foreign Policy* magazine named her one of 2012's

Top 100 Global Thinkers. She served as chief technology officer for the Office of Science and Technology Policy from 2009 to 2011. Upon her departure, spokesman for the department Rick Weiss had this to say about her:

> Beth has been a tireless advocate for opening the federal government to greater collaboration and public participation. . . . She has helped to develop significant advancements in the administration's efforts to utilize technology to break down the barriers between the American public and their government.[42]

Noveck is also author of the book *Wiki Government: How Technology Can Make Government Better, Democracy Stronger, and Citizens More Powerful.* A chapter from that book appears in *Open Government: Collaboration, Transparency, and Participation in Practice*, where she writes extensively about participatory democracy in the twenty-first century. She begins by pointing out the anachronistic assumptions rooted in an earlier age that was based on the notion that even though citizens might express their opinions, they lacked the capability to make informed decisions on complex matters. In fact, Walter Lippmann—an American reporter, political commentator, and author—devoted an entire book to that theory back in 1927, *The Phantom Public*, which inspired John Dewey to write a counterpoint in his book, *The Public and Its Problems*, from which I quoted earlier. Noveck had this to say in retort:

> It turns out that professional status has much less bearing on the quality of information than might be assumed and that professionals—whether in politics or other domains—are notoriously unsuccessful at making accurate predictions. Or as Scott Page, the University of Michigan author of *The Difference* pithily puts it: "Diversity trumps ability"—this is a mathematical truth, not a feel-good mantra.[43]

Of course the difference today from, say, the 1920s is the access that the average citizen has to an incredible store of information, mostly free, over the Internet. Even with limited transparency in government, what we have available trumps even what the *experts* in Lippmann and Dewey's time had available to them! And we've just begun to set free information that has been locked up and impervious to access except for by the most privileged few. Imagine a future where the default status for information is to make it available and only under the most stringent of cases would information be sequestered or redacted. And not only citizens but government as well benefits. Or as Noveck puts it:

> The less those outside the government know about its activities, self-evidently, the greater the need to rely on internal experts. When the public cannot see how decisions are arrived at, it cannot identify problems and criticize mistakes. Accountability declines and so does government effectiveness.[44]

What transparency enables is not just an opportunity for a million sets of eyes to "identify problems and criticize mistakes" but also a global scale of collaborative efforts. Not only do you, the citizen, get to examine information made available, but so do millions of others, and using the tools of social networking and the Internet, you can cooperate with those with whom you would otherwise never have had the opportunity to do so. And, of course, as Noveck points out, this ain't rocket science and it's nothing new:

> Since the early nineteenth century, members of the august Athenaeum Club on Pall Mall in London have penned questions in a shared book, which was left in the club's leather-chaired drawing room for other members—including Dickens and Thackeray—to answer. The book is still there. As Stephen Kosslyn, chair of the Harvard Department of Psychology, explains, working together allows people to utilize many different tools. He says that, because we "simply do not have enough genes to program the brain fully in advance," we must extend our own intelligence with what he terms *social prosthetic systems*. At the most basic level, we need to

pool our diverse knowledge and skills. Even institutions need prosthetic extensions to make themselves smarter and more effective.[45]

Transparency through the backbone of the global brain and
nervous system we call the Internet, enables these *social prosthetic
systems*. And as she goes on to say:

> Deliberative democracy has been the dominant view of par-
> ticipation in contemporary policies theory. At its center is the
> Habermasian[46] notion that the reasoned exchange of discourse by
> diverse individuals representative of the public at large produces
> a more robust political culture and a healthier democracy. . . . It
> has almost become a commonplace that people of diverse view-
> points should talk to one another town-hall-style in public. . . . By
> allowing diverse participants to come together regardless of the
> boundaries of geography and time, the Internet could help over-
> come the hurdle of groupthink—a state in which like-minded
> people fail to consider alternatives adequately and fall prey to
> their own ideology.[47]

All of this is dependent on the fact that information needs to be freed
so that these interactions can occur. Transparency is at the foundation
of this "healthier democracy." But herein lies a distinction between
deliberation and collaboration that Noveck so aptly points out:

> Deliberation focuses on citizens *discussing* their views and opin-
> ions about what the state should and should not do. The ability
> for people to talk across a distance facilitates the public exchange
> of reasoned talk. . . . Collaboration requires breaking down a
> problem into component parts that can be parceled out and assigned
> to members of the public and officials. . . . Deliberation focuses
> on self-expression. Collaboration focuses on participation.[48]

And transparency enables both. However, it is the *action* of
collaboration that is the endgame of transparency. Again, without the

participation of civic engagement described so pertinently by Barber and expounded on by Noveck, transparency in government would be a wasted endeavor—and an expensive one at that! In the end, Noveck makes her case for a collaborative democracy, which, of course, is based on the platform of more transparent governments, and she justifies the costs of delivering that transparency:

> Collaboration offers a huge potential payoff in the form of more effective government. Effective government, in turn, translates into better decision making and more active problem solving, which could spur growth in society and the economy.[49]

⌘⌘⌘

WHAT THEY SAID . . .

Patrick Henry

"They may carry on the most wicked and pernicious of schemes under the dark veil of secrecy. The liberties of a people never were, nor ever will be, secure, when the transactions of their rulers may be concealed from them. . . . I appeal to this Convention if it would not be better for America to take off the veil of secrecy. *Look at us—hear our transactions.*"

Thomas Jefferson

"The way to prevent these irregular interpositions of the people is to give them full information of their affairs thro' the channel of the public papers, and to contrive that those papers should penetrate the whole mass of the people. . . . If once they become inattentive to the public affairs, you and I, and Congress, and Assemblies, judges and governors shall all become wolves."

James Madison

"A popular Government, without popular information, or the means of acquiring it, is but a Prologue to a Farce or a Tragedy; or, perhaps both. Knowledge will forever govern ignorance: And a people who mean to be their own Governors, must arm themselves with the power which knowledge gives. . . . As the people are the only legitimate fountain of power, and it is from them that the constitutional charter, under which the several branches of government hold their power, is derived."

Woodrow Wilson

"Light is the only thing that can sweeten our political atmosphere. . . . It is good for these things to be done in the glare of publicity. When legislation consists in the giving of a silent judgment upon the suggestion of committees, or of caucuses which meet and conclude in privacy, lawmaking may easily become a fraud . . . by rising the multitude to take knowledge of the affairs of government directly, prepare the time when the multitude will, so far as possible, take charge of the affairs of government."

Louis Brandeis

"If the broad light of day could be let in upon men's actions, it would purify them as the sun disinfects. . . . Publicity is justly commended as a remedy for social and industrial diseases. Sunlight is said to be the best of disinfectants; electric light the most efficient policeman."

John Dewey

"There can be no public without full publicity in respect to all consequences which concern it. Whatever obstructs and restricts publicity, limits and distorts public opinion and checks and distorts thinking on social affairs. . . . [Democracy] will have its consummation when free social inquiry is indissolubly wedded to the art of full and moving communication."

Theodore Roosevelt

"The people who say that they have not time to attend to politics are simply saying that they are unfit to live in a free community. . . . Let him make up his mind to do his duty in politics without regard to holding office at all, and let him know that often the men in this country who have done the best work for our public life have not been the men in office . . . above all things he must not, merely because he is intelligent, or a college professor well read in political literature, try to discuss our institutions when he has had no practical knowledge of how they are worked. . . . No spirit can be more thoroughly alien to American institutions, than the spirit of the Know-Nothings."

Benjamin Barber

"Social scientists and political elites have all too often indulged themselves in this form of hypocrisy. They throw referenda at the people without providing adequate information, full debate, or prudent insulation from money and media pressures and then pillory them for their lack of judgment. . . . Masses make noise, citizens deliberate; masses behave, citizens act; masses collide and intersect, citizens engage, share and contribute. . . . The two terms *participation* and *community* are aspects of one single mode of social being: citizenship."

Beth Simone Noveck

"The less those outside the government know about its activities, self-evidently, the greater the need to rely on internal experts. When the public cannot see how decisions are arrived at, it cannot identify problems and criticize mistakes. Accountability declines and so does government effectiveness."

Chapter 3

How Transparency Arouses
Civic Engagement

*"It is clear by now that 1968 will go down as the
year the new politics of the next decade or more
began. . . . And therefore this is the year when the
old politics must be a thing of the past. But if this
is true—and I profoundly believe that it is—then
there is no more important question than what the
new politics is. What are its components, and what
does it mean to the future of the country? The most
obvious element of the new politics is the politics of
citizen participation, of personal involvement."*

—US Senator Robert Kennedy,
speech at a San Francisco press gathering,
May 21, 1968

In my book *Piss 'Em All Off: And Other Practices of the Effective
Citizen*, I write that we have access to more information than any
generation in history, but that the real challenge before us today is to
sort the chaff from the wheat—the brilliance from the bullshit: "The
measure of a well-informed citizen is the ability to do just that, and in
the end it's reflected in the brilliance of thoughtful deliberation rather
than the bullshit of impulsive ranting and raving."[1] In a speech to
the Boston Unitarian Club in April 1903, Louis Brandeis said that no
one could look into the details of Boston's city administration and be
indifferent—that such information would naturally lead to indigna-

tion, and that out of that indignation would come a movement for remedial action. My lament is whether we're actually *capable* of such brilliance, because in the end, transparency is simply an academic exercise if it doesn't engender the "indignation" Brandeis spoke of in his speech. I like to call that indignation "civic enragement," but you get the point.

However, to fully appreciate the impact of transparency in governments we have to connect the dots between transparency and civic engagement, if we are to fulfill what Robert Kennedy referred to as "the politics of citizen participation, of personal involvement."[2] If indeed a new politics is to finally unfold nearly fifty years after that speech, then it will come on the back of an open and transparent government. Yet if transparency is to engender the civic participation our democracy requires, then we need to understand that there are two aspects to making this connection work. First we have to get it right and then we have to get it done. Getting transparency "right" is crucial if there is any hope that opening up government will lead to citizens taking responsibility for government—local and federal—in ways that keep citizens attentive to the affairs of those whom we elect and those who run our government agencies.

Getting transparency "done," on the other hand, means that we convert that knowledge, gained through a more transparent government, into action. The important question here is, what will we do with this newly found information? Sit on our butts and weep or engage in political action? How we respond will determine whether we're capable of fostering our democracy in the twenty-first century or whether we'll all sit back and allow government to run rampant and be hijacked by the select few special interests who have seized control of it.

GET IT RIGHT

When he was speaking to that Boston Unitarian Club back in 1903, I'm sure Louis Brandeis understood both that this civic "enragement" can lead to civic engagement and that often enough that enragement is fueled by the details derived out of a more transparent and open government. However, in reflecting back on his optimism, one needs to temper it with a large dose of pragmatism. In fact, we can derive some of that pragmatic advice from Brandeis himself. In that same month in a statement to a reporter in the *Boston Record*, he was quoted as saying: "What I have desired to do is to make the people of Boston realize that the most important office, and the one which all of us can and should fill, is that of private citizen. The duties of the office of private citizen cannot under a republican form of government be neglected without serious injury to the public."[3] With that "office" of citizenship comes the responsibility to *get it right* before passing judgment, but that ability comes with some hurdles.

The High Hurdles

When Walter Lippmann, a distinguished political columnist and author, wrote *The Phantom Public* back in 1927, he felt strongly that the "public" was no longer able to fully understand the complex issues facing it in a modern world. Lippmann assumed that our future would be in the hands of experts because the public lacked the intelligence and the time to pass judgment on the issues:

> Democracy, therefore, has never developed an education for the public. It has merely given it a smattering of the kind of knowledge which the responsible man requires. It has, in fact, aimed not at making good citizens but at making a mass of amateur executives.[4]

Today, with the tools of communication available to us, we have not only the resources to understand even complex issues but also an obligation to do so. That obligation, as Brandeis exhorted some years before Lippmann wrote his book, is to fulfill the office of citizenship. Should we not, others—so-called experts—will seize control of the dialogue, the solutions, and, eventually, our democracy. And let's not underestimate how complex the issues have become since the days of Brandeis and Lippmann. How does one get one's arms around, much less one's head around, the challenge of understanding issues that seemingly defy the ability of the average person to grasp?

Enter John Dewey, perhaps best known for his writings on education and psychology, but who also wrote extensively on democracy and provided a response to Lippmann in his book *The Public and Its Problems*. Written just after Lippmann's book, Dewey saw education and communication as the solutions to the public's dilemma of an ever-expanding scope and complexity of issues and an ever-lessening amount of time to gain the knowledge to properly understand these issues:

> We have the physical tools of communication as never before. . . . Without such communication the public will remain shadowy and formless, seeking spasmodically for itself, but seizing and holding its shadow rather than its substance. . . . Communication can alone create a great community.[5]

Neither of them could have predicted the explosion of technology in the latter half of the twentieth century that would allow every citizen to become well informed. Nor could either have predicted that the education level of the average American would increase three- to fivefold since Lippmann and Dewey wrote their books. However, even with the expanding education of our populace, barely more than one in four citizens has a college degree.[6] So it's good that we don't have to be *that* well-educated to be well-informed. In fact, much information today is often recast from its raw data to a more understandable format, and the raw data is often available for those who wish to dig deeper.

Yet numerous hurdles to transparency exist on both sides— government and citizens. So, let's first look at the governmental hurdles that stand in the way of achieving full transparency and then we'll examine the hurdles on the citizen side of the equation. And certainly I would be remiss in presenting these hurdles without offering up at least some semblance of solutions in clearing these hurdles. I do this at the risk of seeming to be somewhat intransigent, but rather these solutions should be looked at as catalysts for further recommendations on correcting the shortcomings of transparency in government. No one person has all the answers—certainly not I—and no one answer is the proverbial silver bullet. So allow me to offer these solutions as a departure point for further deliberation on addressing these problems.

The Government High Hurdles

Enter the world of government of any size and you will more than likely encounter a culture shock if you were expecting anything approximating twenty-first-century efficiencies. I'll let Gary Bass, founder and executive director of OMB Watch, now the Center for Effective Government,[7] and Sean Moulton, who has served OMB Watch since 2002, explain the first three of the high hurdles of government when it comes to transparency—policy, technology, and culture.

Bass and Moulton wrote about the governmental hurdles back in 2009; since then, some progress has been made, but not a lot. Also, they speak specifically to the federal government, and there's been progress there because of President Obama's transparency directive when he came into office. Unfortunately, for the most part, that approach hasn't yet trickled down to local governments still mired in their twentieth-century cultures. I'll speak to each hurdle, regarding Bass and Moulton's recommendations and adding my own comments.

Policy Hurdle

"Current laws and policies on public access are inadequate for today's 24-hour-per-day, seven-day-per-week Internet-enabled world.

Too often, the burden falls on the public to request information, and there are far too many loopholes that allow agencies to withhold information. These policies need radical overhaul."[8]

Clearing the Policy Hurdle

As I've implied in my definition of *transparency*, and affirmed by our authors here, our elected representatives and civil servants have a duty to enable transparency, therefore "We need to institute an affirmative obligation on federal agencies to disclose information, what we will call the Right to Know (RTK). Instead of government responding to requests for information, it must *initiate* the disclosure. . . . Anytime the government proceeds to collect information, it should presume that the information will be disclosed in a timely and searchable manner."[9]

Additionally, governments should be required to file a FOIE (Freedom of Information Exception) for information that they deem too sensitive to release, specifying a time frame as to when the data *will* be released. Furthermore, all state and local inspector generals should be charged with the responsibility of challenging FOIEs if sufficient cause is brought by citizens.

Technology Hurdle

"The federal government's use of interactive technology is largely grounded in the twentieth century. The use of Web 2.0 technology and thinking is only starting to make its way into government via the Obama administration, but the hardware, software, and capacity of public employees need significant upgrades."[10]

Clearing the Technology Hurdle

To this end, we have a long way to go on the federal, state, and local levels. With few exceptions, government entities in general have not embraced the technology of the twenty-first century. As such, and recommend by Bass and Moulton, "Building the government's capacity to construct, modify, and maintain websites should be a priority . . . [including changes to] make databases more publicly accessible . . . allow commercial search engines to index all government information . . . provide the open programming interfaces to data that allow the public to build upon government information . . . [and ensure that] the information that is provided must . . . be authoritative and authentic."[11]

To that I would add the requirement that information be released in a timely and efficient manner. Almost all data today comes in a digital form or is transcribed digitally, which means it's available the moment it's captured. The only delay should be if the government entity files an FOIE, otherwise the information should be available immediately in its raw-data form.

Moreover, I would add that we need to require government agencies to convert that information into a useable format that provides a level of comprehensibility that doesn't require a law degree to decipher. Also, governments should be mandated to retain the information in perpetuity. Given the dirt-cheap costs of data storage today, there's no reason to destroy anything or take it off line.

Cultural Hurdle

"Even with the best technology and policies, an underlying culture of secrecy pervades government. No civil servant gets rewarded for improving public access, but they do get attention if they give out information that could be misused. Disincentives for openness are built into the way agencies and [the] whole of government operate. Civil servants need to be given the freedom to disclose information, and they need to be rewarded for doing so."[12]

Clearing the Cultural Hurdle

Addressing the issue of secrecy should conjure up Patrick Henry's admonition that our liberties will never be secure if the transactions of our rulers are hidden from us. Considering that these transactions often need to be exorcised from inside the bowels of government, incentives as recommended by Bass and Moulton need to be created:

> Agencies approach public access in an elegantly insouciant manner; with few incentives to advocate or promote openness . . . several ideas for encouraging civil servants to make transparency an important part of what they do [are]
>
> 1. create new review processes that . . . [include] making public access and other government openness issues par of formal government employee reviews. . . .
> 2. create . . . a sort of transparency report card . . . establish mechanisms for the public to provide better feedback. . . .
> 3. grant awards . . . for the best agency efforts on transparency. . . .
> 4. agency and staff . . . should be required to attend periodic training on Right to Know issues.[13]

To that I would add that we need a national "Bill of Rights to Know" that identifies the role of citizens and our rights to information. In addition, we need to give serious consideration to encouraging *all* states to allow for referred state statutes—legislative measures put before citizens on a state ballot to be voted upon. Currently fewer than half of the states allow for this. To wait for legislators to change their own culture, or to make even just some of the measures mentioned above, would be like waiting for Godot. Citizens in all fifty states need the leverage to impose these changes upon government unwilling to do so for itself.

But wait, there are more government hurdles to be cleared if we're to achieve full transparency . . .

FOIA Hurdle

Nothing comes for free, not even our democracy—and certainly not transparency in government. Let's consider just one aspect of providing full transparency, and that would be the federal Freedom of Information Act (FOIA). Enacted on July 4, 1966, and taking effect one year later, FOIA provides that any person has a right, enforceable in court, to obtain access to federal-agency records, except to the extent that such records (or portions of them) are protected from public disclosure by one of nine exemptions or by one of three special law-enforcement-record exclusions.

This act has been amended five times since its passage in 1966, with the last being in 2002, in the wake of the 9/11 attacks, to limit the ability of foreign agents to request records from US intelligence agencies.[14] Since 1966, every state in the union has followed suit and enacted FOIAs in their respective legislatures. It is by far the most recognizable aspect of transparency and probably the most costly. By the mid-1990s, the executive branch of the federal government alone was processing more than half a million requests at a cost of about $100 million.[15]

In 1996, the e-FOIA amendment was passed, which brought FOIA into the "information and electronic age by clarifying that it applies to records maintained in electronic format."[16] As an immediate result of this passage, the General Accounting Office (GAO) reported that the twenty-five agencies surveyed had logged 119 percent more requests in FY 1999 than in 1998. In a later report, the GAO found that agency requests increased by 71 percent from 2002 to 2004.[17] Though numbers aren't available for all fifty states as an aggregate, you can extrapolate from just the GAO numbers for the federal government to realize that it ain't cheap to provide government information when requested through the FOIA process.

Clearing the FOIA Hurdle

The various Freedom of Information Acts across all fifty states and in the federal government are anachronistic vestiges of twentieth-century politics. They should be rewritten with the premise that all government data belongs to the public and should be released at the time of capture. Underlying the concept of FOIA is that you can have the information if you ask for it and you know exactly what it is that you're looking for, as opposed to simply making the information available as it's created for anyone to access without jumping through hoops to get to it. Additionally this puts a burden on government to respond to requests, which, of course, entails enormous overhead costs as highlighted above.

Almost every aspect of government activities (reports, meeting minutes, e-mails, etc.) is digitized today, meaning that it's available at the time that it happens. To make it available to citizens would simply entail uploading it to a designated repository on the Internet—no transcribing necessary. As I've said, it's not rocket science, though some politicians would have you think so. Submitting a FOIA is a convoluted and often-obscure process, but even where governments have streamlined the system, citizens often get caught up in lengthy delay processes and rejections. And sadly, when information is successfully obtained, it often lacks in comprehensibility. If we continue down the path of FOIA as the primary method for citizens to acquire information about what our governments are doing, we're going to further discourage the type of civic engagement that depends upon access to the knowledge of how our government operates.

As for the exceptions to immediate release, such as ongoing investigations or public safety and security, that doesn't mean the information is to be sequestered for an indeterminate period of time. Rather, at the time that government data is withheld from public access, there needs to be a time frame associated with when the data will be released. And it doesn't need to be an exact date, though in some cases that will be the norm. A criminal investigation, for example, might entail a lengthy process that has no determinate end. Simply stating that the information will be made available upon completion of an investigation or some defined period after the end of the investigation would be sufficient, but leaving it open-ended without any time constraints is not an acceptable strategy.

Cost Hurdle

Of course FOIA is just one aspect of providing for a more open and transparent government—albeit a major one—and just one cost center for governments in providing that data. As the tools of technology have advanced and we've moved from the era of Web 2.0 (social media and online collaboration) to the era of Web 3.0 (allowing data to be shared across applications and readable by other machines—the "semantic" web) and soon Web 4.0 (the ultra-intelligent agent that recognizes you), it is crucial that government continues to move with those tools of technology.[18] But technology and the people to implement and maintain those tools aren't cheap.

Without getting too geek on you, let's just recognize that the Internet is the great equalizer and the fulcrum from which widespread transparency in government is being enabled. That said, how government utilizes this communication juggernaut will determine whether or not we get it right. Here's the thing. At one time, most people had no idea as to what went on inside government. It was simply a black box and we knew little of how it operated. We are on the threshold today, at the dawn of the twenty-first century, of finally realizing the expectations of our founders, to be the deliberative and educated citizens who have their hands on the wheels of democracy and the republic that we've created.

So, whatever the cost, it is the price of doing transparency right. Yet the greater the cost, the more resistance there will be to provisioning the funds necessary to create a culture of transparency in government. And when you come right down to it, the "art" of transparency—making it accessible, comprehensible, and enticing—

is not really a core competency in government. And even where governments have created departments specifically to address delivering more transparency, we're then stuck with a one-solution approach and the hopes that they'll get it right. Don't hold your breath!

Clearing the Cost Hurdle

The state of the art of US government transparency today leaves much to be desired. There are two primary paths to providing the information in a way that is accessible, comprehensible, and enticing—the three requirements of true transparency. Either the government entity can manipulate the raw data or a third party can do so, in which case the government entity is simply what is called an information platform. Neither approach is exclusive, and both can be incorporated as a way to provide the public with information.

When government is the provider of information, it falls upon agencies often mired in a cultural bureaucracy not only to get the data out in a timely manner, but also to manipulate it so that citizens understand clearly what it is they're getting. Good luck with that one. Though large, urban municipalities have more resources to get it done right, that doesn't mean they will. And what of all the rest of the smaller municipalities that make up the majority of urban, suburban, ex-urban, and small-town America? We want more transparency, but at what cost?

The solution lies in government playing the role of information platform and allowing the third-party actors to deliver on transparency. As you'll see later in this chapter, it's being done already and in a very successful and cost-effective way. However, there's a catch. When government abdicates its role of sole provider of transparency and allows others to become the providers, who answers to the citizens? In many cases, the third-party actors are nonprofit organizations that are staffed by volunteers. Certainly they aren't equipped to become a service center for citizens to inquire about the information being presented—nor should they!

However, if we approach this from a purely project-management perspective, government, like any organization that hires private contractors to do work that is not the organization's core competency, would retain control of what is being delivered. To use as an example a project mentioned later in the chapter, if citizens have a question regarding who voted on a particular piece of legislation in Chicago's City Council, they wouldn't call the group that produced the application (Councilmatic) but rather would contact someone in the city department that provides the data and "contracted" the group responsible for delivering the information.

This brings up another issue, and that's the open-source problem associated with government acting as platform provider but allowing anyone to have access to it. That's all well and good, but those third-party actors accessing the data and producing these transparency applications based on the data, such as the Councilmatic example, should be accredited in some way. That is, there needs to be a certification process whereby the city basically gives a "stamp of approval" to third-party applications, thus recognizing that the application is out there and that it accurately represents the data being provided by the city. With such a process, the city department then keeps "ownership" of the application in that it has approved of it and is familiar with it and thus can address citizen concerns and questions related to information obtained through the application. It is also a cost effective way for these transparency applications to be built without government incurring the development costs.

The ACT Hurdle

You might think that putting out accurate, complete, and timely information is a cornerstone of delivering transparency in government, and you'd be right. Unfortunately, that's not always what we get when it comes to government, and, to be fair, it's not always what we get from the media or other institutions on which we depend for information. However, in the end, government, more than any other institution, should be held to a higher standard when it comes to the ACT (Accuracy, Completeness, and Timeliness) of transparency.

Accuracy of information should be a slam dunk, right? Hardly. Expecting perfection, when it comes to ensuring the accuracy of information, is far too much to ask for, as long as humans touch the data. Yet, as we all know, even computers "make mistakes" because in the end computers are nothing more than the sum of the software that runs them, which in turn is designed and installed by humans. Information, government-produced or otherwise, is always subject to error, and those errors can cause havoc when it comes to the expectation that transparency will enable citizens to respond rationally to the information they're given.

Completeness of information is an absolute necessity that, if lacking, can distort the data that governments release (at the very least) and confound those using it (at the very worst), by withholding from the public information that would have contributed to a more accurate analysis. For example, in Chicago recently there was considerable concern about the validity of the arguments given by the mayor and his staff that installing speed cameras throughout the city around schools and parks would improve safety and reduce pedestrian accidents. Reference was made to studies supporting their statements, but the studies themselves could not be produced. The absence of the corroborating studies left citizens and journalists questioning whether the city was accurate in its statements or was simply trying to create cover for a program that was seen to be more of a revenue generator than a safety program.

Timeliness, more than any other factor, has been a bane of government-produced information. Regardless of the fact that almost all data is digitized today, government information has always seemed to lag behind, sometimes far behind, its relevance. That has begun to change because of the digitization of data, but there needs to be a marker with all government data that inform those capturing the data as to its relevance.

Clearing the ACT Hurdle

Accuracy of information can be addressed by ensuring that all data elements are identified by the person who created the information and the person who submitted the information, much like those tags and stickers you find at times on products where the person on the assembly line has attached his name to the widget that he produced. In doing so, if the data just doesn't seem to pass the reasonableness test, or even if there's simply a question regarding the information, then we have a person to contact who can verify it. This data "marker" needs to include the full name of the individual(s) who created and submitted the information and contact information (e-mail, phone, address, social media, etc.).

Completeness of information can be a rather subjective assessment. In the example above, the underlying studies supporting the report released by the city were missing. If it were an online news story, reference to the studies would have been hyperlinked. So too should all references that are integral to the release of government information—whether those references are internal or external to the government entity. Likewise, in this particular example, as with many reports released by governments, there are meetings that transpire wherein decisions are made. All correspondence (minutes, e-mails, etc.) related to those staff meetings should also be included as hyperlinks in reports. Finally, there are going to be instances where government simply fails to associate relevant information peripheral or even crucial to data that is released—whether intentionally or not—but is identified by the public as missing. This can be resolved by our solution for accuracy in that the individual(s) responsible for creating and submitting the data will be associated with the information and therefore available to contact to resolve any questions.

Timeliness of information very often depends on the size of the government entity and the efficiencies of departments, and thus can vary considerably in how often the information is made available. To rectify this, short of legislation requiring timely reporting, which would probably be impossible to comply with and enforce, all information should come with a time marker. Such a marker would be attached to every data element produced by governments indicating the exact time (year:day:hour:minute) that the information was created and was released to the public. In addition, markers indicating the frequency of the data should also be included—this could be a scheduled frequency such as with biannual or weekly reports, or it could be random such as with staff meeting minutes, but the marker should indicate either way.

The Citizen High Hurdles

As extensive are the issues facing us in government getting transparency right, there are hurdles on the citizen side of transparency as well. Though it is government's responsibility to facilitate an open and transparent government, it is our responsibility as citizens to get it right as well. And by *citizens* I also mean those doing our bidding for us, such as journalists (traditional and otherwise) and various civic and community organizations.

A number of hurdles to transparency exist on the citizen side that are seldom addressed because the focus today has been on opening up government—pointing the finger at politicians and government bureaucrats as the impediments. Not that they don't deserve a good deal of the blame, but even if by some miracle we woke up tomorrow morning and we had all the "sunshine in the world" directed on government, there would still be problems. I remind you of my paraphrasing of Colonel Jessup's lines from *A Few Good Men*: "Transparency? You want transparency? You can't handle transparency!"

Can we handle the truth that full transparency in government will deliver? Do we really want to know how the "sausage" of government is made? Are we up for the task of being deliberative, thoughtful citizens rather than knee-jerk reactionaries who act from the gut rather than from the head? These are serious concerns we have to address as we plow ahead at a frantic pace to deliver on the promise of transparent governments. And those citizen hurdles are much more disconcerting and can be more difficult to resolve than those that government faces. Let's examine them.

The Attention Hurdle

Forget the "Millennials" or "Gen X–ers" or the "Re-Boomers." The appropriate label for the generations inheriting our twenty-first-century democracy is the "one-click" generation! Back in 2008, Nicholas Carr wrote an article for the *Atlantic Monthly* titled "Is Google Making Us Stupid?" in which he said:

> When the Net absorbs a medium, that medium is re-created in the Net's image. It injects the medium's content with hyperlinks, blinking ads, and other digital gewgaws, and it surrounds the content with the content of all the other media it has absorbed. A new e-mail message, for instance, may announce its arrival as we're glancing over the latest headlines at a newspaper's site. The result is to scatter our attention and diffuse our concentration.[19]

A few years later, as a follow-up to the *Atlantic* article, Carr would write his seminal work titled: *The Shallows: What the Internet Is Doing to Our Brains* as an in-depth analysis of how human thought has been shaped through the centuries by "tools of the mind," such as the Internet. Coincidentally, also in 2008, a study commissioned by Lloyds TSB Insurance found that "the average attention span is now just five minutes and seven seconds, compared to more than 12 minutes a decade ago."[20]

This is a real concern, since getting transparency right from the citizen's point of view means having the capacity to absorb more than just a few minutes' or few hyperlinks' worth of information in order to get a complete picture. Short of that, we're just hopping from one sound bite of data to another and regardless of how thorough and insightful is the information being released by government, we thus risk reacting to it in an overly simplistic and emotionally charged manner.

Transparency ends right here, at the doorstep of the average citizen, if we're not capable of giving it the attention necessary to sort through the myriad facts, figures, and sometimes-lengthy discourse that we're apt to be presented with. The tendency today is take the "SparkNotes" approach to issues by simply taking someone else's summarized digest as the facts because that takes far less time than going to the source.

At the end of the first chapter, I mentioned that Lawrence Lessig, professor of law and director of the Edmond J. Safra Center for Ethics at Harvard Law School, wrote an article for the *New Republic* titled "Against Transparency: The Perils of Openness in Government." In it, he points out the hazards that come with the lack of an appropriate attention span: "To understand something—an essay, an argument, a proof of innocence—requires a certain amount of attention. But on many issues, the average, or even rational, amount of attention given to understand many of these correlations, and their defamatory implications, is almost always less than the amount of time required."[21]

Clearing the Attention Hurdle

To be clear, the solution does not necessarily lie in trying to change the effects of the most recent tools of the mind. However, it would be in the best interests of civic engagement if governments begin with the premise that citizens have a severely truncated span of attention. With that in mind, information can be presented in a way that accommodates the "one-click" generation, not to mention the less than stellar appreciation for detail of an older generation raised on the "boob tube."

How to do this? Well, governments can begin by always providing short abstracts of the information being presented, which shouldn't take the average reader more than a minute to glance over. Included with the abstract should be an index of the underlying details with total pages indicated so that the reader is prepared for what is to follow. And what should follow is a layered approach to presenting the information so that someone can strip away pieces of the details much like peeling back an onion—going ever deeper the more time one has and the more interest in getting all the facts.

Now this doesn't preclude third-party actors from taking the raw data and creating an interface to the government's data that is interesting and easily digestible by the average, attention-challenged citizen. As mentioned above, this is certainly more cost effective for government in being the platform and not focusing on the delivery vehicle for the information. However, government still has the responsibility to present some of the information. For example, when the City of Chicago puts its annual budget online, it does so in a rather perfunctory way with a series of pdf documents. (Just a note of caution here if you're going to visit this website. The city is notorious for constantly moving documents around. I had to change the URL three times in the process of writing this book. *That* is *not* transparency!)[22] Someone with a reasonable attention span could sort through these. For everyone else, a more summarized, piecemeal approach can be more effective. Maybe you just want to go in-depth looking at expenditures for the Streets and Sanitation Department. You're not going to get that transparent view on the city's website. However, a third-party actor could utilize the city's data portal to capture the budget's raw data and create applications that would allow citizens to do just that.[23] If we're going to get transparency right, we have to find ways to accommodate the fact that citizens are just not going to spend a great deal of time doing their research—particularly when that next exciting hyperlink is a click away!

The Bias Hurdle

Lessig points out another one of the hurdles to transparency in that *New Republic* article I quoted earlier when he says: "Responses to information are inseparable from their interests, desires, resources, cognitive capacities, and social contexts. Owing to these and other factors, people may ignore information, or misunderstand it, or misuse it. Whether and how new information is used to further public objectives depends upon its incorporation into complex chains of comprehension, action, and response."[24]

Let's face it. No one—absolutely no one—is without bias. Everyone has unique interests and desires and, as Lessig so aptly puts it, will respond to information presented to them according to those interests and desires. Human nature being what it is, we have to take this into consideration when putting information into the hands of a diverse and at times somewhat-volatile citizenry. Information often is like art—interpreted in the mind of the beholder. Of course, the implication here is that both governments and citizens have an obligation to recognize this.

Often much is said about the need for government to make more information available but little is said about how that information should be presented. Given the wide diversity of biases and opinions, that shortsightedness can present an enormous problem in how information is perceived by the public. This gets right to the heart of one of our required elements of transparency—comprehensibility.

If, for example, the City of Chicago releases a trove of data on its red-light/speed-camera program, along with corroborating studies, there should be recognition of the fact that citizens will take one or another side of the issue. Some will examine the data from the perspective of supporting the programs from a bias toward pedestrian and vehicular safety. Others will take the information with a huge dose of skepticism that safety is incidental to the real purpose for these programs—revenue.

To ignore the obvious biases is to foment further divisiveness among the public rather than encourage citizens to find common ground. On the other hand, there's an almost-flippant attitude among citizens in how one uses the information presented by governments in their effort to promote more transparency, and instead seek to find nuggets of data out of context to support one's biased opinion. The solution to this bias issue is, therefore, really twofold.

Clearing the Bias Hurdle

Although I've addressed the government hurdles earlier in this chapter, we must recognize that in addressing this citizen-side hurdle to transparency there is a government component to resolving this problem. By ignoring the biases of the public that will consume the information governments present, these same governments only further contribute to those biases. As I've said before, there's no eliminating the human tendency for biases, but that doesn't absolve governments from considering biases when making information available, as a matter of comprehensibility. So what to do?

Governments need to incorporate what I call a "Cronkite Compass." As anchor of the *CBS Evening News* broadcast from 1962 through 1981, Walter Cronkite was one of the most trusted voices in media. As he said in an 1973 interview with the *Christian Science Monitor*, "I'm a news presenter, a news broadcaster, an anchorman, a managing editor—not a commentator or analyst . . . I feel no compulsion to be a pundit."[25] When governments publish information, there must be an overriding consideration given to ensuring that the information is presented as objectively as possible. When it comes to transparency, governments must be "news presenters" and not commentators or analysts.

So, when data on a city's budget is released, for instance, it's imperative that it doesn't come packaged with political overtures such as promoting awards for disclosure, hyping surpluses over deficits, and so on. This is what press releases are for and when those are presented as a result of transparency efforts, they should come with some standard words of caution that the information contained within is an opinion of the individual and can contain hyperbole and exaggerations.

Where the Cronkite Compass comes in is in rating transparency, not from the perspective of quantity or thoroughness of information presented, but rather from the perspective of objectivity. I won't get into the details of the metrics for doing so, but instead leave that task to those more experienced in the art of journalism to make that call. And speaking of journalists' standards, I would suggest that the panel assembled to create and apply the Cronkite Compass would consist of those in the field of journalism—academic and practicing. Then, when citizens access government data, there can at least be a level of expectation that the information is as objective and free of bias as possible and the compass rating will provide an indicator as to what degree of objectivity it is.

As I said at the beginning, this is a two-fold solution and citizens must be responsible enough to recognize their own biases. In my book, *Piss 'Em All Off*, I dedicate an entire chapter to the importance of being an informed citizen and how one becomes so informed. Among the numerous recommendations I posit, one specifically addresses how to deal with the demons of biases and prejudices—one's own and those of others: "It's rare that a story is written without any slant whatsoever, so the lesson here is not to seek only unbiased stories but rather to become aware of the writer's bias and accept it for what it is and how it influences the facts."[26] Here I was speaking of the media, but it applies just as well to governments and the information they release. Sans a Cronkite Compass, citizens need to be aware of when the information they are being given is more fiction than fact, more amplification than authenticity.

But what to do about our own biases? Again, from my previous book:

> If there's any tactic that can help us intelligently inform our own opinions, it is to be well-read. American psychologist Abraham Maslow said, 'I remember seeing an elaborate and complicated automatic washing machine for automobiles that did a beautiful job of washing them. But it could do only that, and everything else that got into its clutches was treated as if it were an automobile to be washed. I suppose it is tempting, if the only tool you have is a hammer, to treat everything as if it were a nail.' If you only get your news from sources that fit your own personal biases, then

the world begins to look just like your own personal biases. We all need to expose ourselves to facts and opinions that don't fit neatly into our narrow view of reality.[27]

This strategy is not meant to eliminate biases but more so to both mitigate and recognize them.

The "More Is Less" Hurdle

We've all been faced with this hurdle one time or another—that nagging, incessant need to dig deeper and deeper into the facts to get to the "real" story. Well, I have a button I keep above my desk that says the following: "How far do you open your mind before your brains fall out?" Sorting fact from fiction and recognizing biases is all well and good, but only like with everything else in life: in moderation. You peel an onion back too far, and all you're left with is tears—and no onion. And when it comes to government information, we can easily become overwhelmed. Governments, local and federal, collect vast sums of data, and sifting through all that data looking for tidbits of truth is probably best left to the investigative journalists of the Fourth Estate, both traditional and emerging media, but also to third-party actors that create transparency applications from the information.

In either case, realize that more information can actually lead to less understanding and in many cases to complete confusion. This is not to say that the data shouldn't be made available and that everything that's feasible to release regarding government data and processes should indeed be released. However, that doesn't mean that we need spend all of our waking hours sifting through it. Nothing will discourage the average citizen and hog-tie transparency more than saddling the public with the notion that in the minutiae of too many facts and details lay the information we need to understand how and why our governments do what they do.

Clearing the "More Is Less" Hurdle

As I discussed earlier, there are advantages to having third-party actors take government data and create transparency applications that present that data in a more digestible and palatable format for the public. In doing so, these actors also do a service for citizens in digging down deep into the bowels of governments to pull out information that otherwise would be far too difficult for the average citizen to find time to do. In this scenario the transparency application provides an interface to all this data and distills it down to a more comprehensible view, whether summarized in text/in visualizations such as graphs or charts. What we as citizens need to become familiar and comfortable with are the various third-party actors, a few of which I'll examine later in this chapter, and the legitimacy and credibility of their products.

There will always be among us citizens who are gluttons for punishment—those who love to sort through all the chaff to find the few strands of wheat. And that's okay. But for most, we want our information distilled and free of excessive details and fluff, knowing that if want to peel away at that onion the specifics are there for us to dig into. Governments can be those distillers of data or just be the platform from which the Fourth Estate and third-party actors can strip away the information and package it such that citizens everywhere can benefit from the transparency they provide. In the end, though, more can indeed be less if it discourages civic engagement, which, after all, is the ultimate goal of transparency in government.

The Distrust Hurdle

The picture painted by the latest study of trust in government is pretty grim, particularly when you consider the long-term trend from the Eisenhower administration to today—and that trend is dramatically negative. The majority of Americans today feel that their government is a threat to their personal rights and freedoms, and, incredibly, less than 20 percent of Americans say that they trust our federal government to do what is right always or most of the time. That last figure is down from 73 percent during the 1950s and has been declining ever since![28] Additionally, a survey conducted in January 2013 by the research firm Public Policy Polling found that the approval rating for Congress ranked "lower than cockroaches, Genghis Khan and Nickelback."[29] None of this bodes well for establishing any sort of credibility when it comes to transparency efforts by governments. Not long ago we experienced a tragic set of circumstances in Syria where hundreds of people apparently died from the use of chemical weapons and President Obama authorized the use of missiles to rain down on select targets in Syria (with congressional approval), because "evidence" showed that the Syrian government was responsible for the use of these weapons, in violation of international treaties.

At that time, dozens of reports to the contrary had been surfacing in both the traditional media as well as in emerging media, such as Truthout.org, a 501c3 organization dedicated to providing independent news and commentary, on a daily basis.[30] Conflicting stories like this do little to further the public's trust in government and fosters the kind of confusion that in the end undermines transparency efforts by governments. Some mistakes are certainly acceptable. After all, we're human, and whether as citizens or as government employees, we're all liable to err. However, when patterns of lies and innuendo emerge over an extended period of time, the public loses trust in all governments.

When trust in government is lost, it doesn't matter how transparent governments try to be, the information that they provide will be suspect, and questions as to the validity of the data, be it a municipal budget or the supposed facts behind supporting an attack on Syria, will arise every time. The result is that governments get immersed in an onslaught of challenges to the authenticity of its data. Not only does this put government in a position of defending itself, but that defense uses resources that otherwise could be devoted to promoting and implementing even greater transparency. Add to that the peripheral damage caused by mistrust of the people we elect: as is reflected in the most recent Public Policy Polling survey, we find a barren landscape in which transparency in government can't even be created, much less thrive and engender civic engagement.

Clearing the Distrust Hurdle

At first blush, this hurdle seems insurmountable. Every day we seem to be face-to-face with yet another story about government distortions or secrets that cuts to the heart of our thirst for more open, honest, and transparent government—and that's just our federal government. I'm sure each of you has a story about your local governments. Here in Chicago we're never at a loss for stories of political intrigue and corruption, which create a barrier between citizens and government so thick it's hard to imagine how transparency of any kind can flourish—but it does.

We have, I suspect, certain resilience when it comes to good government, and despite all the sordid goings-on we encounter from day to day, there seems to be a tacit understanding that *most* people inside government are no different than you and I are. They too are citizens, and therefore they too *mostly* want what is best—an open, honest, and transparent government. Remember what I said a little earlier about changing the culture inside government? Given the right motivations and environment to work in, good government can arise out of the ashes of a Machiavellian political school of thought. But I do emphasize the word *most*, because there are those in government who would love to see things stay as they are.

Yet I believe that from the inside out, we can change government. Government employees, reflecting a new generation of citizens tired of the old politics, can affect change from within by replacing those resistant to change. Whistleblowers, emboldened by more and more legislation to protect them, can bring down those who would otherwise corrupt and debase our political system. And the Fourth Estate, expanded to include citizen journalists and emerging media, can and does shine many lights upon government, which in turn forces those in government to get it right and do right by "We the People."

What I sincerely believe we are seeing today is a trough in government mistrust. I believe we're on the cusp of a blossoming of transparency in government based on a heightened level of civic engagement never before seen in American history. Why? One word. *Communication*! It has so changed the dynamics of the government-citizen relationship that there's no going back. In a somewhat-perverse way, all this distrust, deceit, and distortion of the truth will, in the end, foster a new era of politics—and it's already happening in local governments all across the country.

In the next chapter, we look at best practices from all corners of the United States. The picture presented in those examples show that glass walls are going up where concrete bunkers existed. And those glass walls are going up because those old, impervious barriers to the truth can't withstand the onslaught of so many of us infused with the desire to make government responsive to its citizens who, when all is said and done, give it its legitimacy. The solutions to distrust of government aren't immediate, but they are inevitable as a new generation of citizens, tired of the old way of doing politics, takes control by running for office without the shackles of political parties and enters government jobs with the expectations of *not* doing business as usual. Change is coming, and the old guard will either get out of the way or be run over.

The "Gotcha" Hurdle

When I teach my hands-on course on transparency in government and we examine Chicago's city government, one thing I make clear to my students up front is that they are not doing "gotcha" research. In other words, they're not in it to make some individual or some department look bad. Finding faults is okay as long as it's done constructively with an eye toward how to improve the way government is done and to increase transparency and civic engagement.

At times, I find that public sentiment reflects that gotcha mentality and in particular in the social media, where the sport of hurling invectives and vulgar tirades is commonplace. The rise in popularity of fact-checking websites, though useful in validating the sometimes-questionable statements our political leaders tend to make, have morphed into a competitive battle where one site tries to outdo the other in the now-popular pastime of disputing anything a politician or a government employee may say for the public record. This only fuels further distrust of government and makes it that much more difficult to get transparency right.

Clearing the "Gotcha" Hurdle

There's a balance to be struck here, but at this point it seems we've buried the needle on the side of contentious and combative discourse. It's time we let up on the gas pedal and apply the brakes of civility and decency. For some, firing those proverbial shots across the bow might be entertaining at first, but unabated they lead to a breakdown in the fabric of our democracy. We need to keep in mind that a healthy democracy is tolerant of opinions and invectives on the extremes, but it resolves its problems in the middle where civic decorum and courtesy are practiced.

The sooner we learn that lesson in citizenship, the sooner we'll get beyond fault finding and get around to more constructive criticism. But here's another thing to keep in mind, and this is very important. When elected officials or government employees believe that their every move will be criticized and held up to ridicule, they will be much less cooperative when it comes to opening up government. Think of how you would feel if everything you do at work was not only under constant scrutiny but also subject for public scorn. You'd be a lot less forthcoming about disclosing what you do, and I wouldn't blame you.

Back in 2012, Chicago mayor Rahm Emanuel, just a few months into office, made himself available for that interview with a *Chicago*

Tribune reporter mentioned in chapter 1. Making the entire interview available to the public wasn't the interesting part. What the mayor said about his staff was, and it reflects this "circle the wagons" mentality that exists in government. In response to one question about being more open about sharing what goes on in the mayor's staff meetings, Mayor Emanuel said this: "If meetings that I have—I have a senior staff meeting every day. That's probably the most important meeting of the day, but that's not going to be something you're going to get because I can't have them say, Hey we have this issue here this is what we're doing, OK, and I've got to be able to have that conversation."[31]

In other words, the mayor, who ran on a platform of more transparency in government, is telling this reporter that his staff members won't be forthcoming, open, and honest with him if they believe their every word is going to be made public. That's interesting for two reasons. First, it says something about the mentality of people in government who feel that what they say in an honest and open conversation might be interpreted as being less than ethical or borderline corrupt. To which you might ask, What have they to hide? Well, in Chicago, often plenty! The second point of interest is that the mayor doesn't believe he'll get open and honest opinions from those of his staff, whom he hired, simply because their conversations might become public record. What does that say about his management style and the people he's hired? Again, plenty!

Finally, this example, however distasteful when held up to the light of public scrutiny, shows both the air of contempt that some in government may have for those in public who would second-guess their actions and the air of fear that some may have that no matter what they say or do, some person or some organization will find reason to ridicule and debase their every action. This isn't to say that some of our politicians don't need a verbal lashing from time to time, and we shouldn't be reticent in giving one when the occasion demands it. However, we as citizens looking in from the outside need to be more sensitive to how we level our criticisms and whenever possible do so in a constructive rather than demeaning way. Otherwise, we're going to get a lot less transparency in government than we hoped for.

GET IT DONE

So what follows successful deployment of transparency in government? Once we get it right, or even partially right, what should we expect? After all, this is not an academic exercise. The measure of success is the degree of civic engagement that arises from any particular transparency efforts. But what exactly is civic engagement? How will we recognize it if we come across it? Well, one way is to read my first book *Piss 'Em All Off: And Other Practices of the Effective Citizen*, and I certainly encourage you to do that to get the full picture of what it means to be an engaged citizen. However, short of that, I'll give you here an excerpt of how to distinguish the acts of the Good Samaritan from the responsibilities and actions that come with being an effective citizen:

> Though working [at] a soup kitchen, volunteering in a senior-citizen center, or mentoring at-risk children are all laudable community activities that should be encouraged . . . what differentiates these pursuits from those that serve to enhance the responsibilities of citizenship and therefore strengthen our democracy is the fine line of political action. . . . We could make a case for any socially motivated activity as practicing effective citizenship, but the point is to differentiate acts of citizenship from simply being a caring neighbor.[32]

To be specific to the cause and effect of transparency, that civic engagement is reflected in one's participation in or organizing around any endeavor that *proactively informs* our elected representatives and government employees or that *responds to* the actions of elected representatives and government employees. Again, from my previous book:

In all cases, these activities eventually involve interaction between citizens and elected officials or government agencies. The idea behind taking action as an engaged citizen in a spirited and inter-active democracy is the simple premise that an individual can make a difference—in government, in the people we elect, in the quality of life.[33]

As you might suspect, transparency is the necessary *fuel* for motivating the types of citizens who become engaged in such a way as to affect the quality of government and the democracy it fosters. And to propagate that civic engagement, we need transparent governments so that citizens have the information necessary to *participate* and *organize*. To complete this circle, you can say that information culled from governments that have become more transparent is the *fuel* that triggers the individual behaviors conducive to good citizenship—civic engagement.

If ever there was a time in human history that one person so inclined to make a difference could be successful in doing so, it is today. The quote often attributed to Margaret Mead "Never doubt that a small group of thoughtful, committed citizens can change the world. . . . Indeed, it is the only thing that ever has" has never rung truer than today. Transparency, enabled by the tools of twenty-first-century communication, is empowering the citizen activist in us all and giving new life to an old term. . . .

The Third Estate

Recently there's been some noise around the term *Fifth Estate*. The definition for this new term seems to be one that incorporates bloggers or simply highly networked individuals as the members of this new estate. One definition, and the most encompassing, posits membership in this estate as anyone not in the first four! When Edmund Burke coined the phrase of the Fourth Estate back in eighteenth century, he gave that moniker to the press—the assumption being that the First

Estate was the House of Lords Spiritual (the bishops), the Second Estate was the House of Lords Temporal (those who inherited title), and the Third Estate was the commoners (yeah, the common folk).

By classical definition, the Fifth Estate is somewhat redundant because it includes those already defined as commoners and to some degree the Fourth Estate, but with special skills—online journalistic and communication skills. There's even a magazine titled *Fifth Estate* that has been around since the 1960s and dedicated to the anarchist commoner in us all.[34] And, as of this writing, a movie called *The Fifth Estate* is being released ; it is about the rise and fall of Julian Assange and WikiLeaks.[35]

Personally, I think the use of the term *Fifth Estate* is overkill and unnecessary for our purposes, and I bring this up because I believe that the future of our democracy lies in the hands of the very people that a Fifth Estate would seem to exclude—commoners—at the very moment in history when we're seeing a rise to power of the Third Estate.

Having the technical chops capable of taking government data-sets released in the name of transparency and manipulating that data to make it accessible, comprehensible, and enticing to all of us citizens is indeed a special skill. But that doesn't preclude the fact that people doing this are by definition what has always been considered the Third Estate. And those journalists still practicing as card-carrying members of the Fourth Estate have learned to use the tools of technology, such as blogs, if only to survive. Certainly that doesn't make the traditional journalist a member of the Fifth Estate.

There have been variations in defining these estates of the realm over the centuries, though we seem to have locked into the definitions in play after Edmund Burke's Fourth Estate comment in the British Parliament in 1787. I'll stick with those definitions here and make my case for the Third Estate by paraphrasing Burke's comment in that I find the Third Estate today "more important far than they all."[36] And simply because those who fit into this classic appellation have a variety of online skills from simply being able to navigate the Internet to posting on Facebook to creating applications from datasets doesn't mean we should put them into different categories. In fact, there is power in those numbers, and it would behoove us to see ourselves belonging to one common civic class—the Third Estate.

Taking It to the Streets

Ever-increasing transparency in government will provide the data to create applications that literally put what you want to know, when you want to know it, and how you want know it, at your fingertips—and that's a good thing. One of the basic tenets of successful transparency efforts is to deliver information that citizens find useful at the time that they need it and in a format that fits their lifestyle. For example, the City of Los Angeles, like other major cities' governments, has an intensive restaurant-inspection program and, again like many large-city administrations today, posts the results of those inspections online. Of course, that does you little good when you're walking into a restaurant, so following the tenet of the "what-when-how" utility, Los Angeles requires restaurants to post a standard sign in their windows reflecting the results of their last inspection, which includes in large print the letter grade for that inspection—what you need to know, when you need to know it, and how you would want it delivered.

In Chicago, my hometown, this approach to letting the Third Estate deliver on transparency has not only gotten off the ground, but it has taken wings! And not a moment too soon, given that the city is close to broke at this time. So we may not see a lot of creative stuff coming out of Chicago's Department of Innovation and Technology when budgets are being cut to the bone and further![37] But the truth is that the department doesn't need to do it all in-house, and that's a good thing, because the city saves a lot of money by not having to do all the creative work. Third Estate groups like Open City have partnered with the department to deliver on what the city has preferred to let others do, simply by accessing city data. In this way the city and the Department of Innovation and Technology specifically, act as the "platform" for transparency—providing the raw data and letting others do the work.[38]

Open City is a group of volunteers who create apps with open data to improve transparency and citizen understanding of our government. They host the Open Gov Hack Night[39] in Chicago, a weekly event for developers, designers, data scientists, policy experts, and curious citizens to learn about and work with open data released by governments. One of the creative applications they've developed is Councilmatic,[40] which tells citizens what legislation the Chicago City Council has been passing. Citizens can search, browse, subscribe, and comment on everything the City Council has done since January 1, 2010. You think that doesn't motivate citizens to find out what their alderman is up to? Talk about "shining a light on government"! Margaret Mead would be proud of this "small group of thoughtful, committed citizens" who are indeed changing the world—well, at least the world in Chicago.

And that's only one group. There are individuals and groups sprouting up all over the city, because the directive coming from the mayor is to be more transparent by releasing more and more of the city's information in common datasets through what the city calls its Data Portal.[41] So anyone in the Third Estate with a reasonable capacity for working with the current technology toolbox can spin off all sorts of cool applications that open up the black box of city data and turn it out to citizens by making it much more accessible, much more comprehensible, and much more enticing.

But wait. There's more! You don't have to be a geek to be effective in using this data. An organization that's been around Chicago for many years, well before the transparency breakout, is the Center for Neighborhood Technology (CNT)—"a creative think-and-do tank that combines rigorous research with effective solutions [and] works across disciplines and issues, including transportation and community development, energy, water, and climate change."[42]

Now CNT is directing its attention to "tackling neighborhood challenges with technology . . . [where] community activists and app developers will work together to build tools to make our neighbor-hoods more sustainable, both environmentally and economically."[43] So someone like me, who's a technology challenged community activist, can collaborate with those who are activist challenged but technically astute. Talk about the power of the Third Estate in releasing a wave of transparency in government!

Then you have people like Tom Tresser, founder and "Tool-Builder-in-Chief" of a nonprofit organization called Civic Lab, which is "Dedicated to building, distributing and encouraging the use of new tools for civic engagement and government accountability."[44] Civic Lab intends "to create a space and a place for activists to come together to share, educate and build tools for civic engagement." Open to anyone with a passion for democracy, Civic Lab just recently scored a huge victory in creating an application from the City of Chicago's tax increment financing data that exposed how the hundreds of mil-lions of dollars of city property tax funds were being redirected to billionaire projects throughout the city. Tresser and his group broke the data down in a way the city was reticent to do—by ward—and took the data "to the streets," delivering presentations in wards throughout the city to make the public aware of this "shadow budget" that's been siphoning off funds from the city's schools and parks to give to devel-opers to mainly build commercial and retail projects throughout the city. Transparency spawning civic enragement, indeed!

I could go on and on with similar projects from likeminded groups of citizens—the Third Estate—who are seizing the initiative to use the information gleaned from a still-nascent endeavor in transparency to change the politics of a city that for 175 years has been mired in a "wink and nod" culture of corruption, nepotism, patronage, and back-room deals. And hold onto your seats—it's working! If ever there was an experiment to show how democracy can be snatched from the jaws of a political machine through even a modicum of transparency in government, it is in progress here inside the belly of the beast we Chicagoans simply call "The Machine."

But transparency knows no borders, and certainly there are many such efforts as those here in Chicago prevalent around the country, and one of those efforts worth mentioning here is Code for America (CFA). As its website tells us, CFA "aims to improve the relationships between citizens and government."[45] Its purpose is to "help governments restructure to create low-risk settings for innovation, engage citizens to create better services, and support ongoing competition in the govtech marketplace." This group has taken it beyond the streets and out to the states—all fifty of them.

Through its Peer Network, CFA recognizes that "local governments are changing. Forward-thinking public servants across the country are leveraging technology to innovate the way our cities work—and it's accelerated by the exchange of ideas, solutions, best practices, and even software code between likeminded leaders."[46] CFA's Peer Network "is a professional learning network for local government innovators who share the common goal of taking innovation in their city to the next level. Through the Peer Network, Code for America connects local governments around the country to facilitate peer learning, collaborative problem solving, and the spread of innovation best practices between cities."

Finally, there's the Code for America Brigade. Large metropolises like Chicago not only have their own technology departments but also have a seemingly unending source of citizens looking to develop applications from city data. But most cities aren't the size of Chicago, so wouldn't it be great if these medium-sized cities could tap into what the big cities are doing? Well they can! That's what CFA Brigade is all about. Its online directions run as follows, so that any engaged citizen can make use of CFA's apps:

> All across the country civic hackers are building amazing, open source applications. You can leverage their efforts to redeploy those applications in your city. We've selected a few of the most easily reused and promising apps to feature on the Brigade, and added step-by-step instructions on how to get them running. Pick an app below and then recruit your friends to make it happen.[47]

Code for America alone should give all of us a sense of optimism about how transparency in government is enabling the kind of civic engagement that will transform American democracy in the twenty-first century. Yet there are examples of how transparency is changing the political landscape in every corner of the country, from large cities to small towns, as we'll see shortly. Remember, none of this would have been possible a mere decade ago. With the tools of communication now available, the fulfillment of even a modicum of transparency in governments across the land, and a populace ready for a new way to do politics, we have a perfect storm of democracy brewing in cities and states everywhere—a storm with few "clouds" and lots of "sunshine." Groups like Code for America are where the transformative and creative ideas for our twenty-first-century democracy are being born. As citizens, but particularly as political leaders, we'd best pay attention or be left in the dustheap of anachronistic twentieth-century ideas that no longer work.

Not a Bunch of Onlookers

We were all reminded recently of the fiftieth anniversary of the Reverend Martin Luther King Jr.'s "I Have a Dream" speech in Washington, DC, in 1963. As incredible a speech as that was, it was not the only speech given at the March on Washington. A little-known rabbi who happened to be a close friend of King's, Dr. Joachim Prinz, also spoke. His speech was much shorter but nevertheless was poignant and relevant then as well as for us today. As I continue to remind you, transparency in government is simply an academic exercise if in the end it doesn't foster the actions of civic engagement. Prinz's words delivered that day spoke to that, especially in this excerpt:

> America must not become a nation of onlookers. America must not remain silent. Not merely black America, but all of America. It must speak up and act, from the President down to the humblest of us, and not for the sake of the Negro, not for the sake of the

black community but for the sake of the image, the idea and the aspiration of America itself. [48]

The Third Estate was then, and still is today, composed of the commoners; and the organizations of change I mentioned above are important components of that Third Estate. However, individual citizens are really the bedrock of our democracy and the agents of change that will transform it here in the twenty-first century, once we use the information that transparency reveals. The roots of that civic engagement go as far back in civilization to at least the Golden Age of Athens and the words left us from Pericles's funeral oration to the brave soldiers who died in defense of their city:

> Here each individual is interested not only in his own affairs but in the affairs of the state as well; even those who are mostly occupied with their own business are extremely well-informed on general politics—this is a peculiarity of ours; we do not say that a man who takes no interest in politics is a man who minds his own business; we say that he has no business here at all. [49]

Athenians took their democracy seriously, but then again it was a direct democracy, so transparency was "built-in" and one couldn't avoid what one was inevitably immersed in—social issues and their solutions. And deliberating on those issues and finding solutions were not frivolous exercises in excoriating and denouncing the opinions of others. As Pericles would go on to say:

> We Athenians, in our own persons, take our decisions on policy or submit them to proper discussions: for we do not think that there is an incompatibility between words and deeds; the worst thing is to rush into action before the consequences have been properly debated. And this is another point where we differ from other people. [50]

Commoners we may be, but we are citizen commoners, and the fruits of transparency give us the tools and the information we need to be the "individual [who] is interested not only in his own affairs but in the affairs of the state as well" and to "submit [decisions on policy] to proper discussions" and not "to rush into action before the consequences have been properly debated."

If you need further motivation to get off your butts and avoid being the onlooker disparaged by Prinz, there is the admonishment of John Stuart Mill, delivered in the inaugural address to the University of St. Andrews in 1867:

> Let not any one pacify his conscience by the delusion that he can do no harm if he takes no part, and forms no opinion. Bad men need nothing more to compass their ends, than that good men should look on and do nothing. He is not a good man who, without a protest, allows wrong to be committed in his name, and with the means which he helps to supply, because he will not trouble himself to use his mind on the subject.[51]

Ultimately our civic engagement, inspired by the proliferation of transparency, leads not only to solutions to social problems and an improvement in the efficiencies of government but also to a mitigation of corruption and the winnowing of those we elect who would cause harm; as Mill so aptly put it, "bad men need nothing more to compass their ends, than that good men should look on and do nothing." There simply is no excuse for some level of participation by everyone since each of us has at least one hot button when it comes to social issues and at least one idea, if not more, on how to solve the social problems facing us today and how to make lives better for everyone. And properly motivated, by information acquired through heightened transparency in government, each of us can pursue our roles as citizen activists in a variety of ways.

Face-to-Face

If you like the reality of face-to-face "combat," you can join or start a neighborhood block club, become a member in your local community council, or even participate in a planning committee on topics like zoning or urban development, to name just a few options. The opportunities are numerous, whether you live in a small town or a large city. And if you'd like some civic education to further motivate you, that's available too.

You simply have to see what is offered in your local community. For example, here in Chicago, Civic Lab offers classes on a variety of topics that will make you a more effective citizen.[52] Also, the Better Government Association here in Chicago offers classes on both how to be a citizen "watchdog" and how to submit a Freedom of Information form and learn more about the FOIA.[53] Do a little Internet browsing, and I'm sure you'll find similar civic classes in your own town. And remember to check your community colleges that are also getting into the market of civic education.

Every Which Way from Sunday

Of course, if you prefer fulfilling your civic role virtually, there are plenty of options for the "closet citizen" as well—so many that you could easily overcommit yourself. This is probably a good time to address that topic of commitment. Transparency in government is already proving to be a source for an extraordinary amount of data and that will only grow exponentially in the future. And all that transparency provides more than ample motivation to get involved— but how involved should you get? After all, there's only so much one can do, given all the other responsibilities in life tugging for our attention.

Considering all the other diversions and responsibilities of day-to-day life, it would be difficult, at best, to commit to pursuing one or two of the hot-button issues that keep you up at night. I've seen numerous cases over the years where some have tried to stretch themselves too thin by taking on numerous issues and not succeeded in addressing any one of them. It's easy to get pulled into far more than you should, so my caveat is: Don't! Find the most important issue for you and give it all of your attention, without sacrificing everything else in your life and succumbing to the temptation to take on other social issues. You'll be happier that you focused on one topic or goal, and you can always move on to other issues after a period of time and success, and you'll be a better citizen for it.

I know I won't make friends among community organizations by telling you to parse your time, but I've participated in enough organizations over the years to know that no one asks whether you have other commitments, and no one really cares. Expectations are that you're an adult and you should know your capabilities. As the famous American philosopher Detective Harry Callahan once said, a man's got to know his limitations. I'll add that women do, too. Don't expect to be turned away because you give your time to numerous organizations, and be prepared to be asked to give your full attention to each—having been caught more than once in the web of oversubscribing my own time, I know well that this is likely to happen.

Virtually There

If all that transparency leads you down the virtual road, realize that social media can indeed be a magnet for your attention, so proceed with caution in going down this path. However, for those who don't have the desire for or are uncomfortable with the face-to-face interactions mentioned above, the Internet allows you to interact and form relationships that will more than satisfy your civic-minded pursuits, without ever coming in contact with a living, breathing, carbon-based life-form. Let's look at a few examples.

One that I use all the time with my students when discussing how one person can have an impact are success stories from Change.org. When it comes to politics, you can't reach higher up than the president of the United States. In August 2012, "after more than 135,000 people signed Jerry Ensminger's campaign on Change.org, President [Barack] Obama [had] signed [into law] the Honoring America's Veterans and Caring for Camp Lejeune Families Act."[54] The law "provides health coverage for the military families who drank water contaminated with cancer-causing chemicals over a thirty-year period at the Camp Lejeune military base in North Carolina."

On the other end of the political spectrum, local initiatives can work just as well. Just recently, citizens here in the Rogers Park community in Chicago organized to oppose the construction of a 250-car parking garage that was being considered by a billionaire investor and was supported by the local alderman.[55] Among other tactics, one citizen used Change.org to gather signatures opposing the garage. Over four hundred signatures had been gathered, and this petition was printed and taken to a city zoning committee meeting as evidence of community opposition.

In the past, the only way to get signatures would be to stand on street corners and try to get people to stop so that you could explain to them what you wanted them to sign. Sites like Change.org have changed those dynamics. Granted, there are thousands of petitions on Change.org that are far less effective than the two mentioned above have been, but the point is that platforms such as this give any one of us an opportunity to be the next Jerry Ensminger, and all without leaving the comfort of home! Of course, being civically engaged alone can be, well, lonely. It doesn't have to be, though, if you can reach out to others of similar political sentiment.

Facebook, with its one billion users around the planet, certainly provides more than ample opportunity to connect with those with likeminded interests. One example, on a local level, is a group that has organized here in our community around the crime-fighting tactic called "positive loitering."[56] Its mission statement says that it is "a volunteer association of residents who believe that our collective appearance as a group of non-confrontational 'loiterers' will give a visible and powerful message that the community belongs to all of us.

Part of our non-verbal message is that we are a diverse, organized, and alert body of neighbors who act as the eyes and ears for one another and for our police enforcement services."

You can search through groups that your Facebook friends belong to, and if you are well networked in Facebook, you'll see plenty of groups to join with interests as varied as your friends are. Or you can expand your search for groups by simply going into your web browser and searching for keywords of civic interest. For instance, if you're particularly interested in environmental issues, just plug "environmental organizations" into your search bar, and you'll be more than overwhelmed with the possibilities. Of course, I'd recommend that you narrow down your search to specific issues, such as "environmental organizations Great Lakes," if you live in the Great Lakes region. One of the results from that search would be the Great Lakes Watershed Organization, and if your interest is in water quality, this would be a great place to start.[57] And from there, you'll see even more organizations focused on the water quality of the Great Lakes, any one of which you can join to make a difference right there from your couch.

The Goldilocks Factor

In the end, it is truly up to each of us to manage our level of engagement as citizens. You can see how easy it is to get caught up in the "fire-hose" flow of information from more and more government transparency. There's only so much time in a day, and we have to be careful that being a good citizen doesn't trump everything else in our lives. On the other hand, it's also important to recognize that no matter how busy we may be, we have an obligation as citizens to pay at least of modicum of attention to what our government does and to be ready to respond through our actions when we believe it's necessary for our voices to be heard. Not too much, not too little, but just right.

So why in the world should you care? I mean, really! Just bury yourself in your apartment or house or log cabin in the woods and tune it all out—government corruption, government inefficiencies, government failure to act in the best interest of its citizens. Life will go on. The grocery store, the movie theater, the mall up the road will all be there for you. Open for business just like always. A fixation on fashion, music, movies, and sports might be good for the soul, but it also sucks attention like a black hole sucks light. And with so little attention left over for everything else, I'm afraid that what could lie ahead for our democracy in twenty-first-century America won't be very pretty. So it should give us great pause and concern as to whether we care enough to continue the grand experiment begun over two hundred years ago by a ragtag bunch of youthful patriots. What secures any democracy—the practice of citizenship—depends on every one of us.

Our government is a representative form, and representative democracy works best when you have an engaged electorate—yet its very nature encourages us to become *dis*engaged! We elect surrogates to pass legislation and run our government, and trust they'll do a good job. While we don't need to make a habit of attending city council meetings or reading the minutes, delegating authority does lull us into complacency. Perhaps in a perfect republic we could doze off without a care, but we don't have a perfect republic and we're not perfect human beings—so we can't disengage or our democracy fails.

Sadly, we are disengaging, our democracy is failing, and we are responsible—not self-serving politicians, not all the money that pours into campaigns, not inept and crooked government employees. From time to time, those we've entrusted will inevitably fail us, and so we leave accountability to laws passed and enforcement applied. Yet laws can be circumvented, and enforcement can never keep pace with the circumventing. In the words of Alexis de Tocqueville, the great historian of early eighteenth-century America, "The health of a democratic society may be measured by the quality of functions performed by private citizens."[58]

We *can* take control of our government and squeeze out a lot of the corruption and the waste, but only if we make the conscious decision to do so—to allocate our time wisely, to take advantage of all the information that more and more transparency is making available, and to act on that information. Transparency in government, if we get it right and then get it done, can be the catalyst for a flourishing of American democracy in the twenty-first century. It will usher in, as Robert Kennedy envisioned nearly fifty years ago, a new politics of citizen participation and of personal involvement, but it must be a lifelong commitment to good citizenship, not just a passing interest—a lifelong commitment that requires a personal dedication of time to whatever aspect of civic responsibility inspires us.

Many of us have been victims of irrational exuberance from time to time, when we've been caught up in the thrill of supporting a particular issue or individual—that passing interest. What we have to do is rationally convert that exuberance into an enduring commitment of our personal time. Let me give you an example that anyone who has run a marathon can personally relate to and that everyone else can easily understand.

When people ask me if it's hard training to run that kind of distance, I always have a stock response: the mileage is easy; the time commitment is the tough part. The running alone can consume upward of ten hours a week over a six-month period. A fifteen-to-twenty-mile practice run can take three hours, and that's if you keep a pretty decent pace. And, toward the end, you're doing one of those nearly every week. Add in the recovery time of long showers, icing muscles, stretching, strength training, and naps . . . well, you get the picture. A twenty-hour-a-week commitment is fairly typical.

Most of us have our marathons that we commit to doing, and we find time for them because we perceive that the benefits to our well-being outweigh the costs. For those who don't have their own "marathon," it may be that they just haven't yet discovered what they're passionate about—what gets them excited enough to commit personal time and effort. But we all have the capacity to become passionate about something. All we have to do is find out what that is. However, time is the limiting factor that we have to allocate, and we don't have an unlimited amount to commit—not too much, not too little. Yet, what we sometimes lose sight of is that our democracy creates the environment in which we can make these personal decisions about life, liberty, and the pursuit of happiness. How's that for a benefit? Democracy requires nurturing, and unless we leave time in our lives to do our part, it will not survive; and without democracy, we risk losing everything important to us.

Think about It: The Promise of Transparency

Robert Kennedy was riding a wave of popularity, particularly among the youth of this country, when he addressed the San Francisco press gathering back in May 1968. In the midst of a highly unpopular war in Vietnam, foisted upon our country by his own Democratic political party, Kennedy spoke eloquently on the role of this country on the global stage. Yet the crux of this long and extended speech was really about the adoption of what he called the "new politics" and, likewise, the shedding of the old. Had he not been shot down by an assassin's bullets a few weeks later, he almost certainly would have been elected, and the "politics of citizen participation" would probably have become the foundation of his tenure in office and ultimately his legacy. Instead, Richard Nixon was elected, and the country became hopelessly divided and embattled. But today we have the opportunity to resurrect that dream of a new politics, and the key in doing so is a civic awakening to the responsibilities of citizenship galvanized by nearly unfettered access to information that results from ever-increasing government transparency.

Reflecting back on his speech, you can see that it has all the elements of what transparency can deliver today if we only connect the dots from an open, transparent government to the civic engagement of personal involvement envisioned by Kennedy. This is the real promise of transparency—the new politics of civic engagement and the transformation to a much stronger democracy based on a broad commitment to the obligations of citizenship.

In his seminal book *Strong Democracy: Participatory Politics for a New Age*, Benjamin Barber, America's preeminent political theorist, made an excellent case for civic engagement by associating democracy with "a civic culture nearer to the themes of participation, citizenship, and political activity that are democracy's central virtues . . . [and to] do so . . . without falling victim to either the nostalgia for ancient, small-scale republics that has made so many communitarian theories seem irrelevant to modern life or to the taste for monolithic collectivism that can turn large-scale direct democracy into plebiscitary tyranny."[59] Barber wrote that in 1980, far before the communication revolution that would enable the transparency that would drive the civic engagement that he envisioned for a healthy, strong democracy.

To quote Barber again, "democratic politics has become something we watch rather than something we do."[60] Democracy can take the blows of some dropping out, but most of us have to nurture it. I see our democracy like a symphony, and we're the orchestra—a very large orchestra, indeed—so a few not showing up won't make much of a difference. As more and more drop out, however, the music begins to become discordant. I can't tell you when, but eventually the symphony is simply dissonant. The music dies. At some point, so too does our democracy.

Part 2

Measuring Transparency in Government

Chapter 4

An Analysis of Best Practices in Measuring Transparency

"The times that tried men's souls are over—and the greatest and completest revolution the world ever knew, gloriously and happily accomplished."
—Thomas Paine, *The American Crisis*, no. 13

One way to get a sense of how far we've come in opening up government in just the past few years is to examine some best practices in transparency that have been implemented across the country. These examples also serve to demonstrate the imaginative and often-ingenious applications that can come to fruition when citizens are emboldened with the opportunities of civic engagement that results from governments giving these citizens access to information that had been previously been unavailable to them or difficult to obtain. I like to think of these as so many gardens of democracy where the seeds of citizenship are being sown, and from that comes a flowering of ideas to make government more efficient, reduce corruption, and inspire a new cadre of individuals to run for office as an expression of public service rather than as an opportunity to cash in on a career.

As we look at these "gardens," it's important to keep in mind that civic engagement is not a stepping-stone to direct democracy. Our republic, crafted so wisely by our founders, was designed to be a representative democracy that they envisioned would scale well for a country of such vast geographic boundaries. The motivation toward a more transparent government is not to second-guess or replace our elected representatives with a plebiscite-oriented democracy, but rather to mobilize a vigilance-oriented republic of citizens who are a complement to, not substitute for, those we elect to represent us. Our founders foresaw the need for citizens to have "proxies" represent them in the decision-making process, not only because a direct democracy wouldn't scale well across such a vast land and population but also to allow for a good deal of calculated deliberation.

Given communication tools today, citizens could theoretically vote on everything, participating in all aspects of running the government and deciding on budgetary proposals. However attainable that goal is today given technology and information at your fingertips, that doesn't mean we should do it. There is good reason for a contemplative and deliberative thought process before enacting legislation, approving budgets, or simply making decisions that affect the running of our governments. The alternative is knee-jerk democracy, where the loudest voice, the squeakiest wheel, the most engaged of citizens get what they want, and everyone else falls victim to the tyrannical majority that James Madison and Thomas Jefferson so feared.

Participatory democracy sounds like mom, apple pie, and baseball, but if by *participatory* is meant *direct* democracy, well, I sure wouldn't want to run a country, state, or city that way. Our founders had it right when they provided a buffer between us and our government. Our role is to keep an eye on those who would be our "buffer," not usurp their responsibilities; ever more-transparent governments allow us to do just that—as the following examples demonstrate.

Civic engagement makes our democracy stronger because it creates an environment whereby citizens buy into their government by taking ownership of its performance, but it also secures ownership in our legacy. You see, the American Revolution continues. Our democracy, an unfolding work in progress, evolves. None of this is rocket science, but it is political science, and that's something the average citizen doesn't seem to be very good at. The letters of *The American Crisis* that Thomas Paine so eloquently wrote from 1776 to 1783 were about a revolution in crisis—the American Revolution.

Today we're faced with the crisis of sustaining the democracy born out of that revolution. Were Paine to write today, he would likely find a quote from his first letter more appropriate:

> These are the times that try men's souls. The summer soldier and the sunshine patriot will, in this crisis, shrink from the service of their country; but he that stands it now, deserves the love and thanks of man and woman.[1]

These are indeed the times that try men's souls, but the crisis today is self-inflicted. We have lost our passion for democracy—not its principles, but its practice. As the saying goes, we talk the talk, but we don't walk the walk. We want good government and honest politicians, but most of us aren't willing to do the work necessary to make sure we get them. Sadly, we have become a nation of summer soldiers and sunshine patriots. Few of us deserve the love and thanks of man and woman. Yet my experience as a community activist tells me that we can surmount apathy, exorcise corruption, and reinvigorate our democracy, and the tools of transparency provide us what we need as engaged citizens to do just that.

We all want government we can be proud of and a nation that will lead the world on the stage of democratic principles. The problem is that many people aren't compelled to leave the comfort of home to engage in the practices of citizenship because they don't have an overriding sense that their participation and its benefits outweigh the benefits of simply staying put. Most of us have an innate sense of managing time to maximize our personal well-being and pleasure. If the practices of citizenship don't provide an experience fulfilling enough to outweigh other options to get us off our butts and out of the house, then we aren't going to participate. If done right, transparency in government can be the catalyst to move citizens off their couches and into the streets.

John Dewey, the noted American philosopher and psychologist, in a speech he gave at the Hotel Commodore in New York City,

October 20, 1949, on the occasion of his ninetieth birthday, said that "democracy is an educative process; . . . the act of voting is in a democratic regime a culmination of a continued process of open and public communication."[2] Culmination, indeed. We don't wake up on Election Day—or early voting days—and decide that it's a good day to go out and vote. Voting, as Dewey reminded us, is a barometer of civic engagement. It's what we do *before* election days that very often determines whether we'll show up *on* election days. As we'll see with these selected applications, it's how transparency is delivered that determines its success in driving civic engagement, which subsequently drives turnout on election days.

Democracy demands the vigilance and intelligence of an engaged citizenry. If we're ever to have good government—not perfect, but at least good—then we must all practice the acts of citizenship, and to do that we need to prioritize our time to allow ourselves the opportunity for that practice. As we'll see, technologies of the twenty-first century provide us with the communication channels to enable anyone to obtain the knowledge and share the experiences necessary to be the type of citizen who helps foster a great community and, in turn, a great democracy. However, it's up to each of us to find the time and motivation to utilize these tools.

There never was a time in our history to shrink from service to our country, but circumstances today provide us the opportunities to embolden ourselves to take up the cause of saving our democracy—communication in the service of transparency can do that. Nearly fifty years ago, a president boldly challenged us to ask not what our country can do for us, but rather what we can do for our country.[3] Interestingly, that summons to greatness was given in the context of an inaugural speech focused on national security and our role as a world leader among nations, and the gauntlet that President Kennedy laid down with those words seemed at the time more to do with serving one's country in defense of freedom than anything else.

However, as with many great quotes, it has taken on a much broader meaning of citizenship and its responsibilities. The aspirations of one's civic duties that Kennedy attempted to instill in us seemed to have died with him or at least to have been muted over the years, but now we have the means through more open and transparent governments to resurrect it and infuse those aspirations with a heightened sense of civic awareness. Benjamin Barber, in his book *Strong Democracy*, envisioned a very hands-on electorate capable of a high degree of self-governing, whereby our representative governance is preempted by a more direct form of democracy. He and I part ways at that juncture, but we both share a commitment to the concept of an engaged citizenry with a passion for the democratic principles upon which this country was founded and the practices of citizenship that secure those principles. I believe we've lost that passion, but if these best practices that follow show anything, it's how we can regain it. So let's take a look.

⚬⚬⚬

THE PRACTICES

> "Cherish therefore the spirit of our people, and keep alive their attention. Do not be too severe upon their errors, but reclaim them by enlightening them. If once they become inattentive to the public affairs, you and I, and Congress, and Assemblies, judges and governors shall all become wolves."
> —Thomas Jefferson,
> letter to Edward Carrington,
> January 16, 1787

During the winter quarters of 2012 and 2013, students in my course Political Research Seminar on Transparency in Government had the opportunity to work with staff from the Chicago Inspector General's Office in analyzing the level of transparency in various city departments and then making recommendations for improving transparency.

As a preliminary exercise, the students first spent a few weeks researching transparency initiatives undertaken by other government entities, looking for best practices in achieving civic engagement through those practices. Five of these, what I consider the best examples, are presented in this chapter and reflect efforts of these government entities to keep alive the attention of their citizens by enlightening them through a more transparent government.

A state, a federal program, and three municipalities are presented to demonstrate a wide diversity of applications and methodologies utilized to engage citizens to become more active and knowledgeable in how their governments are run, often with the intent of motivating residents to provide feedback to improve their governments. The order in which these are presented, along with the names of the students who produced the research, follows below. Each is presented in a three-part format of abstract, analysis, and conclusion (with notes).

1. "Maryland's StateStat Website (State of Maryland)," by Elizabeth Franz
2. "Ministry of Infrastructure's 'By the Numbers' Website (Ontario, Canada)," by Brandon DeLallo, Karen Badawi, and Matt Marcus
3. "Mayor's Office of New Urban Mechanics (Boston, Massachusetts)," by Nicole Bronnimann
4. "Reset San Francisco (San Francisco, California)," by George Geiger, Jessi Reber, and Shireen Ali Mirza
5. "Portland's Civic Apps Initiative (Portland, Oregon)," by Phil Boardman, Peter Contos, and Bryan Weber

"MARYLAND'S STATESTAT WEBSITE (STATE OF MARYLAND)," BY ELIZABETH FRANZ

Abstract

Initially developed as an executive tool to assist in driving performance accountability in government, Maryland's StateStat program has progressed to become an instrument of government transparency. Ushered in by then newly elected Governor Martin O'Malley, the StateStat program was modeled after the CitiStat program O'Malley created as mayor of Baltimore but has expanded significantly to improve transparency and promote public engagement.

After legislation to create StateStat was signed by Governor O'Malley in April 2007, the full website and open-data portal were opened for the public in January 2008, at statestat.maryland.gov.[1] Moving from a performance-management tool used by the governor and other government leaders, the current model has grown under StateStat director Beth Blauer to include a dashboard-report view of the administration's major policy goals, an interactive map center, and a plethora of easily accessible datasets. The StateStat site also provides the ability to collect data volunteered by citizens through simple polling questions, preparing the path for further research and policy discussions by state agencies.

Such complex models of data collection and utilization are sometimes thought of as expensive and difficult to maintain. To the contrary, the StateStat site was created with a budget of $361,000, with annual expenses of less than $400,000.[2] While this is still a significant amount of money, the return in savings through performance management by the various agencies and the governor's office more than make up for expenditures. For example, by analyzing the data of the Maryland Department of Public Safety and Correctional Services (DPSCS) collected for StateStat, opportunities to cut overtime for corrections officers were found. By acting on these opportunities and continuing to watch the data, the DPSCS was able to save $12 million in overtime costs over two years.[3]

The original CitiStat model, still currently used in Baltimore, was born of the New York Police Department's CompStat program.[4] Now widely used throughout most mid- to large-sized police departments and in as many as nineteen cities across the United States, the concept of statistics-based management is quickly becoming a style of management preferred by many.[5] The way in which Maryland's StateStat program has made a name for itself is in its broadened use of that performance data to foster and promote transparency.

Employing the reports collected by each participating agency, the StateStat website compiles and presents that data in a clear, concise, and timely manner while tying it to relevant policy goals identified by the administration. Along with the dashboard-view reports of each objective is a section titled, "How Can I Get Involved?" which includes relevant links to various programs or information within Maryland government. Furthermore, the breakdown of data by goal, agency, and other means allows citizens to easily navigate to and view the information most relevant to them. As the average citizen cannot—and probably does not want to—dig through facts and figures for each state agency, these various methods of compartmentalization make the site manageable for the public.

In order to cultivate engagement, there are numerous ways within the site to provide feedback to individual agencies, the StateStat office, and the governor's office. StateStat also connects with residents through its own Twitter account as well as by posting videos on Maryland State's YouTube channel. While the effectiveness of these methods to increase awareness and foster involvement is debated, they are at least steps in the right direction.

Analysis

Maryland's StateStat program was developed through the governor's office as a data-driven performance-measurement and performance-management system. By making the data collected by each state agency available and easily accessible to the public, this system has increased government transparency and accountability on many levels. With collections taking place in fourteen agencies, including Human Resources, Transportation, Planning, and State Police, the administration has been able to compile data across agencies for a more effective analysis.[6]

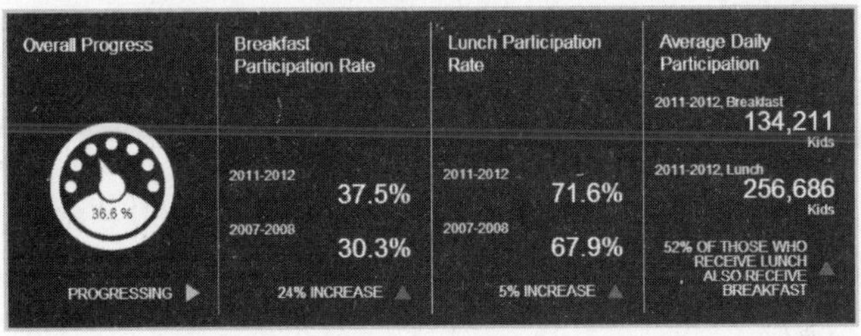

Fig. 4.1. Goal: End Childhood Hunger in Maryland by 2015.
(Courtesy of Maryland StateStat.)

From its roots in the Baltimore CitiStat program, StateStat has progressed by providing dashboard reports for each of the governor's fifteen strategic policy goals. A subunit of the StateStat program, Governor O'Malley's Delivery Unit, assembles data collected through StateStat to create the accessible dashboard reports.[7] The main "Goals" page provides titles of areas for each specific goal with a rating of "Delivered," "On Track," and "Progressing." As a user hovers over each area title, a short description of the administration's goal for that area is displayed. By clicking a goal, a user is brought to the dashboard report for that goal containing an "Overall Progress" rating for that specific goal as well as progress on key indicators used to measure overall goal progress, as demonstrated in figure 4.1.[8] Further charts, graphs, and maps detailing additional indicating factors utilized in judging advancement for that objective are also displayed, along with a short video explaining the need for and current progress of the goal. Additionally, each goal page has sections used to explain how the goal is measured ("Are We Meeting

Our Goals?"), what steps the administration has taken to meet that goal ("Actions Taken Towards Goal"), and links to various information and agencies related to the goal ("How Can I Get Involved?"), including a link to provide feedback to Delivery Unit and StateStat. Finally, to maximize transparency and accountability there is a link to read the administration's comprehensive plan for each goal as well as the links to the specific datasets used to generate the dashboard for each particular goal. By providing information at a variety of depths and in various formats, the StateStat program is able to maximize engagement by allowing users to delve in at the level to which they are most interested and in the format in which they are most comfortable. From its most basic level, publishing the stated goals and levels of achievement allow even the least engaged members of the public to understand the priorities of its government. From the first step of understanding the priorities of one's government, conversations and further engagement can be fostered.

One of the most important features of StateStat is the timeliness of the data. As part of an overall performance-management system, the heads of each agency report to the governor's office on a biweekly or monthly basis. In preparation for those meetings, all data is updated and compiled to provide an executive dashboard report for the governor's office.[9] This same data is then uploaded to the StateStat website to update reports and allow for download of full datasets by the public. Consistently updating the data applied and offered on the StateStat website encourages users to return on a regular basis to follow the areas of most significance to them.

Vast amounts of datasets and reports are compiled and made accessible through the StateStat website. Data templates provided by state agencies for regular meetings with the governor's office are provided to the StateStat office, which drafts executive-view reports and a memo for each meeting.[10] The dashboard reports are, in turn, published on the StateStat website for public consumption. These reports are clearly organized by report date, agency, accompanying charts or maps, and meeting summaries. The viewing order of these reports is sortable by any of the aforementioned categories, allowing citizens to easily select their desired report(s).[11] For example, users can choose to view all of the reports for the Department of Juvenile Services and track month-by-month changes. "Meeting Summary" reports published foster transparency by allowing the public to easily understand the current issue foci of the state administration. Each report is clearly summarized by topic, with various charts and graphs representing data factored into discussions, and they are provided in an easily downloadable pdf. While these meetings are not generally open to the public, this provides an opening into the meetings. The reports remain on the site well after initial publication, affording easy public access of data going back to the launch of the StateStat program in 2007.

For those looking to dig deeper into the data, the StateStat website also contains an open data portal. While it is easy for open data portals to become clogged and difficult to navigate, the StateStat portal allows for easy searching as well as providing categories and topics to group multiple datasets. Using Socrata data platform software,[12] experienced data users filter and manage the data; create maps, charts, or graphs with user-selected data; or export in one of eight different formats. Keeping consistent with other areas of the StateStat site, users can easily suggest or request additional datasets to be published.

While the average citizen probably does not consider downloading datasets or thoroughly analyzing the vast amounts of information, by making the facts and figures easily available to the public, the government is sending a message of open accountability. Additionally, strongly interested folks, watchdog organizations, policy groups, and others who will utilize the data provided will not begin each encounter with their government as a frustrating exercise in bureaucracy—no forms to fill out or lengthy delays in gathering information. By eliminating these steps, those groups can focus more time on active engagement in their area of interest.

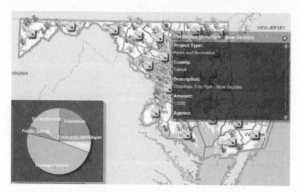

*Fig. 4.2. Maryland State Capital Budget Map, FY 2013.
(Courtesy of Maryland StateStat.)*

Much of the data published is also utilized through the creation of multiple dynamic maps accessible through the "Map Center" of StateStat's website. Currently, the site features twenty-one maps spanning a variety of interests; each is rich and dynamic, depicted as map applications rather than static representations.[13] Most representative of government transparency, the "State Budget Map" provides a breakdown of the state capital budget by county, with the ability to view specific categories of "Economic Development," "Education," "Environment," "Health," "Parks and Recreation," "Public Safety," and "Transportation." Within each of these categories there is an option to "Show Individual Projects on Map." By selecting this option, users are provided with rich graphical icons representing each project. As seen in figure 4.2,[14] simply hovering over a pinpoint on the map brings up a high-level view with project location, description, agency, total capital expenditures allocated, and unallocated spending incurred. This easy-to-understand format is a great beginning for public-interest novices. For those wishing to explore further, the map has additional links to full data tables in each of the aforementioned categories.

The Maryland State data used in creation of the maps available in StateStat's "Map Center" are housed and managed through the "MD iMap Portal." Created by an executive order signed by Governor

O'Malley in December 2009, the iMap portal publishes map services from multiple agencies through a common information-technology infrastructure.[15] The map services provided through MD iMap supply another source of data that can be readily accessed and utilized by the public. As with the full datasets in the open data portal, the average citizen will probably not dig through the extensive metadata. But by supplying the data in ways that interested public members and groups can utilize, the level of transparency is increased.

An interesting and innovative piece of the StateStat website is the effort to collect data from visitors and publish that in a real-time report. The current home page of the website asks a simple multiple-choice question—"Do you know where your food originates?" The informal survey includes four multiple-choice answers and the ability to include your zip code. The site then offers real-time results that can be viewed, including searching answers by zip code. While this simple poll could not be used alone to generate a policy or make a high-stakes decision, it can be used to start a policy conversation or even to drive the need for further research.

Maryland's StateStat program does maintain its own Twitter account to post new information and alerts.[16] The account is also advertised as a place to ask questions—or tweet questions—to the StateStat office. This Twitter account could be far better managed and operated to further promote its use, but having the basic structure, as they do, is good groundwork that can be built on.

StateStat also takes advantage of Maryland State's YouTube channel to post videos promoting the site.[17] As previously mentioned, each of the fifteen policy goals of the administration has its own page on the StateStat site with updates and progress reports. Part of this initiative includes a short video explaining the root concern the policy is looking to address, why that goal is important, and the steps taken toward achieving the objective. These videos are important in grabbing the attention of citizens uninterested in charts and graphs or in digging through data. By utilizing various forms of media, StateStat is encouraging all members of the community to partake in their government. Current participation levels are not as high as expected, but this is recognized by the leaders of the program, and hopefully future efforts will be made to increase engagement.[18]

The bare bones of StateStat begin with simple, off-the-shelf technology such as Microsoft Excel and PowerPoint.[19] New technology has been used for the map-creation portal, dashboard reporting, and other areas,[20] but most of the technology is basic in nature but complex in the ways in which it is used. By using basic technology, StateStat is further proving that a relatively low-cost initiative can have broad policy impact while increasing transparency.

Conclusion

Data collection and publication efforts have had an enormous impact on the state of Maryland. StateStat has advanced a culture of transparency for government employees as well as citizens of Maryland. From its origins in Baltimore's CitiStat program under Martin O'Malley, the performance-measurement and performance-management style has proven to be an effective tool for government and citizens.

Under then mayor O'Malley, Baltimore saved an estimated $350 million through efficiencies and other discoveries made through CitiStat, as well as received the Innovations on American Government Award from Harvard University.[21] The newer model of StateStat has still been a money-saving endeavor for Marylanders, but the savings are not always as quantifiable as with the work done on the city level. One of the first projects of the newly launched StateStat program was to address employee overtime within state government.[22] While the concept of reducing employee overtime is quite simple, the StateStat model helped flush out hidden causes for that overtime. In the previously noted example of overtime at the DPSCS, data collection and analysis provided the opportunity to address the root causes of overtime and address those issues.[23] In another situation, when the state was able to close an underutilized juvenile detention facility, it used a portion of the savings to fund more effective community youth programs.[24] As efficiencies are discovered and cost-saving steps are put into place, taxpayers will feel less frustrated with the use of their tax dollars. No one likes to feel like his or her money is being thrown away.

"Perhaps the greatest value of this model of governance is that it brings government closer to the people it exists to serve."[25] This quote from Governor O'Malley is reflective of the StateStat model. As the data is collected, applying it to easily understood, specific policy goals is an important factor in encouraging citizen participation in government. The dashboard-view reports and interactive "Map Center" are clear examples of government transparency at work for its citizens. Full datasets and metadata to back the high-level information form an additional, important layer of transparency needed to keep government accessible and accountable.

The best ideas come from groups comprised of a diversity of individuals. Making efforts to include as many from the citizenry as possible increases the chances of having all of the best ideas brought to the table. The models followed by Maryland's StateStat program—dashboard reporting views, an interactive map center, and easily accessible data—are strong moves to increase transparency and public engagement.

"MINISTRY OF INFRASTRUCTURE'S 'BY THE NUMBERS' WEBSITE (ONTARIO, CANADA)," BY BRANDON DELALLO, KAREN BADAWI, AND MATT MARCUS

Abstract

The Ontario Ministry of Infrastructure[1] (MOI) initiated the "By the Numbers"[2] website as part of the Canadian Open Data Pilot Project.[3] This was done as part of the Government 2.0 Initiative[4] that was created and implemented to increase citizen engagement in federal government. Additionally, as part of the goal of increasing citizen engagement, it means quantitative and qualitative data is available to increase disclosure and transparency. This twelve-month trial project launched in March 2011 and running through January 2012 continues to receive community feedback to improve the services and content served via the Open Data website. This truly is the definition of government engaging the citizenry for the betterment of the political establishment.

Part of the goal of the Open Data Project is that the Canadian government makes data available for both noncommercial and commercial use. The mission is to provide "a catalogue of government datasets that are available for users, developers and data suppliers to find, evaluate, access, visualize and reuse federal government data. This pilot site is the first step in providing access to reusable government data."[5] The Open Data project "is about offering government data in a more useful format to enable citizens, the private sector and non-government organizations to leverage it in innovative and value-added ways."[6] The Open Information Project is "about making information about the Government available to Canadians on a proactive and ongoing basis—it's about sharing knowledge and ensuring accountability."[7] Finally, the Open Dialogue project is about enhancing Canadian citizens' engagement in government policies, programs, and priorities.[8] The Canadian federal government sponsored the program under the overall theme of enhancing community engagement and information distribution to maximize governmental transparency.

The Ontario MOI, in compliance with this project, provides a breakdown of the expenditures for ongoing infrastructure projects with its "By the Numbers" website. Although this is not the only website in compliance, its straightforward approach to data transparency makes it an interesting website for analysis. This website provides details of the dollars spent on infrastructure projects in Ontario, Canada, using mash-ups, charts, and graphs.

As part of the Open Government Initiative there are "Open Data," "Open Information," and "Open Dialogue" subsets designed to maximize information release and community feedback. The MOI's "By the Numbers" website allows for at-a-glance and in-depth analysis of distribution of the investments.[9]

Additionally, high-quality maps representing the general locations of various infrastructure projects are available for analysis (one such map is rendered on the title page [of the website]). The MOI, in keeping with transparency, displays a list of the specific projects it is responsible for while indicating their type: cultural, transit/transportation, or water/environment. Although this data is not specifically found on the "By the Numbers" website, the MOI makes this information easily available. Finally, as part of this initiative, the presence on social media cannot be ignored. The MOI is present on Twitter[10] and Facebook,[11] allowing real-time updates and another avenue for integration into its voting community's lives.

Self-promotion of the government creates a believable reality that the government is indeed listening to its citizenry and working toward change. Presenting information via social media such as Facebook and Twitter, as well as government websites, demonstrates the type of exposure the government is initiating in an effort to engage the citizenry. Through easy-to-read graphs, maps, social media, and user feedback for improvement, this initiative and certainly the "By the Numbers" website creates buzz using twenty-first-century tools.

Analysis

The Open Data Pilot Project through the Canadian government is an initiative designed to ensure that the government is more in line with transparency and disclosure by providing open data, open information, and open dialogue. "The Open Data Pilot seeks to improve the ability of the public to find, download and use Government of Canada data."[12] This project is accomplished through the use of innovative technology to create greater economic opportunities for its citizens. Users are invited to search the catalog and download datasets to gather as much publicly available information as they would like.

Commitment to this initiative is demonstrated through an MOI website link detailing the expenditures in easy-to-read graphical representations, labeled "By the Numbers." The Open Data Pilot Project is an ongoing Canadian government initiative that the MOI is complying with to share information relating to its ongoing infrastructure projects. In addition to committing to smarter infrastructure investments, the MOI is committed to ensuring the right infrastructure is built in the right place in a way that is transparent, open, and fair, while ensuring it gets the best value. Its commitment to this initiative is demonstrated through a website detailing the expenditures in easy-to-read graphical representations, through its "By the Numbers" website.

This dissemination of information is distinct due to the nature and detail of the transparency. Additionally, instead of dumping facts and raw data in some Excel[13] or Adobe[14] document onto a website and stamping itself under the auspice of disclosure, the MOI works to ensure the public can read and react to the data. Additionally, website-user feedback is requested to make improvements. The data is displayed for all to see, which allows for individuals and companies to track the progress of infrastructure stimulus projects in their community and across the province. Additionally, this allows for a robust and continually improved method for increased consumption of government-generated data. The raw data is displayed in graphs and charts that are meant to target the average citizen, instead of requiring an advanced business degree to comprehend.

The goal of this website, to offer increased transparency, translates to improved accountability to residents as it pertains to federal-provincial infrastructure stimulus funding. The contributions of the province and federal government are broken down as they relate to projects, tracking construction progress and providing regular updates on new investments.

Open Data Project, through its community-facing website, offers numerous sources of data for public analysis. The website hosts maps of the province, showing projects by community, enabling citizens to see where their money is going and to which projects. The website has a job-creation and community-investment portal, which allows job seekers an opportunity to find out about the employment available. There are project search tools, including a postal-code search, which allows for multiple ways to search the datasets. This increases the chances the data will be searched, viewed, digested, and comprehended. In addition to the raw data, there are links to news articles, videos, webcams, and photos about the projects, allowing citizens to keep up-to-date on the status of projects.

The Canadian federal government in partnership with the Ontario Province has invested close to $11 billion for more than 2,600 infrastructure projects across the province.[15] This has been ongoing since February 2011 in an effort to stimulate the economy and create jobs. As with any major government expenditure, there are concerns that the distribution of capital could lead to project cost overruns, abuse, waste, and fraud. As more individuals are aware of how their tax dollars are disseminated, it gives them greater bargaining power with their elected officials as well as insight into how their government is run. This level of disclosure and transparency empowers citizens to actively seek solutions within the government structure to improve efficiencies.

Ontario's Ministry of Infrastructure website falls under the purview of the Canadian Access to Information Act of 1985.[16] In an attempt to promote government transparency, Ontario increases local residents' access to the multifaceted portfolio of public services in an efficient and cost-effective manner. Hundreds of reports, agendas, meeting minutes, and other city-vital information are created for city staff and officials. Rebranding the same information in a new and user-friendly format allows for the distribution of "digestible" data to the public.

The MOI extends far beyond the scope of infrastructure. It works directly with several local ministries to include citizen engagement and participation in governance. The website is a communication tool reaching Canada's most populous province/territory of Ontario, containing over 12 million residents.[17] The website facilitates the operation of government and the disbursement of government information and services to local residents by utilizing numerous technological innovations. This includes graphical user interfaces[18] (GUIs) that directly manipulate a graphical element to perform an action. For example, by clicking on a graphical icon to perform an action along with text navigation allows a website visitor to communicate and interact with city departments and employees.[19] Additionally, instant access is provided via instant messaging (IM), e-mail alerts, Twitter, Facebook, and direct text navigation to the "Government of Ontario News"[20] feed webpage. Another appealing feature is the ability to view audiovisual presentations and number "crunching" in easy-to-read tables and charts.

As much as the above referenced "tags," GUIs, and text navigation seem to be mundane computer lingo, their function is paramount to any user's ability to access information. They provide internal classification structure so that information in databases can be stored, queried, and shared. Therefore, once tagged, it can be used and shared anywhere, anytime. This is a major achievement in communication innovation, providing real-time relay of various data. Technological advancement will also usher in a culture change by shifting information from being stored away for internal government purposes into a broader view. Government data can continue to be unfettered, and put out in real-time. Improving transparency through online information will be a great benefit to researchers, reporters, and ordinary citizens, and will make it easier to follow the government money trail. Digital technology represents a way for government to become more transparent and proactive in dealing with citizens and businesses. Many government agencies today are reactive in nature. They wait for people to request information or services. However, the Internet allows government agencies to customize information and push material out to the people. From a resident's perspective, registering a particular interest in a subject puts your name on a list to receive information when new information becomes available.

Importantly, the website provides citizens the ability to monitor their elected officials; consider if they have delivered on promises made, completed projects, and applied funds in an open and beneficial manner; along with several other visual "taps" on the local government. Ultimately, computer access and utilization enhances social inclusion. A better-informed constituency helps create a better dialogue between residents and government officials and results in better policy decisions as well as being a time saver for both the government and the local residents.

The data available at your fingertips on Ontario's "By the Numbers" initiative differentiates itself from many of the Canadian Open Data websites in that it does not rely on stakeholders to manipulate raw government data into usable formats, but rather attempts to do so itself. Infographics, the context-relevant graphical framing of data, has become more mainstream among Internet users and media content consumers in recent years. Ontario has taken provincial data streams and created multiple infographics that are quickly and easily reviewed by constituents for an at-a-glance review of current government infrastructure and stimulus programs.[21]

For stakeholders who wish for slightly more in-depth analysis of the investment programs, clicking on any one of the budget categories links to additional infographics (in multiple formats) that further provide graphical explanations of provincial data.[22]

Local governments have a tendency to be internal-facing with their data output, as such reports and data are often generated for review by an auditing or oversight body that has the time and expertise to review raw data, not constituents and other stakeholders with varying amounts of available time and education levels. The use of technology here is twofold; Ontario's approach addresses that issue by releasing essential government data in a manner easily reviewed by most constituents and, should the viewer desire more in-depth data, provides several layers of additional analysis. This approach is likely to satisfy many stakeholders, and those who prefer either raw data or highly detailed analysis have other avenues available to them for such information. Room for improvement definitely exists with Ontario's relatively basic use of charts and graphs in lieu of more context-relevant infographics, but the effort represents an important and necessary baseline.

While compiling and boiling down data is the primary task Ontario tackles, the secondary challenge is in finding an effective and appropriate medium to bring this data to stakeholders. Again, Ontario has made a solid first step in developing outreach efforts across new mediums. The government created a Twitter account specifically designed to push out news and information regarding provincial infrastructure initiatives in mid-2011.[23] While the effort resulted in regular updates and messaging pushes throughout the summer of 2011, it appears to have tapered off since then, with little or no updated information. The strengths and weaknesses of Twitter as a medium have become evident in the past two to three years. The site is great for short-form messaging updates, promotional pushes, and, depending on the context, website traffic generation. It is not, however, the best medium for sharing even slightly complex data or information due both to its character limitation and its primary focus on text only. On the other hand, Facebook would appear to be an ideal medium for local governments seeking to share concise data with citizens and stakeholders. Facebook users are far more likely to share relevant data within their geo-groups. This means that if Ontario were to publish its data on Facebook and perhaps create a limited, geo-targeted, outreach campaign to identify likely thought-leaders, they would be able to rely on existing social networks of users from the Ontario area to share the data among themselves and perhaps encourage interaction and debate regarding the findings.

Conclusion

Contributing to Ontario's socio-political-economic success is the province's commitment to its citizenry, with a focus on infrastructure, education, employment, and overall state of physical and mental health. The mission is partially achieved by communication through providing electronic access points to government programs and infrastructure projects. Educator John Dewey proposed that democracy is a community process.[24] Through the experience of participating in democratic decision-making processes, citizens could truly learn the value of democracy and acquire the capacities of full and meaningful participation.

The argument could be made that an average citizen is concerned with matters that directly impact his or her life. For different individuals, that means different things. One important value the MOI provides its local residents is the ability to visualize federal- and local-government budget allocation, thus increasing confidence in the political establishment. Another value to local residents is that the MOI willingly submits to strict scrutiny by various groups and individuals. The consideration that certain situations merit journalistic attention further heightens public awareness of certain mainstream events. Yet the media is known to carefully and purposefully select data to promote their interests (ratings). Deciphering the accurate information from the invalid is an acquired skill.

Advantageously, residents are able to directly locate or become informed regarding their individual needs or interests from the convenience and privacy of their home, office, school, or public library, or on-the-go via web-enabled mobile devices. With a "click," any user is able to obtain or request the information he or she is seeking, in more than sixteen languages, from numerous federal- and local-government departments.[25] For example, one can register one's newborn, apply for a Social Insurance Number, or apply for government financial-assistance programs,[26] while another user may be interested in tracking government infrastructure projects for financials, transportation, housing, employment, healthcare, education opportunities, or exposé.

Subjectively speaking, the greatest value the MOI extends its local residents is empowerment. The status quo is not the only option. Ultimately, the website cultivates the invaluable opportunity of systematic political literacy, and collective action, setting an exemplary alternative practice of how government can become truly transparent, educate its citizens, and stimulate resident participation in democracy. Knowing what you stand for, and what you are against, enables an informed decision at elections.

In leveraging already-existing technologies and putting easily accessible information on government websites, Ontario's initiative goes a step further and has allowed its citizens to gain a level of knowledge, over time, about government spending efforts that was previously not available to them. Moreover, by leveraging emerging technologies and mediums, government can reach and communicate with younger/different constituent groups to create new levels of engagement. In a time of measurably increased distrust in government at all levels, two-way engagement with stakeholders to promote transparency and governmental efficacy data should be in nearly any administration's interest. The Canadian government conducted a nationwide feedback response study based on the Open Data initiative and is scheduled to publish the results in March 2012.[27]

Also important to note, data is conceivably of importance to other governmental bodies and nongovernmental organizations (NGOs) at the provincial and national level. By making this data available in varying levels of detail and complexity, it certainly serves the interest of the public. Additionally, it likely serves internal interests as well by making information available to other departments at its own level, as well up-slope and down-slope along the governmental food chain, in a highly efficient manner. Too often, government institutions suffer from the right-hand/left-hand dilemma, where information provided by one department is inconsistent with information provided by another, creating both tension within and outside the administration as well as duplication of effort. The Ontario example allows for the creation of multisource, single-output technological solutions that can be used both externally to constituent groups, NGOs, and the media, as well as at the intragovernment level.

"MAYOR'S OFFICE OF NEW URBAN MECHANICS (BOSTON, MASSACHUSETTS)" BY NICOLE BRONNIMANN

Abstract

The Mayor's Office of New Urban Mechanics (MONUM) is an office in the Boston municipal government that seeks to foster civic engagement and transparency by using technology to give citizens the means of interacting and participating in the improvement of city services. It was created in 2010 by Mayor Thomas Menino and is currently under the co-management of Chris Osgood, an urban-policy specialist, and Nigel Jacob, an IT developer.[1]

The goal of MONUM is to transform the way that citizens interact with local government and local-government services by creating and promoting technology that makes civic participation both easier and more appealing. The office calls itself "the City's innovation incubator" and focuses on "building partnerships between City agencies and outside institutions and entrepreneurs to pilot projects in Boston that address resident and business needs."[2] It functions as an "in-house R&D shop for the city,"[3] with an emphasis on technological innovations in three major areas: civic engagement, sustainable city growth and management, and education.

Most related to transparency in government are the projects concerning civic engagement, a concept MONUM calls "Participatory Urbanism."[4] MONUM wishes to reshape the citizen-city relationship into one that is more directly interactive. It wishes to make problem solving for the community a process that is both collective and collectivizing. Transparency, in the eyes of MONUM's leadership, is a "characteristic of a good civic solution."[5] Therefore, "by creating new ways into civic issues"[6] through technology, greater transparency is achieved.

Citizens Connect, Participatory Chinatown, and Community PlanIt are three major projects under the "Participatory Urbanism" branch of MONUM that particularly demonstrate this belief in action. Citizens Connect is perhaps the simplest and also the most successful. It is a smartphone app that allows citizens to submit maintenance requests with attached photographs to the city and track the city's response time to these requests.[7] Meanwhile Participatory Chinatown and Community PlanIt look at how civic engagement can be transformed into a web-based "game," that is easy to use and, unlike many other community-engagement programs, enticing to users. Participatory Chinatown was a video game developed to involve citizens in urban planning. In a simulation of Boston's Chinatown, players assumed the role of avatars representative of various community members. They performed tasks relating to these avatars' needs and then assessed their strategies and what they believed the development priorities of the neighborhood should be, based off of their experiences.[8]

Community PlanIt was a partnership with Boston Public Schools, in which a points-based online game was used to procure citizen feedback concerning a new metrics system for evaluating public-school performance.[9] Importantly, both Participatory Chinatown and Community PlanIt concluded with an in-person meeting between the players and the city decision makers responsible for real-life implementation of the project in question (developers in the case of Participatory Chinatown and Boston Public Schools district officials in the case of Community PlanIt). The highly attended meetings[10] included many citizens who would otherwise not have attended a community meeting regarding the topic. However, because of the "game" that had both informed and engaged them regarding the issues, many felt that they had a stake in the process.

Through these projects and partnerships, MONUM is not only able make the processes of urban planning and management more accessible but interactive and engaging as well. The list of projects undertaken by MONUM, while extensive, does certainly not exhaust the projects that could be developed in the future. Equally important as the individual projects is the idea of directly engaging "constituents and institutions in developing and piloting projects that will re-shape City government and improve services."[11]

MONUM's website[12] outlines its projects and focus areas in greater detail, in addition to providing multiple portals for immediate citizen feedback.

Analysis

Citizens Connect App

The Citizens Connect app is an example of a project that creatively uses technology to enable citizens to report city service problems and allows for greater transparency regarding how and at what pace the city resolves those problems. Before the launch of Citizens Connect, the only portal for seeking city services was a "hard-to-navigate" website and a call center that "didn't respond in a timely manner to citizen requests."[13] Because of widespread discontent with this process, Citizens Connect was one of the first projects undertaken by the office of New Urban Mechanics.

The app it created was innovative in the use of technology in two primary ways. First, after looking at other cities' apps, MONUM made the choice to have the Citizens Connect app highly focused on one citizen-government interaction (the reporting and resolving of service problems). Other cities had previously launched apps that tried to cover every area of local government and ended up creating what was essentially a miniature version of a "hard-to-navigate" site that already existed. MONUM believed that a very tailored app would allow for an easier and more appealing user experience.[14] Second, because MONUM developed the app to eliminate time-intensive and inefficient processes, the service requests that users submit are immediately placed in the work-order queue of city workers.[15] Communication is stream-lined in that users can submit detailed descriptions of the issues they report (which range from graffiti to potholes to excessive trash), along with GPS coordinates and pictures.[16]

Fig. 4.3. Citizens Connect App.

In the realm of transparency, the app has also changed the way that citizens can track city responses to their requests. When users submit a case, they are first informed how quickly it will take for the case to be closed. The case is automatically sent to the "My Reports" folder of their app (left-hand side of figure 4.3), which allows users to keep track of the requests they have submitted. Then, when city workers do respond to the request, the date and time of the resolution is recorded. This allows users to easily see the response time between the time of the request and the time of the resolution, not only for their reports, which are neatly organized in their "My Reports" folder, but for the reports of their fellow citizens as well, which are seen in the "Recent Reports" stream (lower-right side of figure 4.3). There is even a direct connection to Twitter in the app, which allows users to "tweet" their reports, thereby publicizing it within their networks (left-hand side of figure 4.3).[17]

The Citizens Connect app has changed the process of responding to city service requests in Boston. Instead of calling a call center, which would give unrecorded and often-inaccurate estimations of how long it would take to respond to a request, users of Citizens Connect can track and document how quickly and efficiently the city is operating. It is designed to be both immediately relevant to their lives and user-friendly. Because it is a smartphone app, Citizens Connect can easily become embedded into residents' daily routine. Coming across a problem, a citizen can take a quick picture and send it directly to the city, making engagement easier and minimizing the amount of time citizens must invest to be engaged. Moreover, with the turnaround time of their reports being automatically recorded in the app, citizens can hold the city accountable from the palm of their hands.

Participatory Chinatown

Participatory Chinatown is one of the most unique best practices found under the New Urban Mechanics office. Made possible by a partnership with Emerson College and funding from the MacArthur Foundation,[18] Participatory Chinatown was a video game piloted in 2010 that engaged citizens from all walks of life in urban planning. The goal of the project was to "transform the planning practices shaping Boston's Chinatown—from disjointed transactions between developers and communities to a persistent conversation shaped by participatory learning."[19]

The project worked by making the complex balancing of priorities in any development project into an interactive multiplayer game. The developers of the game targeted individuals within the Chinatown community to be the players, focusing on bringing to the table voices that were often underrepresented in development conversations—such as "youth, recent immigrants, and young professionals."[20] Players within the game took on the role of different avatars representative of the neighborhood—ranging correspondingly in terms of income, race, family size, and, of course, community needs. In a virtual environment simulating Boston's Chinatown, players completed tasks such as finding a job, a house, and a place to socialize. After these tasks, they were then asked to assess and rank developmental priorities.

What made Participatory Chinatown more than a just a video game but in fact an exercise in open government was the way that feedback from the players was collected and used. The game was played in groups of community members and structured around a combination of "physical deliberation, virtual interaction, and Web-based input."[21] Players had the opportunity to discuss their personal opinions regarding how the future of Chinatown should be shaped, both in small groups of their fellow citizens and with representatives from the city as well. Every one of their comments was recorded and shared with the decision makers of the project.[22]

Citizens responded to the game with a surprising level of engagement. During the testing period, venues for playing the game, usually large auditoriums, were repeatedly filled over capacity with community members wishing to play. They were citizens who otherwise would likely never have attended a single community meeting regarding development plans. Bilingual specialists were available at every session so that even residents who had previously faced a language barrier when voicing their concerns and opinions were able to participate in the game and shape their community.[23]

Participatory Chinatown was awarded the Games for Change 2011 Direct Impact Award[24] and is a model that could be replicated in any urban-planning project. The game underlines a larger trend toward "gamification" in civic engagement, not only making widespread and active participation in community decisions more possible but incentivizing citizens to do so by providing a more appealing medium. There were still, however, many improvements that could be made to the game, such as the creation of a portal through which citizens could see the ways their comments were used and the weight they were given in making the final development decisions. For now, though, it remains an innovative first step to a more collaborative strategy in urban planning.

Community PlanIt

MONUM's partnership with Community PlanIt and Boston Public Schools is a project much in the same vein as Participatory Chinatown, though it uses a different platform and addresses an entirely different area of government. The purpose of the Community PlanIt collaboration was to engage the community in reevaluating the metrics used by Boston Public Schools to measure school performance. New Urban Mechanics took on the project specifically because of its potential "to explore how on-line platforms can complement in-person community meetings—as well as reach an audience that might not attend a community meeting."[25]

This thirty-five-day project was launched in the fall of 2011, in immediate response to the district initiative to create a new system for measuring school accountability in six key areas: growth, proficiency, achievement gaps, attendance, school environment and safety, and student/family engagement. It was similar to Participatory Chinatown in the way that it "gamified" the process of collecting citizen feedback. Players earned tokens by answering questions and completing activities regarding their views on the different performance metrics. A representative question from the game, for instance, was the following: "How much do you agree with the following statement: Some students should get more than 4 years to graduate—and schools should be given credit for getting these students to graduate eventually? Explain your answer in a comment."[26] Players could deposit the tokens they earned from answering such questions into the six aforementioned accountability areas, based on which they felt was most important. Moreover, with each token they ascended higher on the "Community Leaderboard," visible to everyone.

About 450 players participated in the game, all coming from the primary stakeholder groups: students, teachers, parents, and administrators. In the thirty-five-day online period, they generated close to five thousand comments on the platform. Like Participatory Chinatown, the game culminated in a community meeting. In addition to the players of the game, district officials attended and listened to discussion on what metrics of school performance mattered most to these key stakeholders. Utilizing the Community PlanIt platform changed the nature of this community meeting. Participants included many citizens who would normally not attend meetings, such as students. The game had briefed them on the issues at stake, so they were able to come to the meeting informed, with their comments already permanently recorded on the platform. With this record of their deliberations and decisions, citizens then had the ability to compare how the results of their conversations translated into actual changes in the Boston Public Schools school-accountability system. Still lacking is the automatic presentation of this data to participants, but hopefully future civic interaction platforms will incorporate this feature.

What is particularly innovative about collaborative civic engagement of this kind is that it touches on many different aspects of transparency. First, it presents users with the underlying facts and figures regarding a government decision—for instance, what metrics have been used to judge school performance in the past. Second, it does so in a way that users find appealing—participants are incentivized through the structure of a "game." Third, the online and in-person components illuminate the processes that are behind government decisions and actively engage an informed citizenry in participating in these decisions. With a tool such as Community PlanIt or Participatory Chinatown, citizens have a straightforward and real method for learning about and impacting local-government decisions.[27]

Conclusion

The Mayor's Office of New Urban Mechanics is supporting projects that have the potential to change the way urban planning and management is operated in Boston and, indeed, in cities everywhere.

For the benefit of citizens, MONUM develops projects that give them greater voice and action in shaping their communities. Instead of a dead-end call to a city call center, citizens can easily monitor city service problems and response times through an app on the phone. Instead of the same few people showing up to a community meeting about an upcoming government decision, platforms like Community PlanIt and Participatory Chinatown bring to the table underrepresented citizens who, through the structure of a game, have been informed about issues concerning their neighborhoods and have been incentivized to participate in the deliberative process. Because citizens are given a larger role in developing city policy, they become more aware of and engaged in local affairs.

Governments, meanwhile, are able to draw on the expertise of their constituents and receive more accurate measures of public opinion. In the case of Participatory Chinatown, the Boston government was able to make more informed decisions about the kinds of services that were most needed and would be most used by residents of Chinatown. The Community PlanIt collaboration enabled the Boston Public Schools accountability team to know what performance metrics really mattered to the schools, parents, and students in the district. Finally, the Citizens Connect app streamlined the city's own operations by essentially creating thousands of on-the-ground city inspectors who could send reports directly to city workers. These projects together create a more efficient process for garnering public feedback and foster a more engaged citizenry. Because citizens who are engaged are more likely to be invested in the success of their communities, this contributes to a positive cycle of economic and sociological improvement for cities. This is perhaps the reason that Mayor Michael Nutter of Philadelphia announced in October 2012 that he was also creating an office of New Urban Mechanics to explore this method of engaging the public to find solutions to city challenges.[28]

The three "Participatory Urbanism" projects that have been mentioned as well as the driving ideology behind the New Urban Mechanics office point to "third-generation transparency,"[29] a type of transparency that goes beyond informing the public that they simply have the right to know data about their government and also goes beyond targeted efforts to make relevant data available to citizens. Third-generation transparency is "collaborative transparency"[30]— it is a partnership between citizens and government that empowers citizens to directly weigh in on and shape community decisions. Government takes on a role that is "facilitating rather than controlling"[31]—it provides the channels for citizens to collaborate with city officials and invests deeply in attracting citizens to those channels.

New technologies, including online platforms that can manage and document thousands of diverse opinions and interests, are fundamental in making this new type of transparency possible. The White

House Open Government Initiative calls this crossover between open government and civic technology "open innovation"[32] and has cited MONUM as a sterling example of it.

Perhaps this concept of "open innovation," the foundational driver for MONUM, is best encapsulated by the office's mantra, a quote from Mayor Menino: "We are all urban mechanics."[33] In this interesting phrase, the city of Boston is compared to a machine and citizens are its operators and overseers. This is not the typical way that the relationship between a government and its constituency has been envisioned, but many city governments and residents are seeing it as the model for the future. If the innovation occurring in offices like MONUM is shared and widely adopted, government has the potential to become a *tool* managed by *all* citizens, who are empowered through technology to use it, manage it, and—when necessary—fix it.

"RESET SAN FRANCISCO (SAN FRANCISCO, CALIFORNIA)," BY GEORGE GEIGER, JESSI REBER, AND SHIREEN ALI MIRZA

Abstract

Reset San Francisco was created in 2010 by Phil Ting, the assessor-recorder of the County and City of San Francisco. Ting was appointed to his position in 2005 by then-mayor Gavin Newsom. Ting launched the initiative and corresponding website in order to garner input and ideas from citizens to create a more effective and efficient city government. For a period of time, Reset San Francisco was paid for by the mayoral campaign for Phil Ting. However, since the mayoral election, the website has been funded by the Phil Ting for Assembly 2012 campaign. The website's FAQ section guarantees that the project will continue after Ting leaves his position, although it does not clarify or expound on by whom or how the website and project will be funded.

Reset San Francisco (RSF) is a reform-driven website that aims to inform residents of San Francisco about governmental issues by providing a resource that allows constituents easy access to information. Using the latest technology of the Web 2.0 platform, the site comprises multiple links directly to information that would otherwise be tedious and time-consuming for residents to pursue. The website covers a broad range of issues that directly affect the average citizen on a daily basis, while offering an innovative way for them to contribute ideas for reform.

RSF empowers the residents of San Francisco by providing them the platform for creating an online profile. The profile is similar to many social-media websites, the person becomes a virtual individual. Once a profile is created, the San Francisco resident is able to read opinions, contribute to current conversations on issues, or present a new topic for discussion. RSF provides the opportunity for San Franciscans to discuss issues that are most important to them while providing input that is read by city residents; presenting opinions for subscribers to have a well-rounded understanding of other residents' opinions.

The site is forum-based and is broken down into nine "issue pages": "Transportation," "Education," "Better Government," "Environment," "Tax Reform," "Neighborhoods," "Public Safety," "Jobs," and "Housing." Each issue page contains discussion topics started by users. Each issue page includes its own reset blogs and discussion boards for the particular focus within the topic. These pages also include resource links for further reading under the heading "Worth a Read." There are polls on the issue pages that provide instant feedback of opinions and views of other RSF members and participants. Lastly, the page uses videos titled "Ask an Expert," present on both the home page and the individual issue pages. The videos work to clarify the motivations behind the site, as well as to help new visitors understand the layout. They also help to ensure that a member of RSF can get the most out of the website by providing different methods of communicating information.

The website also includes a variety of links to separate, outside resources. One section of RSF is dedicated to innovative initiatives in other cities or areas, in collaboration with Government 2.0. There is also a section for current San Francisco news. Including these outside links encourages residents to visit the website for additional content that can also be accessed in multiple languages, including English, Mandarin, Spanish, Vietnamese, and Russian. This feature creates more accessibility by a larger percentage of the population, as it works to counteract the potential to disenfranchise and isolate non-English-speaking residents of the city. Also of note, the site is very easy to navigate. The user-friendly interface allows citizens without much computer or Internet knowledge equal access to the features of the website. All of these aspects assist the viability and success of the project by increasing page views in hopes the website will reach a broader audience.

Analysis

A. Transparency and Civic Engagement

The RSF is designed to encourage civic engagement and produce greater transparency in regards to the projects and goals of the city government. The copious discussion boards are the primary aspects that encompass input of the general public. The discussions support different views, allowing the residents to voice varying opinions. The opportunities to voice contrasting opinions aim to stimulate the citizens of San Francisco to share their stories to promote a healthy dialogue of suggestions for improvement. This also serves as an educational tool, as the website could not possibly include such a wide variety of information without the input of the city's constituents. Shared personal experiences and stories can contribute to better understanding of multiple issues.

The discussion boards encourage sharing ideas between residents, creating opportunities to come together in solidarity. The discussions can help formulate a more well-rounded point of view for an individual; it can also motivate residents into action. Finding shared perspectives that support and validate opinions allows residents to join together to potentially influence positive change.

RSF aims to create and support civic engagement by educating San Franciscans about the current state of the city government and related issues. The issue pages provide focused information, creating a site that is both easy to navigate and simple to use as a tool to gain more understanding of government activity. The easier a website is to use, the more efficient and successful it will often become. It is difficult to reach out to new visitors or moderately interested citizens if they must work hard to garner information. The issue pages summarize the common concerns for the residents to understand city government with optimism of influencing change. This helps to easily educate newcomers to widely discussed issues so that they can become educated, involved citizens. The site works even harder to create a welcoming environment by offering four different language options. Interested parties can view the website in the language with which they are most comfortable. This function works to make the site accessible to as many people as possible. The more residents that participate in the project will make a greater possibility for effecting change and creating improvements.

One of the best portions of RSF to highlight transparency is the "Better Government" section. This section describes the efforts of other cities and municipalities to create greater transparency and more responsive government policies and programs. Sharing these efforts with San Francisco's residents can help them integrate the changes into the government of San Francisco. These examples may encourage brainstorming in San Franciscans and even help them come up with their own ideas for greater transparency. The "Better Government" page asks residents directly for their ideas on how to improve their government. No one is more integral to producing change than the citizens who would be directly affected by any results. It also works to discourage any pessimism that may arise;

it is difficult to claim nothing will ever change when presented with evidence to the contrary.

Engaging the residents of the city is the main goal of RSF. The website capitalizes on social-media tools to encourage this participation. A resident can inform friends, family, and neighbors by sharing information from the site through any number of types of social media. This can work to educate those citizens who may not be inclined to search out additional knowledge on their own. As with many other aspects of the website, the access to social-media tools encourages more participation, which certainly helps create more transparency by involving more people. A larger base of concerned citizens creates more pressure on the city government to enact change.

When the website was first launched by Phil Ting, there was some question of the motives behind the creation of the project, as it does not wholly fall under the realm of assessor-recorder job description. Most likely, the website serves to act both as a resource for the citizens and as a campaign tool for Ting. For example, in an article for the *SF Weekly*, consultant Jim Ross, who is not affiliated with Phil Ting or Reset San Francisco, stated, "I think Phil truly cares about policy and having a true discussion. But . . . any citywide politician right now wants to establish themselves on a variety of issues."[1] Regardless of the motives, RSF results in a valuable asset for San Franciscans.

B. Innovation for Residents

The Internet phenomenon continues to grow, and more and more individuals are obtaining access to the global network and are learning how to efficiently navigate it through different mediums. As web-navigation skills continue to rise among average citizens, the common use of the Internet has provided them with the ability to access information more efficiently than ever. By utilizing technological innovations, Reset San Francisco has empowered residents to be more involved in San Francisco's government, in turn modernizing the democratic method of constituent involvement.

1. Crowdsourcing

The featured concept of RSF is the application of a technique known as crowdsourcing.[2] As defined by *Business Week*, crowdsourcing is obtaining needed services, and gathering ideas, by soliciting information from a collection of individuals in an online community. According to a 2006 article in *Wired* magazine, crowdsourcing has become the alternate means of cheap labor alongside outsourcing.[3] Originally used as a business technique, it solicits information from the general public about consumer products, and ideas for better business practices. RSF has applied this tool to promote better government. This featured business practice is applicable in a political situation as it reinvigorates the democratic process. San Francisco's constituents are not only more informed about government activity but also can collectively contribute ideas through different forms of media to make their government more effective.

2. Media

Media techniques utilized by RSF are mainly focused on group input of government issues through blogs, electronic newsletters, and social media. With regards to RSF blogging, the constituents can create a discussion forum that focuses on a government issue and solicits feedback from any participant who would like to provide input. Residents create an RSF profile, which will be explained in detail below, and automatically receive electronic updates of the discussion to which they have contributed. The ability to share information through different forms of media has become the most efficient way to appeal to residents for becoming more involved. By making significant government information available via the Internet, RSF returned to a practical means of communicating information between constituents, not on a global scale, but in a communal setting for residents of San Francisco.

3. Bridging the Gap of Social Strata through Modern Technology and Social Media

Reset San Francisco's most innovative accomplishment is utilizing mediums of social and professional media to communicate important information of government activity. The social-media revolution has captivated individuals of all age, socio-economic, and educational strata. From corporate executives to a community of high-school students, the evolution of professional and social media has attracted millions of individuals whose Internet-navigation skills vary from beginner to advanced levels. By utilizing these media outlets, RSF is bridging the gap of social stratum to understand and/or be involved in government activity. This creates an equal understanding of government issues between these groups and allows the individuals to take part in the discussions and voice their opinion. It takes very little skill to access the general social-media sites (Gmail, Facebook, etc.), and the channel of connecting people on various levels of the Internet is innovation at its finest via the RSF.

C. Use of Technology

Under principles of Gov 2.0, RSF uses modern mediums of Internet technology that creatively engage constituents of San Francisco. These resources help residents become familiar with the operations of the city's government, discuss issues that are pertinent to their goals, and create and share original content with friends and family to build a larger network of citizen activists.

1. Learn

RSF partners with other California transparency projects such as California Common Sense, a Stanford University–based non-profit focused on "government transparency through opening city financial data to the public."[4] The CACS tool offers a high-tech visualization of the last ten years of San Francisco's historical debt, deficits, surpluses, revenues, and expenditures. Not only does it show the changes in amounts over time, but it breaks down the contributions to those totals, such as public works, public protection, and general government administration. You can hear Phil Ting speak about their partnership on the RSF YouTube page and the importance of "demystifying the state budget"[5] in order to empower the average citizen.

In addition to the partnership with CACS, RSF also has a running feed of news stories pertaining to the city of San Francisco. Many of them are arranged by topic and can be found on the left column on the site, but users may also access the stories through the various social-media platforms RSF is connected through, such as Facebook and Twitter. Users may also access pre-researched resource material on the designated discussion topics under the "Worth a Read" icon for more background information. Last, under the "Toolkit" icon, RSF connects users with several governmental and non-governmental websites that provide data and information on the happenings in San Francisco, including SFGOV blog, SFgate, Bay Citizen, and Flipboard.

2. Discuss/Create

The most attractive feature of the RSF site is the use of a personalized profile for users. Citizens are allowed to create an account in order to utilize what they've learned, to generate content and comments, and to connect with others. They can bypass a login by also directly connecting through Facebook. In addition to the personalized profile, RSF also makes use of polls strategically placed throughout the site that evaluate the opinions of citizens on different government initiatives and display results in real time. Under the "Smarter Ideas" tab, RSF implements an interactive feature where users may suggest specific solutions to governmental problems and have fellow users comment on the feasibility. In the past they have targeted this feature to only city employees, but now it is open to all users.

Fig. 4.4. Social media bandwagon. (Illustrated by Matt Hamm.)

Furthermore, under the "Ask an Expert" icon, users may stream live conversations and chat in real-time with government employees as well as the RSF team. RSF runs an Ustream link where experts hold a live broadcast where a diverse crowd can join online and have a conversation. This feature is only used on special occasions but significantly helps connect those that cannot physically come into town hall meetings, such as the disabled, or even those who would like a face to an interactive website.

3. Connect/Share

Like many modern organization web pages, RSF makes use of a Facebook fan page. In a city with the population of roughly 776,000, RSF has garnered around 14,000 likes, that's about 2 percent of the city population. RSF has also managed to get about 500 Twitter followers and several hundred views on its photo-sharing page on Flickr. In fact, a user can choose from over three hundred social media sources to share his or her personal content created through the site as well as the site's plethora of information and resources provided for the user. Share options are visible on multiple platforms, and each post has at least the option of three types of social media outlets to share through.

The site also boasts hundreds of views on its YouTube channel.

There are several videos about the organization as well as a step-by-step introduction on how to use all the features of the site and interviews with the team of RSF. There are also user-generated tutorials on questions asked by fellow users of RSF on governmental practices. And if a user doesn't feel connected enough, he or she may share professional networks with other users and city officials through LinkedIn and sign up for RSS-feed e-mails when the site is updated.

Conclusion

A. *Value to the Constituents*

RSF empowers constituents with an online community in which they may express what they would like changed or "reset" in the San Francisco government. In doing so, it serves as "a movement to improve processes for, participation in, and accessibility of government by utilizing advancements in technology."[6] This is done by providing utilities in which citizens can obtain meaningful data and analysis on their city government. Whether this be raw-data analysis in the form of the CACS initiative, streaming news reports of city and government happenings, blog posts informing constituents of similar initiatives and creative transparency innovations throughout the country, or highlighted issue tabs with preexisting background information in which to flourish further discussion. The primary goal of RSF is to supply constituents with as many tools as possible in order to empower and build a network of activists.

Furthermore, with the tools provided by RSF, constituents can unite as a community on issues that matter. Users of RSF may create and discuss content as well as share the content on a wide variety of mediums. These are tools through which constituents can take ownership in their activism and produce wider networks to garner physical change in the government. Additionally, these tools provide a tangible method of positive public discourse in which real results are achieved.

B. Value to Government

The value of this program to the San Francisco government is that it connects constituents of all different social capacities to be involved in the political process. This raises the political awareness of the San Francisco population. Residents of diverse backgrounds and age groups become aware of the issues that are elevating or hindering their government. Voter turnout would rise significantly, which would fare better for the elected officials who seek constituent votes to retain their position. Ultimately, the entire city would benefit from more involvement.

As discussed, the RSF's use of the Internet through social and professional media provides a unique guide to understanding and contributing innovative ideas to government. As the business concept of crowdsourcing was designed, the community's input is cost-free to the government. This in turn enhances government operation by soliciting suggestions for being better representatives. When the community feels that it is a part of its government, citizens feel more compelled to be involved in political processes that affect their city, and possibly the state. As the goal of the RSF, the revolution of electronic resources and social media has provided a platform for making San Francisco more transparent regarding government activity and city information and creates accountability for government issues that have not been addressed. Ultimately, the democratic process is reinvigorated and upheld to its highest standards by allowing the residents to practice their democratic rights by informing and being informed.

"PORTLAND'S CIVIC APPS INITIATIVE (PORTLAND, OREGON)," BY PHIL BOARDMAN, PETER CONTOS, AND BRYAN WEBER

Abstract

Portland's Bureau of Technology Services began working to launch CivicApps back in September 2009.[1] It has since become a dynamic collaboration between public and private sponsors with a focus on unraveling the complexity of Portland's newly released public data into a format that is useful. CivicApps is an innovative program that hopes to combine public data (such as information on Portland's Fire Department and EMS); technology involving apps for mobile devices; and civic engagement, by encouraging citizens, businesses, and developers to brainstorm, plan, implement, and improve applications based off the mountain of public data Portland uses. Citizens are encouraged to postulate ideas on ways to make the datasets meaningful and then are allowed to comment and rate the ideas. Those that have overwhelming public support are taken to businesses and developers who are encouraged to make the idea a reality through open-source programming. CivicApps has created a buzz around transparency in Portland and has been a motivation to continually expand the scope of the project as more citizens begin to realize the application's usefulness.

Project innovation has brought the Portland community together to create useful projects using government data. Some of the most talked-about projects use Fire/EMS, crime, power-outage, government-program, and community-created data to create applications on a platform that is easy to use and understand for the average citizen. In order to ensure usefulness, the City of Portland promotes the program by increasing awareness and rewarding development so that more citizens use and contribute to the applications. By doing this, Portland hopes that CivicApps becomes the most important aspect of city government by increasing efficiency within government and empowering its citizens.

CivicApps is a government-sponsored initiative led by Trimet, which is Portland's public transportation system, and the Portland Development Commission, which is a department involved in economic development. However, the initiative has also drawn in private co-sponsors,[2] which include Bridgecity Studio, Webtrends, Microsoft, Software Association of Oregon, Alto Law Group, Capybara Ventures, Perkins Coie, Oregon Entrepreneurs Network, Portland Ten, Swider Medeiros Haver LLP, Souk, NedSpace, Widmer Brothers Brewing, Hopworks Urban Brewery, and Open Source Lab at Oregon State University.[3]

The CivicApps initiative is a model for increasing transparency and civic involvement, utilizing volunteer resources rather than government money. In an era of tightening city budgets, this method of creating a bridge between citizen involvement and transparency efforts is an attractive solution. The collaborative partnership, which includes the software and entrepreneurial community in the city, creates a three-way connection between government, business, and individual citizens, and develops the kind of excitement that drives growth in the business sector as well as increased responsiveness by the government and a greater sense of satisfaction by Portlanders.

Analysis

CivicApps is an initiative created by Portland to promote "open and transparent government, open data, and partnership opportunities between the public, private and non-profit sectors, academia and labor."[4] To actualize this goal, the city partnered with citizens to transform open government data into user-friendly Internet and mobile applications.[5] The CivicApps website has gained attention from the media due to its innovative concepts and interesting features.

The CivicApps website is comprised of three key areas: data,[6] ideas,[7] and applications.[8] At the time of the website's launch, Portland was one of a handful of cities to offer government datasets in an easily consumable format. It was also the first to provide datasets from inter-jurisdictional agencies.[9] The data available is provided by various government websites, such as www.portlandonline.com, www.oregonmetro.gov, www.pps.k12.or.us, and www.trimet.org, which provide information on Portland for a broad horizon of subjects like education and public transportation.

However, just making the data available does not achieve transparency. Transparency requires the data to be in a format that is easily accessible, easily understood, and meaningful. While the datasets were easily accessible, they were not meaningful to those who lacked the technical knowledge to parse the data. Rather than working on making the data more open through internal projects, the city engaged its citizens and encouraged them to provide the most meaningful use of the data.[10] They accomplished this by holding an application-creation contest when the website launched. This was innovative in its own right, as Portland was one of the first cities to sponsor such a contest.[11]

In addition to the open submission of applications that made novel use of the datasets provided, the CivicApps contest included an additional component that set the contest apart from its predecessors. The initial phase of the contest was an idea challenge. Anyone could submit an idea for an application through a user-friendly form,[12] even if he or she lacked the resources or knowledge to develop the application. This opened up the contest to a wider audience and encouraged citizen engagement by offering prizes for the best ideas.[13]

Once the idea-generation phase of the contest concluded, the application phase began. Developers could submit an application based on one of the ideas from the first phase or could submit an application of their own design. The city government sponsored events in coordination with the application phase to further engage the community. One outstanding example is CiviCode Day, which was a collaborative conference between developers and stakeholders to discuss and share ideas.[14] In addition, the city held numerous "hackathons" and "coders nights" where Portland hackers could get together and collaborate on writing the code for apps.[15] These events created quite a bit of excitement and engagement within the open-source community of Portland as well as with citizens who collaborated with them to suggest ideas.

The openness of the application-submission process further aided the city in achieving transparency. Any fully functional applications that complied with the rules of the contest were accepted and made available to the public. Because there was no filter on application submission or retrieval, the city achieved a measure of transparency through lack of censorship. Furthermore, the developers for the apps are outside, third-party developers not employed by the government. In theory, because they were not directly employed by government agencies, they would not have a conflict of interest in presenting data as openly as possible.

The website also had two other features associated with the contest that had a latent effect on government transparency and citizen engagement. First, the contest was open-ended, meaning that ideas and applications could be submitted beyond the contest's original deadlines. Second, the website allowed the community to rate the merits of the ideas and applications in addition to the official judging panel. This encouraged an ongoing dialogue within the community and has kept citizens engaged in improving the flow of information from government agencies. Indeed, at the time of this writing, generation of ideas and applications has continued well over one year past the initial deadlines of the contest.[16] For example, the city sponsored a "hackathon" to create an application programming interface (API) for the city-council agenda more than six months after the contest had ended.[17] In addition, the community-provided ratings provide valuable feedback on what data and ideas people find most valuable, furthering the conversation.

Perhaps the most innovative facet of the CivicApps project and the one most economically valuable to the citizens of Portland was the contest's emphasis on tenets of the open-source movement. The contest was created as part of a larger agenda by the city to embrace the open-source community.[18] The rules of the contest stipulated that all applications submitted be licensed under an OSI-approved license.[19] While there are various licenses approved by the OSI (Open Source Initiative), they all share common elements that would benefit the people of Portland. Namely, OSI-licensed applications must be freely redistributable, provide source code, and allow derivative works.[20]

Historically, a lack of financial resources has been the largest barrier to innovation.[21] Because the applications created by the CivicApps contest were freely redistributable, the city would have to spend no more than $25,000 and the local economy could receive a potential boost of millions of dollars in addition to providing innovative uses of its data.[22]

By requiring source code and the ability for people to derive new applications from existing applications, the contest bootstrapped its own momentum. By providing the source code for the applications, novice developers and those without development knowledge could use existing applications as tutorials for creating new applications. And because these applications allowed derived works, developers could modify or improve existing applications.

Finally, a majority of the apps created through the CivicApps website have also increased civic engagement on their own. Some of the more notable ones include:

- Washington County Fire/EMS Twitter: Collects all the recent data on fire engines and ambulances being dispatched, collects them, and posts them on a Twitter accounts that anyone can subscribe to so they can see the activity from their mobile device. This gives citizens an opportunity to see how these services are working, and also allows them to understand the needs of their own neighborhood.[23]
- Portland Crime app: Allows citizens to view and track crimes by area and frequency, it can also help citizens identify crime hotspots across the city simply by using their cell phone. This

provides transparency so that people can see where crimes are occurring, how frequently, and what types of crime are being committed. It allows a better understanding of how safe different areas of the city are as well as provides information for personal decisions on the risk involved in going to different parts of the city.[24]

- Reporter app: Allows members of the community to report infrastructure repairs, potholes, blocked storm drains, and burned-out streetlights as they see them. This really makes citizens a part of the city team. Now, when people are out for a walk, they can immediately report on items that need attention. It allows city services to be deployed more efficiently and makes these services more responsive to the people who live in the city.[25]

- Super Cat City Alerts app: Gives real-time data on city power outages.[26] This creates more transparency in the energy infrastructure so that it can be determined what areas of the city may have more frequent power outages due to aging infrastructure, promoting equity as it becomes more obvious if some areas are repaired more quickly than others. It promotes a sense of being connected to the knowledge base of the city and mitigates the need for people to call the city for information by providing the data in an easy-to-consume format.

- Accessibility Maps: Provides a map of accessibility features, such as ramps and sidewalk cuts, citywide.[27] This app provides transparency and desired information to those people who are interested in accessibility within the city. It may serve as a map to understand if there are areas of the city that still need an increase in ramps or other features. It can also serve as a roadmap for those who need accessible paths as they travel through the city.

- Disaster Relief app: Allows mobile users to send emergency beacons to a real-time map in the event of a disaster. Notices about supplies and terrain reports can also be sent. This app is for use by the government, by medical teams, and by individual citizens. For example, in the event of an earthquake, a citizen can send an emergency beacon with his or her location and status. This app provides transparency and increases government responsiveness in times of emergency and disaster.[28]

- Show of Hands app: Allows for real-time polling over mobile devices and also provides contact information, such as e-mail, Facebook, Twitter, and phone numbers for elected representatives. This app promotes civic engagement by allowing citizens to create polls to understand the views of others in the city, and also by promoting ease of access to elected representatives.[29]

CivicApps seems to be gaining in energy, as more ideas are being suggested and coded into apps. Many of the ideas come with a list of steps that would be needed to create the app, and the website allows visitors to vote on which apps they would most like to see written. Some of the ideas currently listed on the website are:

- Project Funds Finder app: This would encourage citizens to "crowd fund" government projects that are being abandoned for lack of funding. Alternatively, it could allow small businesses to turn to neighborhood clientele to help fund small expansion projects.[30]
- Civic Connect: Would allow public agencies to post about public-involvement opportunities, such as volunteer work or open positions on their board of directors.[31]
- City Cash Flow: An app that would indicate how much money was going in and out of various city departments.[32]

By putting data in easily understood forms, making it readily accessible to all citizens, and leveraging the innovation of its citizens, Portland is laying the groundwork for a more open and engaging city government.

Conclusion

Across the nation, municipalities are getting motivated to attract and keep citizens in order to grow; this creates competition between cities, and in order to entice people to its town, the city needs to create a competitive edge. Innovation and technology has long been the cornerstone of the American economy, but lagging way behind in the information age are our archaic government practices. In order to create this competitive edge, many governments are trying to break new ground and eliminate some of the problems associated with living in big cities by answering such questions as the following: Where does tax money go? What are government employees paid to do? What services does this town offer me? Using innovation and technology, local governments like Portland's and CivicApps are seeking to answer a lot of these questions by promoting transparency.

CivicApps has spurred civic engagement on several layers, in ways that have not yet been seen by most governments. The government releases its data but doesn't just let it sit there; Portland actually invites and encourages its citizens to become a part of the city. Citizens and businesses alike have come together to create efficient ways to compile data that they feel is necessary and to deliver it to those who are likeminded.[33] For the average Portland citizen, overwhelmed by the amount of data, developers have used access to government datasets to make everyday life easy. Trying to find a bike rack to lock up your bike, wondering when construction will happen on your street, or if there is a wheelchair-accessible curb near your place of work, developers are taking into consideration the needs of Portland's citizens and creating innovative ways of making their lives easier. The realization around Portland is that it's good for the community, it brings people together in ways they didn't think were possible, and even the mayor stresses that it's a "really efficient way to deliver economic development and government services."[34] Both citizens and government officials are excited about this kind of innovation and how it can better the lives of each person in Portland. In fact,

Portland is beginning to think outside of just their town by trying to integrate with the state of Oregon, the Pacific Northwest, and possibly internationally.

As optimistic as the community is about transparency in government and the release of government data, there comes a time when there will be a backlash, and somewhere you have to draw the line on the release of data. An ongoing court case in Oregon involves the release of data for individual employees and retirees by the state pension system.[35] In this case, although not specifically geared toward CivicApps but on the topic of transparency, Oregon's Public Employees Retirement System "released the names and monthly benefits of 110,000 retirees in November. A second batch of information will be released in March, including retirees' years of service, retirement date, final average salary and the method used to calculate benefits."[36] This type of transparency caused an eruption in anger from citizens and can change the course of reform. Governments wishing to make reform in the form of transparency will also need to take into account some of the privacy issues it may encounter upon the release of the massive amount of data that it collects. Even though there may be different opinions about what data the government should release, as well as when and how the government releases its data, as long as optimism surrounding transparency exists, municipalities will strive to please their citizens by releasing relevant data to the public.

Chapter 5

Critical Factors in Measuring Transparency

"But what is government itself, but the greatest of all reflections on human nature? If men were angels, no government would be necessary. If angels were to govern men, neither external nor internal controls on government would be necessary. In framing a government which is to be administered by men over men, the great difficulty lies in this: you must first enable the government to control the governed; and in the next place oblige it to control itself. A dependence on the people is, no doubt, the primary control on the government; but experience has taught mankind the necessity of auxiliary precautions."

—James Madison,
The Federalist Papers, Number 51

If men *were* angels, we wouldn't need to bother figuring out how to measure transparency in government because we wouldn't need a transparent government! We would have complete trust in those whom we elected to govern us because they would govern as angels, fully without question to their integrity or ethics. Of course that's not the case, so our founders wanted to ensure that safeguards were in place to protect "We the People" from those who are less than angels.

Federalist Paper Number 51 is about checks and balances in government, which is elaborated upon in that essay as the "auxiliary precautions" to be put in place because our founders feared that dependence on the people as the primary control of government may not always be effective. How prescient they were! We have struggled for over two centuries just to give everyone the right to vote, much less to give voice to the concerns of the disenfranchised and marginalized citizens. Securing control of our government has been even more elusive.

The "Principal-Agent" Relationship

However, as we have entered the twenty-first century, the power of the people to control our government is far superior than at any time in our history, and not a moment too soon. Those checks and balances of the executive, legislative, and judicial branches of government put in place by our constitution have proven to be not as effective as we would hope, particularly when political parties seize control of two of those branches and appoint the third—be it federal or state.

By creating a high level of transparency in government, the kind that so many throughout our history have advocated for, we empower citizens with the information necessary to control our government such that Madison's quote is actually turned on its head. In the end "the people" are the auxiliary precautions in controlling a government when the built-in checks and balances fail, and transparency is the people's tool that enables that control.

To fully appreciate the need for measuring transparency in government, one needs to first understand the concept of information asymmetry. Nobel laureate in economics Joseph Stiglitz explained it well in a lecture he gave back in 2001 In that lecture he explained information asymmetry as follows:

> Information imperfections are pervasive in the economy: indeed, it is hard to imagine what a world with perfect information would be like. Much of the research . . . focuses on asymmetries of information, that fact that different people know different things:

workers know more about their ability than does the firm; the person buying insurance knows more about his health, whether he smokes and drinks immoderately, than the insurance firm; the owner of a car knows more about the car than potential buyers.[1]

This information asymmetry is also relevant to government transparency and brings up what is known as the "principal-agent" problem—referring to situations in which it is difficult to monitor the behavior of one's agents. Think of it this way: In a representative democracy such as we have, rather than a direct democracy, the people we elect to represent us are our agents. They do our bidding for us in the halls of the legislatures of government. In effect, we hire them to do government for us, much like we'd hire a painter to paint our house. Even if we had the skills to undertake painting the exterior of our house, we often choose not to because we don't have the time—so too with government. But government is far more complex than slapping a bucket of paint on a house, and it's much more than just voting on legislation. So it makes a lot sense that we elect these proxies to do government for us. But how to ensure that we're getting "what we pay for"?

The answer lies in fully transparent governments that mitigate the information-asymmetry issue related to the principal-agent problem. The more we know about the behavior and actions of those representing us in government, the better. However, it's one thing to articulate clearly what our expectations are for a more transparent government by precisely defining *transparency*, as we've done earlier in this book. It's another thing to define the metrics whereby we can measure that transparency. We talk a good talk when it comes to transparency in government. We all seem to want more of it—politicians for purposes of getting reelected and citizens for purposes of knowing what those politicians are up to. Yet when it comes to walking the walk, we all seem to take a seat. If transparency in government is to be the great empowering civic tool of this century, then we not only have to define it, we have to measure it.

Do an Internet search for "measuring transparency in government," and you're likely to be disappointed. Aside from a few links to stories on foreign governments and links that don't work, you'll find a number of academic articles speaking to the minutiae of measuring the effectiveness of specific government programs, accounting practices, and theoretical papers that should be regulated by the FDA as sleep aids. One of my favorites is one from the World Bank with the inauspicious title: "Transparenting Transparency: Initial Empirics and Policy Applications."[2] This is not to denigrate the work of those who produced some of these studies, in fact, some I've used as references and material for this chapter.

What I found amazing, though, was the fact that not one of these studies took the time to develop and offer up a clear and concise definition for *transparency* before jumping into the deep end of the metrics pool. Yes, some did throw out a cursory sentence or two in defining it, but it was more an act of getting it out of the way so that they could move on to the more obtuse subject of developing their measures by which they could evaluate something that they really hadn't taken the time to explicitly define in the first place! Of course, you don't have that shortcoming here, unless you skipped chapter 1.

However, there's no sense reinventing the wheel when so many have made attempts at trying to get their arms, if not their brains, around a rather-elusive topic. It certainly was much more convenient to gather bits and pieces from each of these studies mentioned in this chapter, even though each had the limitation of addressing very specific slices of transparency or measuring aspects of transparency that really fall outside the realm of government. Yet, there were many diamonds in the rough, and when found, they were incorporated into what would eventually become a much more encompassing measure that would be developed here—with recognition, of course, as to their source.

What Are We Measuring?

Jerry Brito, a Senior Research Fellow at the Mercatus Center of George Mason University, gave a lecture back in March 2011[3] in which he made an important distinction regarding transparency in government. It was in response to an earlier speech that he heard given by Cass Sunstein, Office of Information and Regulatory Affairs administrator in the Obama administration, speaking at the Brookings Institute.[4] As Brito relates, Sunstein had said the administration was making huge strides on open government, and he cited the new product-recall database from the Consumer Product Safety Commission as a great example of open government. That perplexed Brito in that Sunstein mentioned a tire-safety-ratings database from the Department of Transportation, the toxic-release inventory from EPA, nutrition labeling, newly released FAA flight-delay information, and OSHA workplace-death tallies.

As Brito went on to say, though these data are public, these data-sets are not really about open government, and they are certainly not about transparency. Even Sunstein had said disclosure is a "high-impact, low-cost" form of industry regulation. Industry regulation, prodded by disclosures, though a worthwhile cause, is not what we envision here when describing transparency in government. However, Brito further points out that the disclosure Sunstein speaks of keeps actors accountable for their performances, and thus nudges them to behave well.

So, if disclosure works for regulated industries, it should work for government too, and for Brito that is what open government is about—government disclosing its own actions, not simply the actions of those it regulates. Therefore, Brito finds it dangerous to be satisfied with the current type of open government. To that I'll add one other point to this discussion that relates back to our definition of *transparency*.

Remember, transparency is not simply disclosure, it is so much more, as I pointed out in chapter 1, and government transparency is just that—transparency in government disclosing its *own* actions. Our agents will have the upper hand if they can control the information available to us, the principals. Think of it like this: If you have to disclose your performance, you will have an incentive not to work against the interests of the principal who hired/elected you. This is true as well with those who work in government—those who are hired by those we elect. In the words of Louis Brandeis, "sunshine" is, indeed, the best disinfectant, especially in this classic principal-agent relationship born out a republic form of government. So, let's look at how we *might* measure that "sunshine."

THE RESEARCH

One of the joys of teaching at the university level is the opportunity to work one-on-one with students in an independent-study format, where a student proposes a topic that he or she would like to research under the guidance of a professor. During the 2012–2013 school year, an especially bright student, Matt Marcus, from my Political Research Seminar on Transparency in Government course, asked to do an independent study with me. Because he had been through my course, he and I agreed that his research would be directed to unraveling all of the various attempts by organizations to measure transparency—however broad or limited in scope.

Marcus explains in his overview of this project that as demands increase for more effective state-government transparency efforts, so too do the number of tools designed to measure such efforts. These tools provide a critical service in cutting through the growingly popular rhetoric of transparency and attempting to first identify the specific components that are necessary for such transparency, and then measuring them in their implementation. As the number of such measurement tools grows, however, so does the complexity for those government stakeholders in trying to interpret and synthesize complex and often-contradictory definitions, methodologies, and grading systems. The goal of Marcus's analysis was to examine a number of mainstream transparency evaluation efforts and to identify those measurement best practices that could serve as a simplified and cohesive system for grading states on their efforts at promoting transparent governance.

The evolution of Internet technologies and cultural shifts toward decentralized information have led to an environment where a number of tools and indexes have been developed—often in tandem—that are dedicated to measuring and grading the transparency efforts of state governments. This in itself is fundamental evolution in the concept of democratic governance at this scale. Two decades ago, the effort required for an average citizen to stay informed of the day-to-day mechanics of his or her state government in real time would have made such an endeavor nearly impossible to accomplish. The generally accepted requirement of representative government that its citizenry be well-informed was a duty historically imposed upon the Fourth Estate.

The rise of the digital age, the evolution of Internet technologies, as well as the cultural evolution of digital users have created an environment where states can provide government data and information directly to stakeholders without relying on the media as a constant intermediary. This digital evolution has also allowed for the development of digital tools and indexes designed to measure how states are performing in these efforts and where opportunities for improvement might be found. If government transparency is critical to a well-informed public, then measurements of government transparency are equally critical—for they allow stakeholders to compare their state's efforts to the rest of the country and pressure for those changes or innovations that might improve efforts.

Marcus's analysis focused on evaluating those tools, index, and grading systems, dedicating to measuring state transparency efforts and developing a set of comprehensive best practices. In doing so, he came up with five key organizations that highlight some of those mainstream efforts at developing a set of metrics at the time of his research (2012). The result of this research provided some clarity as to some metrics that could be useful in creating a transparency index but, more important, demonstrates the wide disparity in applying a coherent and consistent set of standards in determining the extent of transparency evident in government. If anything, what is primarily gleaned from this research is that even analyzing a mere five organizations focused on transparency, there are many divergent paths with many divergent goals. To be blunt, Marcus uncovered what he wasn't necessarily looking for—a variety of methodologies in such disarray as to obfuscate any possibility of creating a truly usable and effective transparency index based on a common denominator of metrics. To his credit, he coaxed out of his research a modicum of factors that will contribute to the final metrics presented in the next chapter. However, it's important to show in this research that there is confusion in the present field of transparency metrics, and this reinforces even more so the necessity for a large dose of coherency. What follows is directly from Marcus's research for me.

"GRADING GOVERNMENT TRANSPARENCY: A SEARCH FOR BEST PRACTICES," RESEARCH AND ANALYSIS BY MATT MARCUS UNDER THE DIRECTION OF PROFESSOR DON GORDON, NORTHWESTERN UNIVERSITY, DECEMBER 10, 2012

SUNSHINE REVIEW

http://ballotpedia.org/wiki/index.php/Transparency_Checklist
(Note: In July 2013, Sunshine Review merged with the Lucy Burns Institute)

Strengths: Well-defined criteria, "wiki-style" content allows for evolving data, emphasis on proactive transparency efforts.
Weaknesses: No emphasis placed on quality of transparency or presentation, narrowly focuses on information published on government websites, "wiki-style" content allows editing by

unverified sources, confusing scoring system based on multiple third-party datasets.

The Sunshine Review was founded in 2008 and evaluates state-government transparency efforts by monitoring the information made available on their websites. The organization offers the following as guidance as to how it defines government transparency:

Openness, accountability, and honesty define government transparency. In a free society, transparency is government's obligation to share information with citizens. It is at the heart of how citizens hold their public officials accountable. Governments exist to serve the people. Information on how officials conduct the public business and spend taxpayers' money must be readily available and easily understood. This transparency allows good and just governance.

To further develop its definition, the Sunshine Review divides transparency efforts into three "buckets": proactive disclosure, FOIA, and campaign-finance disclosure. In order to develop its grading index, the organization sent out surveys to a number of "better government" style organizations to request their input on identifying what specific types of information are important for a government to disclose. It then took the most common survey responses and created a "ten-point transparency checklist" that it uses to grade states. This checklist includes the following areas:

1. Budgets
2. Open Meeting Laws
3. Elected Official Information
4. Administrative Official Information
5. Building Permit and Zoning Information
6. Audits
7. Contracts
8. Lobbying

9. Public Records
10. Tax Information

The Sunshine Review only reviews the information that is made available on a state's website, and it does not interpret or evaluate the form in which it is presented; in its own words, "Sunshine has approached transparency with an attitude of *if it's there, then it's transparent*."[5] This approach has the merit of efficiency and, to some extent, objectivity, but it is also highly problematic.

To begin with, we should ask a question that the Sunshine Review should have asked before developing its transparency checklist. Namely, *transparent for whom?* Transparency cannot be seen as virtuous in a vacuum, but as a means of creating an educated citizen base. If citizens are the primary government stakeholders, then it is arguable that sending surveys to better government groups, even if they are not partisan aligned, is more likely to return data points that such a group finds useful, rather than information specific to constituents. More important, and a theme that we will see throughout these reviews, better government groups and similar NGOs are professional organizations often with salaried staff and skill sets specific to their organization's mission. The way in which information can be presented to them, assuming that it is available, is vastly different than the way information can be presented to the general public. Referring to Professor Gordon's definition of transparency, government information must be made *enticing* to the public so that citizens might be encouraged to consume it. Better government groups and the like have no need for enticement, as consuming such information is a key reason for their very existence. By tailoring their checklist to the needs of such groups, the Sunshine Review risks developing a yardstick that measures transparency in a manner vastly different than it should in order to meet the needs of state-government stakeholders.

As noted earlier, the Sunshine Review limits its analysis of states to what is made available on public government websites. On one hand, it could be argued that states should make all information available on their websites. But the Sunshine Review is not making such an argument, rather it seems to have limited the scope of its analysis for the sake of efficiency. In this case, narrowing the scope of the output of this information may have also narrowed the scope of the input. There are other "buckets" of information and types of data that arguably should be included on the Sunshine Review checklist but might not be suitable for disclosure to public via a website. There are also other forms of government transparency that have less to do with disclosure of information and more to do with internal controls—this would include things like ethics oversight and whistleblower protections.

Interestingly, the Sunshine Review–publishing platform is built on the *Wikipedia* software model. While there are certainly risks involved in using this type of open publishing platform—primarily that partisan or other nonobjective parties might alter the data in some way—it also allows for audience participation in the publishing process and a method of evolving data support that no other model incorporates.

UNITED STATES PUBLIC INTEREST GROUP (US PIRG)

http://www.uspirg.org/reports/usp/transparencygov-20-0

> Strengths: Compelling scoring system, objective in-house data collection, grading includes perspective on trending.
> Weaknesses: Narrow focus on budget-only transparency, no emphasis on proactive transparency efforts.

The US PIRG transparency study, funded by a grant from the Ford Foundation is compelling in many ways. The report begins with the following statement:

The ability to see how government uses the public purse is fundamental to democracy. Transparency in government spending pro-

motes fiscal responsibility, checks corruption, and bolsters public confidence.

While this is a strong argument in favor of transparent governance, it does little to define what that transparency actually consists of. What it does accomplish is to narrow the focus of the US PIRG report to fiscal- and budget-transparency efforts. And, with this focus, the report is outstanding. To begin with, it evaluates transparency from the perspective of the average citizen, and as a result (and unlike any other study) emphasizes the importance of presentation and usability. To that end, the report makes the argument that, "practically speaking, public information isn't truly accessible unless it's online."[6] This is a strong, affirmative position to take on transparency efforts and one that is lacking from, for example, the Sunshine Review. Moreover, US PIRG digs into the difference between simply making information available online and making it accessible online to the average user. The organization describes this as the difference between "transparency 1.0" and "transparency 2.0," and the bar that it sets is a simple one; in order for a state-government website to meet the standard of transparency, its website must present comprehensive information compiled onto one website, and gaining access to any specific piece of information should require no more than one click of a mouse. Also important are user-friendly search tools and the ability for a user to download any available data.

The data for the grading component of the US PIRG report was compiled entirely in-house by its research team and then sent along to the state transparency administrator for comment prior to publication. State efforts that were in development at the time of publication were included in the notes. That said, there are a total of thirteen graded elements on the US PIRG report card, all limited to fiscal transparency and all focused on information available on state websites. While, as noted, this is a strong analysis with a robust methodology, there is a danger in viewing the report as anything approaching a holistic report card on state transparency efforts. By not defining government transparency, US PIRG leaves it to the audience to understand that there are a great many factors not being discussed in its report. Considering that it went out of its way to identify citizens as the primary end user for transparency efforts, this may be asking too much.

What the US PIRG report accomplishes, in addition to its primary goal, is to establish several lines in the sand with regard to state transparency efforts. First, it makes the argument, as does this analysis, that any measure of state transparency should view constituents as the primary audience, and second, that simply putting information out there is inadequate. Finally, the internal methodology that US PIRG adopted sets the bar for any next-generation grading index.

UNIVERSITY OF ILLINOIS INSTITUTE OF GOVERNMENT & PUBLIC AFFAIRS (IGPA)

http://igpa.uillinois.edu/content/transparency-state-budgeting

Strengths: Compelling and original grading indicators, incorporation of existing third-party grading tools, emphasis placed on using established statistical-analysis tools.

Weaknesses: Narrow focus on fiscal transparency, no emphasis placed on proactive transparency efforts, narrow focus on transparency for academic and financial stakeholders.

The IGPA report is less interested in grading state transparency efforts and more focused on how those grades are developed. Its focus is on methodology and correlative data analysis. Also important to note is that, along with several other referenced indexes, the IGPA narrows its focus to state-government fiscal transparency. Unlike several of the other indexes, however, the IGPA calls attention to this fact and, in fact, offers a definition for government transparency from the Alt-Lassen Index, which will be discussed later in this analysis:

> *Government transparency includes but is not confined to fiscal transparency. According to Alt, Lassen and Rose (2006: 30–31): "Broadly defined, government transparency is the overall degree to which citizens, the media, and financial markets can observe the government's strategies, its actions, and the resulting outcomes . . . one important aspect of transparency [is] fiscal (or budget) transparency."*

Also discussed within the IGPA review are those elements that make up a more holistic transparency effort, which includes ethics rules, FOIA requirements, regulatory frameworks, procurement and employment practices, codes of conduct, and public performance audits.

The strength of the IGPA report is in digging through the data currently provided by state governments to analyze if it is truly transparent. Its conclusion is that state fiscal transparency data is often so obfuscated by the time it is presented for public consumption that calling such presentation transparent is misleading. It found that state accounting tricks, inter-budget transfers, and off-book gimmicks made any attempt to grade transparency efforts difficult. To back up this argument, the IGPA looked at three modern grading systems of state fiscal transparency (the Alt-Lassen Index, Good Jobs First, the Sunshine Review) and found no significant correlation between them.

The IGPA's conclusion was that better measurement tools would be necessary, generally following the model of the Alt-Lassen Index, but also found that those indicators it identified for state fiscal obfuscation generally decreased as the number of desirable transparency efforts for that state increased. While the IGPA report does not include an analysis as to how its reform efforts would affect different stakeholder groups, its conclusion nevertheless rings true. If states are providing inaccurate or deliberately confusing data, private citizens are the least likely to be able to see through such tricks. By recommending a dataset for promoting true transparency efforts, taxpayers, as primary stakeholders, would also be the primary beneficiaries of such reforms.

CENTER FOR PUBLIC INTEGRITY (CPI)

http://www.stateintegrity.org/

> Strengths: Broad focus on transparency efforts, inclusion of enforcement gap, comprehensive question set, internal peer review.
>
> Weaknesses: Question set developed by narrow set of stakeholders, dataset developed by third-party freelance reporters, focus on corruption risk rather than transparency promotion, limited emphasis on proactive transparency efforts.

The CPI's State Integrity Investigation is, perhaps, the largest of studies discussed in this analysis. As a joint venture between CPI, Global Integrity, and Public Radio International, this study measures a wide range of state-government transparency efforts, weights them, and then assigns a letter grade to each state. Unique among discussed measurement efforts, the CPI Index includes an enforcement-gap weighting to its grading methodology.

The CPI Index evaluates states in fourteen categories:

1. Access to information
2. Campaign finance
3. Executive accountability
4. Legislative accountability
5. Judicial accountability
6. State budgeting
7. Civil-service management
8. Procurement
9. Internal auditing
10. Lobbying disclosure
11. Pension-fund management
12. Ethics enforcement
13. Insurance commissions
14. Redistricting

Combined, these buckets represent a comprehensive analysis of state transparency efforts. The buckets were broken down into a series of 330 statements that were sent to volunteer researchers, generally local journalists, in each state. The responses were compiled, weighted, and each state was assigned a letter grade.

The CPI's methodology, while robust, exhibits several weaknesses that could be resolved by adopting practices used in other measurement studies. Primarily, the use of local journalists as researchers and scorers represents a fundamental liability for the study. Journalists are certainly an educated group when it comes to state transparency efforts, and there is no doubt that the CPI endeavored to work with committed and skilled reporters, but it also skews the objectivity of the study in a manner not easily resolved. Reporters, as members of the Fourth Estate, are a key government stakeholder group and have much at stake with regard to transparency efforts. Important, though, journalists approach their research efforts in a different manner than do average citizens. Where a journalist is willing to dig for answers, a typical citizen may give up. Journalists are also far more exposed to government technical verbiage than are other stakeholders. Had the CPI Index data questions taken perspective into account, it likely could have tailored its questions to provide weight for other stakeholders, however, it did not. Also notable, a review of the state-level graders indicates a wide disparity of experience, background, and employment level. This raises a significant risk of inconsistent data across the states, and it is unclear what weighting or averaging methodologies could do to resolve such a disparity.

A more broad criticism of the CPI Index is that it adopts a similar approach to the Sunshine Review's policy of "if it's there, it's transparent." None of the 330 data points CPI measured reflect *how* information is made available to stakeholders and in what form. Rather, CPI takes the position that its index reflects a way of measuring the risk of corruption for states rather than stakeholder-focused transparency efforts. While corruption and transparency may seem like opposite sides of the same coin, the objectives involved in measuring each differ greatly.

One aspect of the study that stands out is the inclusion of an "enforcement gap" in the weighted grading. This gap is meant to measure the difference between transparency laws on the books and how those laws are actually enforced in each state. This effort is unique among the studies included and stands out as method of grading the practical implications of transparency efforts. CPI documents do little to detail how this gap was measured, but it appears as though the journalists responsible for providing primary research data on existing state laws also provided responses with regard to enforcement. If this is the case, it seems likely that the research data is highly weighted toward these journalists' personal experiences with state law enforcement.

ALT-LASSEN INDEX

http://www.imf.org/external/np/res/seminars/2005/arc/pdf/alt.pdf

Strengths: Detailed and comprehensive methodology, strong emphasis placed on identifying factors that lead to transparency efforts.

Weaknesses: Primary focus on fiscal transparency, limited emphasis on efficacy of transparency efforts or proactive measures.

Of the measurement indexes and tools discussed, none includes a more strenuous methodology or focus on stringent statistical analysis than the index by Dr. James Alt (Harvard University) and Dr. David Lassen (University of Copenhagen). The Alt-Lassen Index brings an aspect to transparency evaluation that the other indexes discussed do not, the element of time. The index studies state-government fiscal transparency over three decades in order to identify the systemic results for stakeholders—primarily taxpayers and institutional investors. The result is twofold. The study not only makes a compelling argument for long-term transparency in state-government fiscal matters but also has developed a robust index in the process. It is the index that will be the focus of this discussion.

The Alt-Lassen Index presents a far more technically robust measurement of state fiscal transparency measures than other measurement tools discussed. They tend toward a focus on established enterprise-level account best practices, but they integrate well into a greater fiscal-transparency scheme. The nine-point checklist includes an emphasis on multiyear expenditure forecasts, streamlined appropriations bills, and published performance measures—all internal mechanisms and controls that help to create a foundation for fiscal transparency in competitive political environments.

Using cross-sectional data for the 1990s from the National Association of State Budget Officers and the National Conference of State Legislatures, the authors code nine dichotomous budget procedures and create an index equal to the number of items for which each state had the more transparent procedure. The nine items are:

1. Is the budget reported on a GAAP (Generally Accepted Accounting Principles) basis? (Yes = more transparent, since shared language facilitates communication)
2. Are multiyear expenditure forecasts prepared? (Yes = more transparent, since more information about plans and the expected consequences of action is disseminated)
3. What is the frequency of the budget cycle? (Annual = more transparent than biennial, since more frequent action means more up-to-date information)
4. Are the revenue forecasts binding? (Yes = more transparent, since binding estimates increase the costliness of being misleading)
5. Does the legislative branch have (or share) responsibility for the revenue forecast? (Yes = more transparent, since legislative or consensus forecasts involve more officials, reducing the likelihood that estimates are misleading or manipulative)
6. Are all appropriations included in a single bill? (Yes = more transparent, since a single location facilitates monitoring)
7. Does a nonpartisan staff write appropriations bills? (Yes =

more transparent, because the staff has less partisan incentive to be misleading)

8. Is the legislature prohibited from passing open-ended appropriations? (Yes = more transparent, because published figures will be closer to ultimate outcomes)

9. Does the budget require published performance measures?(Yes = more transparent, because these create more explicit standards and information for judging politicians' actions)

SUMMARY

Rather than ask which of these indices offers the best solution to measuring state government transparency, this discussion will focus on those elements that could be transplanted from each in order to develop the most efficient and effective measurement model possible. This model should meet the following requirements, while embracing the Gordon definition of transparency:

- Provides simplified transparency grading by state.
- Justifies that grading with supporting "buckets" of data.
- Designed to meet the needs of multiple stakeholders.
- Primary emphasis placed on usability for citizens/taxpayers.
- Allows for some level of stakeholder participation.

The CPI Index provides a comprehensive breakdown of data "buckets" that should be leveraged for creating a new grading system. With the addition of one additional category used by the Sunshine Review (open meetings), the categories would include:

- *Access to information*
- *Open meetings*
- *Campaign finance*
- *Executive accountability*
- *Legislative accountability*

- *Judicial accountability*
- *State budgeting*
- *Civil-service management*
- *Procurement*
- *Internal auditing*
- *Lobbying disclosure*
- *Pension-fund management*
- *Ethics enforcement*
- *Insurance commissions*
- *Redistricting*

Combined, these fifteen categories are robust enough to offer detailed analysis of each state's ongoing transparency efforts, while small enough in number to be digestible to most audiences. The set of questions used by the CPI Index should also serve as a starting-off point. The 330 questions are both detailed and comprehensive. An analysis of the referenced measurement indexes can provide additional support.

To begin with, several questions specific to the open-meetings category should be added. These would focus on state laws specific to open meetings, notice requirements, secret voting, and publication of minutes. The robust fiscal-transparency measures identified by the Alt-Lassen Index should also be included as well. These data points include:

- *Whether or not the state budget is reported on a GAAP basis.*
- *Are multiyear expenditure forecasts prepared?*
- *The frequency of the budget cycle.*
- *Whether or not revenue forecasts are binding.*
- *Whether or not the state legislature shares responsibility for revenue forecasts.*
- *Whether or not the state uses single-bill appropriations.*
- *Whether or not a nonpartisan staff drafts appropriations bills.*
- *Whether or not the state legislature is prohibited from passing open-ended appropriations.*

- *Whether or not the budget requires published performance measures.*

Next, the IGPA-recommended transparency indicators should be adopted as well. These include:

- *Identifying the share of total spending that comes from special funds;*
- *Year-to-year variation in special fund expenditures;*
- *The magnitude of net transfers between general and special funds;*
- *Year-to-year variation in general-special net transfers.*

Finally, a set of stakeholder-usability questions should be developed that align with the US PIRG "transparency 2.0" positioning. This should be extrapolated to include questions as to state transparency efforts not only specific to website-data availability but all information availability—including the open-meetings inclusion and non-digital FOIA requests. Some of these questions would include:

- *Is all state-published data available on a single website?*
- *Is all state-published data downloadable in user-manipulated formats?*
- *Is key state-governance information provided with a summary explaining the data in language the average taxpayer could understand?*
- *At what frequency is information updated?*
- *Is information published on social-media platforms?*
- *Does the state government make efforts to promote its transparency website(s)?*

A key topic that should be discussed is that of data collection. As discussed, the CPI Index relies on state-level journalists to provide index data. This approach is somewhat problematic. The effort by

US PIRG to manage all research in-house is commendable, but also open to the argument that it does not approach research from the perspective of the intended audience. The best approach would be a combination of efforts that focused on localization of effort. One of the most important outcomes of a new index would be to gain an understanding as to how state transparency data was being presented to nonexpert stakeholders.

What better way to measure this aspect than to go directly to end users? An effective research approach would be to standardize the dataset questions and then develop a state-by-state collection of universities willing to assign such a task to their political-science departments. This research base could be augmented as needed by a dedicated internal research staff when more technical expertise was needed, particularly with questions of fiscal policy.

METHODOLOGY

There is perhaps no more complex component of the referenced grading/measurement models than their grading methodology itself. Ironically, since each tries to argue for simplified state transparency, their own methodologies are difficult to dissect and often go unpublished. A simplified grading model would take each of the data points and assign them to one of the fifteen "buckets" identified above. Each question would be awarded a points value of 1–10; yes/no questions would either be awarded a 0 or a 10, depending on the response. Totals would be added and averaged in order to create a 1–10 rating for each bucket, with the fiscal and budget receiving an additional weight for a total of 20 possible points. An additional 40 points would be reserved for questions specific to the presentation and usability of data. At a glance, the scoring breakdown would look like this:

- Access to information (1–10)
- Open meetings (1–10)
- Campaign finance (1–10)

- Executive accountability (1–10)
- Legislative accountability (1–10)
- Judicial accountability (1–10)
- State budgeting (1–20)
- Civil-service management (1–10)
- Procurement (1–10)
- Internal auditing (1–10)
- Lobbying disclosure (1–10)
- Pension-fund management (1–10)
- Ethics enforcement (1–10)
- Insurance commissions (1–10)
- Redistricting (1–10)
- Usability and Presentation (1–40)

Total Points: 200

Assigning a letter grade to each state would then be a simple matter.

A: 180–200
B: 160–179
C: 140–159
D: 120–139
F: 119 and below

If there is one key takeaway from this analysis, it should be that developing a comprehensive measure of state-government trans-parency efforts is a work-intensive task that likely requires the efforts of a dedicated team of engaged individuals, and possibly a group of enthusiastic citizen volunteers across the country. The task is worthy of the effort. If there is a second key takeaway, it should be this: there is currently no state in the union that would currently earn the grade of A under the proposed methodology, nor should there be.

Current efforts at measurement, while robust and well-intentioned, place far too much emphasis on technical legal protections and raw-data production while nearly ignoring the reason for such data production in the first place. To the extent that current measurement and grading tools are driving state-reform efforts, they need to begin driving efforts in the direction of usability and constituent-based objectives.

[End of Research Paper]

∽∾∽

SO NOW WHAT?

Given the pace of change today and in particular the acceleration of solutions being offered to deliver transparency in government, as shown by Marcus in just the few examples above, we appear to be caught up in a cacophony of quick fixes that muddle rather than illuminate the very transparency we're trying to measure. Much of this futility is driven by a lack of a common definition for *transparency*, which we developed in the very first chapter. Yet, given a common definition, there is still a great deal of work to identify the elements that will form a basis for developing metrics that capture the essence of that definition. That's the challenge to be met in the final chapter.

If we're to devise such an index that is widely acceptable, then first it must shine its light directly on those elements that illuminate whether transparency, according to a commonly accepted definition, is being served by government (Focus). Second, it must be easily measured in order to accommodate a crowdsourcing system of judges who are dispersed across all fifty states (Uniformity). Third, it must be practical in that adherence to improving one's score actually creates better government (Sensibility). Finally, the index must be easily understood so that citizens don't need a degree in math or statistics in order to comprehend the results (Simplicity). In other words, our index should take all the FUSS out of the difficulty in measuring transparency in government!

In Dr. Alt's paper, identified in Marcus's research, "The Causes of Fiscal Transparency: Evidence from the American States,"[7] Alt explores the theoretical framework for measuring fiscal transparency. In doing so, he quotes George Kopits and Jon Craig of the International Monetary Fund (IMF) from their research paper wherein they defined *fiscal transparency* as "openness toward the public at large about government structure and functions, fiscal policy intentions, public sector accounts, and projections. It involves ready access to reliable, comprehensive, timely, understandable, and internationally comparable information on government activities . . . so that the electorate and financial markets can accurately assess the government's financial position and the true costs and benefits of government activities, including their present and future economic and social implications."[8]

Kopits and Craig are strictly speaking to a slice of government transparency—that which impacts fiscal responsibility. However, in positing their definition, they make all the important points that are applicable to transparency in general, and that is that the information specific to fiscal policy (Focus) must be comparable (Uniformity) so that the electorate can accurately assess the government's financial position (Simplicity) and the true costs and benefits of government activity (Sensibility). As Alt goes on to explain, citing a variety of sources, this is why we must get it right when we measure transparency: "Transparency is an issue only when there is imperfect information . . . transparency can have both information and incentive effects. In a simple sense, more transparency means 'more information transmitted.' This is generally beneficial, for a variety of reasons including trust, predictability, reduced noise in markets, credibility, and coordination."[9]

Expanding on these reasons, Alt explains that

Trust increases when transparency means "tell them what you're going to do." If a politician has a history of having nothing to hide, then when he needs someone to take something on faith, he is more likely to get it. Transparency reassures people that he has not abandoned long-term goals, which could give him greater flexibility. Greater disclosure makes your actions more predictable when transparency means "give them details and justifications." In the political market, voters get a clearer view of performance, and can make more effective use of votes. Generally better observability is welfare-improving, as it reduces transaction costs in the broadest sense.[10]

Trust, reassurance, and predictability are all sorely missing in government today. As Alt so aptly put it in his paper back in 2005, "voters can make more effective use of votes."[11] And isn't that why we're doing this—measuring transparency—in order to drive civic engagement so that "voters get a clearer view"?[12] And if we're successful, democracy will be enhanced and flourish in this the twenty-first century.

Chapter 6

The Transparency Index

"If the broad light of day could be let in upon men's actions, it would purify them as the sun disinfects."
—Louis Brandeis, letter to Alice Goldmark,
February 26, 1891

Given all the possibilities of measuring transparency in government pointed out in the last chapter, the task of coming up with an index does seem to be rather daunting. Furthermore, even given a rather-abridged and uncomplicated set of metrics, the challenge of who is to do the measuring also must be met. As Marcus alluded to in his research, we really don't want governments rating themselves, so we have to think about who can best provide an objective application of the metrics once the index has been finalized. Both of those issues will be addressed here, but first let's revisit our definition so we can distill what was presented in the previous chapter within the context of what it is that fits into our interpretation of what transparency in government should deliver. Transparency is

the principle by which those affected by administrative decisions and legislation are made aware of the basic facts and figures as well as the mechanisms and processes of their government. This information must be presented in a way that is accessible, comprehensible, and enticing, thus motivating citizens to engage in the dialogue necessary to improve the efficiencies of government and mitigate corruption. It is the duty of our elected representatives and of civil servants to act in such ways as to enable this transparency.

If we're to break down this definition into its discrete parts in order to come up with categories by which we can build an index, we would have the following:

1. Content

    a. Facts/Figures
    b. Mechanisms/Processes

2. Characteristics

    a. Accessibility
    b. Comprehensibility
    c. Persuasiveness (whether it's enticing)

So basically everything that government does, be it municipal, state, or federal, can be distilled into two measureable categories of content and characteristics. Aside from drilling down into those two groupings, we have a fairly simple context that can clearly be disseminated in a graded format to the general public—that is, how much of its information does a government make available (content) and how well does government perform in delivering that information to its citizens (characteristics)? As the saying goes, "the devil is in the details," and certainly that's the case here.

Grading in each of the two classes is dependent on how a government is measured in the subcategories, and those in turn are dependent on the details underlying each of those. But the key here is that for those who simply want to know how their government is doing on being more transparent, the answer lies in just two graded categories—content and characteristics—which encompass the full spectrum of transparency.

READ THIS FIRST!

Allow me to express some strong caveats here before moving on. First, what you're about to encounter here is a completely different approach to measuring transparency in government, unlike anything undertaken in the past by any organization. As Marcus's research has shown for those institutions that currently try to measure transparency, their efforts are all mostly subjective and accommodative in that they measure what is already being done rather than setting a standard of excellence for what *should* be done to achieve full transparency, and *then* apply the metrics necessary to measure it. And by no means was this meant to be an academic exercise any more than this was meant to be a hard-and-fast solution. Ideas generated from these metrics are meant to serve as the basis for creating a foundation whose purpose is to further the cause of transparency through the application of metrics that are anything but static.

If all we're interested in is measuring what governments are already doing, then we're allowing them to create the standards—and governments are hardly the ones we should be looking at to provide those specifications. If all we're interested in is measuring what governments are already doing, then it's not transparency we're interested in measuring but rather their futile efforts that we're vindicating—efforts that too often fall far short of real transparency. And if all we're interested in is measuring what governments are already doing, then we are complicit in the act of dumbing down government transparency such that we have merely capitulated to accept a lowest common denominator of transparency—one that promotes mediocrity at the expense of the extraordinary.

Second, what you're about to encounter here sets a very high bar for achievement, and as it should be—and the metrics here go far beyond what we have done in the past. As citizens we have groveled for years under the umbrella legislation of the Freedom of Information Act (FOIA), which was born in an age of a right-to-know mentality and thus at the time was considered groundbreaking. Indeed, it was—

fifty years ago! It would be akin to saying about the civil-rights movement today that we're satisfied with the fact that Rosa Parks moved to the front of the bus and now all African Americans can take a seat wherever they want on any public mode of transportation. No need to do more. As momentous and historic was the act of Rosa Parks, so too was the passage of the first federal FOIA. Yet that doesn't mean we should be satisfied to stop there. Measuring transparency in governments based on response to FOIA requests would be like measuring advances in civil rights based on how many African Americans now ride at the front of integrated buses and trains. Really, it's that primitive!

Finally, what you're about to encounter here initially comes at a one-time high transition cost to governments. But then again, transparency programs in place today built on systems designed for a twentieth-century right-to-know mentality comes at a *recurring* high cost. A most recent General Accounting Office (GAO) report places the cost of processing a single FOIA request at upward of $4,000! And the federal government alone processes over a half million requests a year![1] Transitioning away from a FOIA-based transparency program to one based on the release of all government data, short of those deemed too sensitive to release immediately, would remove government from the roll of handmaiden to an ever increasingly curious citizenry. Give citizens the tools to research and extract rather than ask a gatekeeper to provide the data. The metrics devised here are based on that premise. The metrics devised here assume the elimination of all FOIAs. The metrics devised here are for a twenty-first-century right-to-know mentality. So let's take a look under the hood and examine the details of the information that make up those metrics.

THE METRICS

> *"Democracy is founded on the principle that the moral authority of government is derived from the consent of the governed. That consent is not very*

meaningful, however, unless it is informed. When a government makes decisions in secret, opportunity for corruption increases and accountability to the people decreases. This is why government transparency should be a priority. When official meetings are open to citizens and the press, when government finances are open to public scrutiny, and when laws and the procedures for making them are open to discussion, the actions of government enjoy greater legitimacy."

—Jerry Brito, "Hack, Mash & Peer: Crowdsourcing Government Transparency," October 21, 2007

Let's first be clear on what we're *not* measuring. As you saw in the examples from the last chapter, there are plenty of efforts dedicated to measuring integrity and accountability, legislation and enforcement, and levels of corruption in government—all of these are commendable achievements in grading government integrity, accountability, legislation, enforcement and corruption. However, none of these measure transparency as we've defined it here, for which the primary purpose is to create civic engagement. To create metrics and publish those results simply to create a scorecard that states can compare themselves to is laudable and certainly useful as catalyst to drive more transparency, and, one could say, in that regard, would be a great accomplishment. Yet if driving more transparency through these metrics doesn't produce a more engaged citizenry, then the index is just another "beauty contest."

Finally, the assumption throughout is that Freedom of Information Acts are a quaint anachronism of a twentieth-century mind-set regarding a citizen's right to know and that all government information, short of individual privacy guarantees, belongs to the people. Why is that? A citizen's right to know is based on the fact that "We the People" are the government and in a democracy such as we have, We the People give legitimacy to that government. Ultimately, everything that our governments do is a result of its citizens giving them the authority to do what they do. Freedom of Information Acts turned that notion on its head, in that they require citizens to request that governments provide them the information that they seek, which belongs to citizens in the first place! So, for purposes of developing an index, all of the metrics are based on this notion of ownership and the irrelevancy of Freedom of Information Acts, and for each metric I've noted the "Graded" criteria.

Content

Facts/Figures

GRADED—The Catalog

Exactly what data does a government gather and produce, and how much of that data is released to the public—and not just through a FOIA request? First we have to consider the repository of information that any government has in its possession, which is actually an enormous hurdle to clear. Think about this. Unless you know exactly what you're looking for, with the knowledge that government provides the data you're seeking, how do know what's available? What if you went into a library looking for a book on cooking, but there was no catalog and no Dewey Decimal System to order the books on the shelf. Even if you knew exactly what culinary book you wanted, how would you find it?

So before we can even think of measuring how transparent a government is when it comes to making facts and figures available, we first need to know what information exists. In other words, the first step for all governments is to catalog what they have—*all* information, not just what's made available to the public. Try asking for a list like that. I guarantee you that you will be disappointed every single time. Yet we can't get past square one in measuring transparency if we don't have it, because without it we don't know what we're measuring!

GRADED—The Chronicle

A list in and of itself is a good start but highly inadequate if not accompanied by a depiction of what each item is. This consists of a number of components when it comes to government information.

1. What? Each item in the list must have a short abstract. It doesn't help listing an item if you have no idea what it is simply from the name associated with the information.
2. When? Not everything is always immediately available, but everything should eventually be available. Create Date, Available Date, Pending Date* are the options.
3. Where? Like the library's Dewey Decimal System, every piece of information needs to be identified as to where to find it. It doesn't even need to be online, but it needs to be somewhere!
4. Who? Here's where we associate responsibility with information. We must know who produced the data and whom and how to contact when there are questions.

*Pending documents are those that government has deemed to be exceptions, such as litigation cases that may be current and therefore information cannot be released yet. However, all pending documents must indicate a date to be released or "N/A" for those not scheduled yet.

Now we're getting somewhere! What we're developing here is what I call a "common denominator of disclosure" based on the concept of catalogs and chronicles. If there is to be any hope of producing an index common across governments, it must begin by holding all governments to a universal standard of citizen expectations. Transparency cannot drive civic engagement if citizens don't have confidence that their government is providing full disclosure as to the data that is available. Therefore, it begins here. However, the relevance of the facts and figures must also be put into context, and that's why government must also provide access to the mechanisms and processes that create the data. Let's look at that using our common denominators.

Mechanisms and Processes

GRADED—The Catalog

If we think about the raw data that governments produce using the analogy of a Hollywood movie, then the mechanisms and processes are the prequel in that it answers the question, How did this all come to be? Budgets, for example, don't just fall out of the sky. There is a process template by which budgets are created—policies and procedures—and mechanisms that are utilized, such as meeting minutes, e-mails, phone calls, and so on, that disclose the decision making behind the process. When legislation is passed, contracts made, judicial decisions arrived at, there is a prequel to each that incorporate policies and procedures in how each is to be done and a trail of minutes, e-mails, phone calls, and so on, that serve to document the decision making that went into each—all of which is digitized today, or, if not, ought to be!

Without the mechanisms and processes, the facts and figures are simply that—a bunch of facts and figures, however relevant, devoid of any context showing how the data was produced. Without the mechanisms and processes, we can never answer the question "Why?" So if we're to measure transparency, we must include the disclosure of the mechanisms and processes associated with the facts and figures. Listing these in a discernible way requires that association. In other words, the way to list the mechanisms and processes is as a subset of the facts and figures list—all one catalog. Otherwise the list of mechanisms and processes would have little meaning outside of the facts and figures that they have created. Of course there would be redundancy here because the same mechanisms and processes can produce numerous facts and figures. In that budget example, many of the line items in the list of facts and figures would have the same mechanisms and processes as their subsets.

GRADED—The Chronicle

Again, a list of mechanisms and processes in and of itself is a good start but is highly inadequate if not accompanied by a depiction of what each item is. This too consists of a number of components but looks very much like our chronicle for facts and figures.

1. What? Each item in the list must have a short abstract. It doesn't help listing an item if you have no idea what it is simply from the name associated with the information.
2. When? Not everything is always immediately available, but everything should eventually be available. Create Date, Available Date, Pending Date* are the options.
3. Where? Like the library's Dewey Decimal System, every piece of information needs to be identified as to where to find it. It doesn't even need to be online, but it needs to be somewhere!
4. Who? Here's where we associate responsibility with information. We must know who produced the processes and developed the mechanisms and whom and how to contact when there are questions.

*Pending documents are those that government has deemed to be exceptions, such as litigation cases that may be current and therefore information cannot be released yet. However, all pending documents must indicate a date to be released or "N/A" for those not scheduled yet.

Characteristics

Remember, providing all that content mentioned above is only an act of disclosure, regardless of how well it's done. In the parlance of transparency, it's a good start, but disclosure is not transparency. Hopefully you're tired of hearing that, which is a good thing, because that means you are hopefully coming to understand the difference! As good as it gets regarding disclosure, we still have a way to go to get to transparency, and to get there we have to ACE disclosure and provide the metrics to measure it.

In considering the characteristics of transparency, we need to think in terms of applying each—Accessible, Comprehensible, and Enticing—to the content described above: facts and figures, mechanisms and processes. Each of the three characteristics will extract transparency out of the disclosure of content if successfully applied. Measuring transparency, then, is dependent on how well each characteristic is applied to content.

Accessibility

In chapter 1, I said that "accessibility should be effortless given the Internet. Every piece of knowledge seems to make it there, and most of it is free. And getting to information is as easy as opening a laptop, a tablet, or a smartphone and doing a search in any number of easy-to-use browser tools. It's getting to the point that if information *isn't* digitized, it doesn't exist!" However, that doesn't mean that the hundreds of thousands of myriad government entities have become all digitized, and even if they have achieved that holy grail of documentation, what about all that history?

The fact is that converting to an all-digital environment is a fairly inexpensive venture today. Going back and capturing all that history is another matter. Sometimes you just draw a line in the sand and leave it at that. In Illinois, there are fairly stringent campaign-finance disclosure laws regarding the reporting of contributions and expenses, all which are posted online now. However, you can only go back to 1999. After that, you're on your own, digging through paper. Given the expense of transcribing/scanning old documents and given the number of offices/candidates in the state of Illinois—over 42,000 elected offices and a multiple of that in candidates—going into the way-back machine can be a pretty expensive undertaking.

One could set a time frame of how far back a government should go to be aggressively transparent, but in the end it would be a crap shoot to try to wrap transparency in the context of digitized history. You could give "extra credit" for a long reach back or even any reach at all, but what is more important is that governments bite the bit of digitization and at least move forward from this point on. Grading on history is something we'll leave aside and instead focus on the present when it comes to establishing metrics.

Also, web navigation and design is an art form in itself, and though some government websites are more intelligently designed than others, it's not the intent to recreate or include these metrics here—navigation and design are best left for any number of those geek sites to do that. However, the website grading rubrics are an important factor in overall accessibility, so one or more of these sites would be utilized to provide an overall score on navigation, search engine optimization (SEO), social media, compliance, and other important factors that go into determining a site's ease of access (usability factor). This can then be included in the accessibility score.

The focus on grading the characteristic of accessibility will be on ratios, which can be quite telling, based on the Chronicle for each. A number of ratios can be coaxed out of these metrics, which will then reflect favorably or unfavorably on the level of transparency. There are four graded categories that map to the four components listed under the Chronicles of Content for facts/figures and mechanisms/processes: Availability, Location, Timeliness, and Approachability. How these categories map to the components are shown in parentheses.

GRADED—Available(1,2)

Based on the list provided under Content, we can extract the accessibility score based on the availability of content for both facts/figures as well mechanisms/processes and a combination of both. We can best express this availability as the ratio of available content to unavailable content:

1. Total Available Content : Total Content (Current and Historical—1 year comparisons)
2. Total Pending Content : Total Content (Current and Historical—1 year comparisons)
3. Total Unscheduled Content : Total Content (Current and Historical—1 year comparisons)

GRADED—Locatable(3)

Based on the list provided under Content we can extract the accessibility score based on the location of content for both facts/figures as well mechanisms/processes and a combination of both. We can best express location as the ratio of available content located online to available content located offline:

1. Available Content Online : Total Available Content (Current and Historical—1 year comparisons)
2. Available Content Offline : Total Available Content (Current and Historical—1 year comparisons)
3. Available Content Online : Available Content Offline (Current and Historical—1 year comparisons)

GRADED—Searchable(1)

Based on the list provided under Content, we can extract the accessibility score based on the "search-ability" of content for both facts/figures as well mechanisms/processes and a combination of both. We can best express search-ability as the ratio of available content that is searchable within the documents as opposed to available content that is not searchable, such as scanned documents not converted to text.

1. Available Searchable Content : Available Non-Searchable Content

GRADED—Timely(2)

Based on the list provided under Content, we can extract the accessibility score based on the timeliness of content for both facts/figures as well mechanisms/processes and a combination of both. We can best express timeliness as the ratio of when content (online and offline) was created/occurred to when it was made available:

1. Date Content Created/Occurred : Date Content Made Available (Online/Offline)

GRADED—Approachable(4)

Based on the list provided under Content, we can extract the accessibility score based on approachability of the authors associated with content for both facts/figures as well mechanisms/processes and a combination of both. We can best express approachability as the ratio of contact information provided for content (available and unavailable) opposed to content where contact information is not provided:

1. Contact Information Provided : Contact Information Not Provided (Available/Unavailable)

Comprehensibility

Again, in chapter 1 I posited the question that even if government had overcome the barriers to access and in the spirit of best practices made all its information easily accessible, would we then have full transparency? As I said, it's easy enough to put that 150-page city budget on the Internet, a mere click away from accessibility, in a portable document format (pdf) that makes it easy to read or print out. It's another thing entirely to present that information in a way that is comprehensible. No doubt accountants and experts in public policy could analyze such a document expeditiously, but all the rest of us would muddle through a few pages and give up. Just making information accessible doesn't make it useful.

Information has to be presented in a way that the average citizen can digest, and how well that is done reflects upon the comprehensibility of the information presented and thus its usefulness to the average citizen. Like good art, though, comprehensible information is in the eye/mind of the beholder. Obviously, there's no way to interpret information in a way that pleases everyone, so measuring the comprehensibility component of transparency may at first seem to be a *fool's errand.*

Yet newspapers and periodicals are published every day that successfully communicate to the average reader. One could make the case that the *New York Times* is a far cry easier to read than *Scientific American*, but each recognizes whom its audience is and thus tailors its stories in a narrative that its audience understands. Of course no one, including this author, has any expectations that governments will rewrite every piece of narrative that they release to suit the most common denominator of an audience of citizens. And let's be clear that what we're talking about here is information released as narrative and not as facts and figures, which present a completely different challenge in comprehensibility.

So how *do* we measure comprehensibility? The answer, as I just alluded to, is actually twofold, depending on whether the information is facts and figures or it is the narrative of those mechanisms and processes behind the facts and figures. For the former, we're working with numbers, graphs, discrete facts, and so on. With the latter, we're working primarily with text in the form of reports, policies and procedures, memorandums, meeting minutes, and the like. Each presents a different challenge in achieving comprehensibility, but they both share a common set of metrics to be graded for transparency. Finally, in both cases the assumption is that we're only measuring comprehensibility of available content. If the content hasn't yet been made available to the public, then there is nothing to measure.

GRADED—Objectivity

Facts/Figures: Unless the data has been "cooked," there should be no question as to objectivity of the facts and figures. What would be of concern, though, is the veracity of the data. So the standard to meet here in terms of objectivity is that the information is correct, that it hasn't been modified to suit someone's agenda, and that errors in transferring or transcribing the data aren't excessive. If not, objectivity suffers because one's ability to interpret the data is compromised by the fact that what is made available isn't true to its source.

Mechanisms/Processes: Ensuring objectivity here is a bit more challenging because we're working with narrative in most cases. Now, that said, consider also that we're working with two distinct types of information—that which is taken verbatim, such as meeting minutes, correspondence, speeches, interviews, and so on; and that which is manufactured for internal or public consumption, such as policies and procedures, budgets, contracts, legislation, press releases, and the like. This distinction is important because in the former, information can often be redacted because it's deemed to be sensitive conversation relating to current circumstances, even though the information has been made "available."

The level of redaction is an important factor in determining comprehensibility because an excessive amount of missing dialogue certainly impacts one's ability to understand what was said and therefore objectivity suffers greatly. In the latter, it's highly unlikely that, given that the information was made available, that there is any reason to redact any of the text—a budget isn't made available until it's ready, a contract isn't made available until it's finalized, legislation isn't made available until it's passed, and so on. Thus, achieving a high level of objectivity in the latter should simply be a matter of ensuring that errors in transferring or transcribing the data weren't excessive or subject to modifications from its source.

GRADED—Presentation

Facts/Figures: The presentation of facts and figures very often lends itself to visualization techniques—fitting the old adage that a picture is worth a thousand words, or, in this case, a graph may be worth a megabyte of data. And of course anything that lends itself to a clearer understanding of the information being presented will contribute greatly to more transparency. Simple graphs of various styles that fit to the data being presented are one way to add clarity to otherwise-mundane facts and figures. In addition, there are interactive mapping tools that create a more hands-on experience, allowing one to actually manipulate the presentation of the data based on the input given as well as supporting what-if scenarios. And more techniques for visualization are coming out every day. Transparency is well served by all of these tools that enhance the comprehensibility of the data.

Mechanisms/Processes: The presentation of documents creates a different challenge since visualization tools don't always work well in this space. However, annotation and audiovisual tools can be used to enhance one's comprehension of the information being presented. Annotation software is simply what it sounds like—a Post-It notes for online documents. Given the obscure nature of much government information, such as budgets, contracts, and legislation, it's helpful if notes can be added to elucidate in simpler terms what is often ambiguous, confusing, and downright unintelligible—think about the legalese of legislation as one example. Another helpful tool is to provide an audio or video complement to the information being presented when it's helpful to have someone take you through a veritable "tour" of a document—think about budgets and how complex they can be. Trying to make your way through even a small municipality's budget can be nothing less than daunting without a little hand-holding.

All of that said, there is room for the application of visualization tools, when it comes to presenting information such as budgets, for example. Instead of just providing the information in a document format, other presentations can be used, such as spreadsheets and graphs, to illuminate and interpret the data contained within the verbiage of the document. Once again, transparency is well served by all of these tools that enhance the comprehensibility of the data by lending a degree of interpretation to the data presented.

GRADED—Extraction

Facts/Figures: One of the key factors enhancing the comprehension of facts and figures is providing the option to extract the data so that either the individual citizen or third-party groups—the Fifth Estate I mentioned earlier—can manipulate the data to create greater clarity. A case in point, going back to the example of the Illinois Board of Elections (IBOE) campaign data, one can download an entire history of a candidate's campaign contributions and expenses. In this case, bringing the data into a spreadsheet, a citizen could then manipulate the data by sorting it or doing what-if analysis. Providing a few of the standard file types as extraction options increases the usability of such a function.

Short of the IBOE offering visualization tools on its site, which it doesn't, simply providing a download capability for the data increases transparency and enhances one's ability to interpret the information. And, of course, third-party groups can utilize this feature to extract the data in order to put it into their own applications that present an interpretive view of the information—hopefully adding clarity. The Developing Governmental Accountability to the People (DGAP) site is a good example of how IBOE data can be manipulated to show aggregate categories of contributions.[2] In this way, the IBOE is more a "platform provider" that makes the information available for others to extract, manipulate, and present in a format that can be delivered as an application on a variety of devices. All of this lends to improving transparency through greater comprehensibility.

Mechanisms/Processes: One would think that extracting documents as opposed to numbers wouldn't be of much help in adding clarity to an otherwise-perfunctory presentation of information such as budgets, contracts, meeting minutes, correspondence, legislation, and so on. However, the trend today seems to lean toward providing these documents in Adobe's portable document format (pdf), which can be read and also downloaded by simply using the save function, as long as one has the Adobe Reader software on one's device. When the option of providing the documents as pdfs is made available, it enhances comprehension because it not only creates a much more readable document with its structured layout but also allows for a limited degree of research through its search tools, which is especially useful for lengthy documents.

Enticement

You'll recall that as important as accessibility and comprehension are to creating transparency from mere disclosure, the information must also be presented in such a way that citizens actually *want* to examine it. Otherwise, transparency is simply an academic exercise if it doesn't drive civic engagement; and engagement we get—or possibly even enragement—if our efforts in transparency draw citizens to delve into the information being provided. To pass the enticement test, information must be presented in a way that's interesting, intriguing, and relevant, regardless whether it's facts and figures or mechanisms and processes. The information must motivate individuals to engage in dialogue directed toward improving the efficiencies of their government and mitigating corruption. This is why enticement is so critical in distinguishing full disclosure from transparency. As I've said before, it's the raison d'être of transparency.

GRADED—Interactivity

Some of what was mentioned as ways to enhance comprehension also serve the purpose of making the information more enticing. Tools such as visualization applications that bring the data alive or video clips that create a multidimensional presentation of the information accomplish this. These certainly serve the purpose of grabbing attention. Reading about a $600 million budget deficit, such as we had in Chicago in 2011, is one thing. Seeing it pictured in a graph is something else. However, if we want to leverage the attention and transition to action, there must be interactive tools available to get citizens to "participate."

For the 2012 budget in Chicago, an application was set up to draw citizen recommendations for improving efficiencies in government. Prior to that, the previous mayor would have a few citywide community meetings whereby he and his staff would listen to citizens who showed up mostly complain and occasionally offer suggestions. If you couldn't make the meeting . . . oh, well. Any methods for giving citizens an opportunity to interact with city government, especially as an addendum to the information being provided, will not only drive participation on the website but also can often lead to citizens organizing offline. In the example of the city budget, recommendations were categorized so that you could add to someone's idea or simply vote on the idea. Any method to provide citizen comments, questions, or responses to the information being presented all enhance the possibility of transparency inspiring citizens to engage.

GRADED—Social Media

Taking that idea one step further, which the city didn't do, action groups could be organized around a recommendation if individuals were given the option to "participate" by joining social-media groups on Facebook, Yahoo!, or Google Groups and the like. This could eventually lead to offline meetings of those interested in promoting a particular idea to improve city services and efficiencies in delivering them. However, it's also crucial to note whether links to various social-media platforms are being utilized (Facebook, Twitter, Pinterest, RSS feeds, etc.) on the government site and in relation to departments or even initiatives presented in the name of transparency.

Going back again to the City of Chicago budget initiative to gather citizen recommendations for improvements, if social-media links were provided, the message would have spread far wider than simply those who visited the city's website. Just the notion that one could send out a tweet when one entered one's recommendation would drive further civic engagement and bring more people to view the information on the city's budget site. Adding any or many social-media options to a website takes transparency from being one-dimensional to being multidimensional and in so doing greatly enhances the possibility that it will lead to the kind of enticement that will drive civic engagement.

GRADED—Streaming

Audio and video tools certainly can enhance transparency through greater comprehension, particularly when considering the differences in how people learn and absorb information—reading, listening and viewing, or a combination. When we consider the ways in which transparency can drive civic engagement by making the information more enticing, audio and video also play a major role, but in a special way—through live and stored streaming of events.

C-SPAN is probably thought of as the granddaddy of live streaming in the political arena, but more and more state and municipal governments are undertaking projects to deliver live streaming of events. A few years back, for example, the City of Chicago city clerk's website began offering live streaming of City Council meetings and stored videos for future viewing. It appears that the intent is to eventually offer streaming of all committee meetings as well. Given the often-acrimonious behavior and controversial issues facing the council, watching these events is much more impactful than simply reading a transcript of them. In particular, it can be quite revealing to see how one's alderman speaks and behaves in council—akin to a video report card that literally shines a light on government. All of this documenting of council activity is good for transparency in pulling aside the curtain of political intrigue and gamesmanship, which in turn drives civic engagement because it makes government less obscure and more palatable to the average citizen.

However, that's only one of many examples of how streaming audio and video can be utilized to incentivize citizens to become engaged in their government. Opening up community meetings to be recorded live through a webcam and streamed over the Internet means that citizens who are unable to attend meetings either because of scheduling conflicts or simply because they feel uncomfortable going to meetings can participate actively or passively by viewing the broadcast. Recording these meetings for everyone to view at any time not only serves greater transparency but also drives civic engagement in allowing citizens to "attend" who otherwise would never have had the opportunity to participate. Another example here in Chicago where this can be utilized, but isn't currently, is broadcasting CAPS (Chicago Alternative Policing Strategy) meetings. CAPS has been around for over twenty years in Chicago and has been quite successful in giving citizens an opportunity to cooperate with local law enforcement to mitigate crime in their neighborhoods. However, it's also dependent on numbers, and the more citizens who participate, the better. Streaming these meetings and allowing for interactive input from those viewing online would greatly increase the level of participation, not to mention markedly improving transparency in the area of public safety—a key government service—and again lead to the kind of enticement that will drive civic engagement.

THE JUDGES

> "One thing I have learned in my research is that in order to judge a program's results, you need to understand what it is trying to accomplish. Only then will you be able to measure whether the program has achieved those aims."
>
> —Jerry Brito, March 9, 2011, testimony to House Committee on Oversight and Government Reform[3]

In October 2007, Jerry Brito, Senior Research Fellow at the Mercatus Center of George Mason University, delivered a working paper called "Hack, Mash, & Peer: Crowdsourcing Government Transparency."[4] Brito also currently serves as an adjunct professor of law at George Mason University, where his research focuses on technology and Internet policy, copyright, and the regulatory process.[5] In that paper he devotes a section to addressing the advantages of crowdsourcing. In 2007, crowdsourcing was just getting its online legs and was still a rather nascent social-media approach to civic action. Today, it's an integral part of social media, impacting everything from raising funds for start-ups to starting revolutions. In fact, it's become so commonplace today that definitions of the term are now offered in most dictionaries, such as this one from *Merriam-Webster*:

the practice of obtaining needed services, ideas, or content by soliciting contributions from a large group of people and especially from the online community rather than from traditional employees or suppliers.[6]

The term itself seems to have been coined by Jeff Howe in an article about innovation in business he wrote for *Wired* magazine back in 2006.[7] Howe, a professor of journalism at Northeastern University in Boston, Massachusetts, and a former Nieman Fellow at Harvard University who previously worked as a contributing editor at *Wired*, said this about crowdsourcing at the time:

> Technological advances in everything from product design software to digital video cameras are breaking down the cost barriers that once separated amateurs from professionals. Hobbyists, part-timers, and dabblers suddenly have a market for their efforts, as smart companies in industries as disparate as pharmaceuticals and television discover ways to tap the latent talent of the crowd. The labor isn't always free, but it costs a lot less than paying traditional employees. It's not outsourcing; it's crowdsourcing.

There's even an industry organization and a website for crowdsourcing that was founded in 2010 and whose mission is:

> to serve as an invaluable source of information to analysts, researchers, journalists, investors, business owners, crowdsourcing experts and participants in crowdsourcing and crowdfunding platforms. . . . A neutral professional association dedicated solely to crowdsourcing and crowdfunding. As one of the most influential and credible authorities in the crowdsourcing space, crowdsourcing.org is recognized worldwide for its intellectual capital, crowdsourcing and crowdfunding practice expertise and unbiased thought leadership.[8]

As a tool for civic engagement, crowdsourcing.org appears to be a godsend. However, as Brito points out in a more recent paper from March 2011:

> Spending-transparency sites like USASpending.org and the Recovery.gov site are also useful because they disclose government's actions. They allow citizens, watchdogs, bloggers, and reporters to access

the raw data of the business of government; make creative uses of that data, including making interesting mashups; and crowdsource accountability. However, these types of sites are not perfect. As the Sunlight Foundation and others have pointed out, the quality of the data available can be sorely lacking.[9]

As Brito points out, the downside to using crowdsourcing is, well . . . the crowd!

In his research paper for me (detailed in chapter 5), Matt Marcus briefly addresses the apparently herculean task of actually measuring transparency in each of the fifty states, given a standard set of metrics:

What better way to measure this aspect than to go directly to end users? An effective research approach would be to standardize the dataset questions and then develop a state-by-state collection of universities willing to assign such a task to their political-science departments. This research base could be augmented as needed by a dedicated internal research staff when more technical expertise was needed, particularly with questions of fiscal policy.

Of course, what Marcus is pointing to is what in academic circles is called "peer production" or another term for crowdsourcing. Brito, in his 2007 paper, went on to say this in praise of crowdsourcing:

The idea is to allow a large group of persons to create, by making small individual contributions, a good that would traditionally have been produced by a single individual or an organization. Usually, the goods in question are cultural or informational products. *Wikipedia*, the online community-written encyclopedia, is the most often cited example of successful crowdsourcing. Thousands of volunteers labor for no monetary compensation to write basic reference articles for every topic under sun. The result is an encyclopedia that is much more extensive than anything a traditional organization with a limited number of writers and editors could produce. This sort of collaboration is possible because the Internet has dramatically reduced the transaction cost of interaction between individuals. Persons engaged in collaborative projects such as *Wikipedia* are often motivated by incentives other than cash compensation, including gaining a positive reputation within a community, and the intrinsic joy of creation and participation.[10]

So what does all of this talk about crowdsourcing have to do with measuring transparency in government? At this point, I imagine the answer to that question is obvious. An undertaking to measure transparency using the standard metrics recommended in this book— and I'm sure more to come later—across all fifty states, much less the hundreds of thousands of municipalities, is nothing short of the herculean effort that Marcus alluded to in his research paper. But herculean efforts are exactly the forte of crowdsourcing initiatives and, I believe, the solution to undertaking a project of this magnitude.

However, as Brito lamented earlier, crowdsourcing is not perfect, due to nothing less than the crowd selected. There are cases that don't require much thought from the crowd, such as SETI's initiative to look for intelligent life in the universe, SETI@home, which is "a scientific experiment that uses Internet-connected computers in the Search for Extraterrestrial Intelligence (SETI). [Anyone] can participate by running a free program that downloads and analyzes radio telescope data."[11] Anyone can serve that purpose.

In our case, however, there is a need for a disciplined, academic approach, and what better place to recruit a "crowd" than on university campuses, where professors and students alike can be organized at select institutions across the country in each of the fifty states? There certainly is no lack of talent, and providing the framework within which governments can be measured would simply be a matter of creating an instructional manual that would ensure a common and equitable application of the metrics. The immutability of most college institutions and the access to a vast student network would coincide well with a project such as this, meant to continue for years to come and requiring a large contingent of an affordable and intelligent talent pool dispersed across the country.

THE INDEX

Summary of Metrics

1. CONTENT

    A. Facts/Figures

        (a) Catalog (0–10)
        (b) Chronicle What (0–10)
        (c) Chronicle When (0–10)
        (d) Chronicle Where (0–10)
        (e) Chronicle Who (0–10)

    B. Mechanisms/Processes

        (a) Catalog (0–10)
        (b) Chronicle What (0–10)
        (c) Chronicle When (0–10)
        (d) Chronicle Where (0–10)
        (e) Chronicle Who (0–10)

2. CHARACTERISTICS

    A. Accessibility—Available

        (a) Total Available Content : Total Content (Current/ Historical—1 year comparisons) (% as a whole number 0–100)
        (b) Total Pending Content : Total Content (Current/ Historical—1 year comparisons) (% as a whole number 0–100)
        (c) Total Unscheduled Content : Total Content (Current/Historical—1 year comparisons) (% as a whole number 0–100)

B. Accessibility—Locatable

    (a) Available Content Online : Total Available Content (Current/Historical—1 year comparisons) (% as a whole number 0–100)

    (b) Available Content Offline : Total Available Content (Current/Historical—1 year comparisons) (% as a whole number 0–100)

    (c) Available Content Online : Available Content Offline (Current/Historical—1 year comparisons) (% as a whole number 0–100)

C. Accessibility—Searchable

    (a) Available Searchable Content : Available Non-Searchable Content (% as a whole number 0–100)

D. Accessibility—Timely

    (a) Date Content Created/Occurred : Date Content Made Available (Online/Offline) (% as a whole number 0–100)

E. Accessibility—Approachable

    (a) Contact Information Provided : Contact Information Not Provided (Available/Unavailable) (% as a whole number 0–100)

F. Comprehensibility—Objectivity

    (a) Facts/Figures: Information is correct and complete as presented (0 or 10)

    (b) Mechanisms/Processes: Level of redaction (% as an inverse whole number 0–100)

G. Comprehensibility—Presentation

   (a) Facts/Figures: Visualization tools used (0–10)
   (b) Mechanisms/Processes: Annotation and audiovisual tools used (0–10)

H. Comprehensibility—Extraction

   (a) Facts/Figures: Provide download capability (% as a whole number 0–100)
   (b) Mechanisms/Processes: Provide documents as pdfs (% as a whole number 0–100)

I. Enticement—Interactivity

   (a) Interactive tools available (% as a whole number 0–100)

J. Enticement—Social Media

   (a) Options for social-media groups/applications (% as a whole number 0–100)

K. Enticement—Streaming

   (a) Live and stored streaming of events (% as a whole number 0–100)

THAT'S A WRAP

"If we do this right, transparency in government

will be the enabler that drives the civic engagement

necessary to sustain resilient urban communities as

gardens of democracy in the twenty-first century."

—Don Gordon

Notes

FOREWORD

1. Lord Acton to Bishop Creighton, in appendix to *Historical Essays and Studies*, by John Emerich Edward Dalberg (Lord Acton), ed. John Neville Figgis and Reginald Vere Laurence (London: Macmillan, 1907), available at "Acton on Moral Judgments in History," Forum at the Online Library of Liberty, http://oll.libertyfund.org/index.php?option=com_content&task=view&id=1407&Itemid=283 (accessed January 13, 2014).

2. Ibid.

CHAPTER 1: WHAT TRANSPARENCY IS AND WHY IT MATTERS

1. *Oxford Dictionaries*, s.v. "transparency," http://www.oxforddictionaries.com/us/definition/american_english/transparency (accessed January 2, 2014).

2. Ibid., s.v. "transparent," http://www.oxforddictionaries.com/us/definition/american_english/transparent (accessed January 2, 2014).

3. Ibid., s.v. "disclosure," http://www.oxforddictionaries.com/us/definition/american_english/disclosure?q=disclosure (accessed January 2, 2014).

4. Transparency International, http://www.transparency.org/whoweare/organisation/faqs_on_corruption#transparency (accessed December 27, 2013).

5. US National Archives and Records Administration, "The Charters of Freedom: Constitution of the United States," http://www.archives.gov/exhibits/charters/constitution_transcript.html (accessed December 27, 2013).

6. Amy Crawford, "For the People, by the People: What I Saw When I Participated in One of the Truest Forms of Democracy," *Slate*, modified May 22, 2013, http://www.slate.com/articles/news_and_politics/politics/2013/05/new_england_town_halls_these_experiments_in_direct_democracy_do_a_far_better.html (accessed December 27, 2013).

7. Benjamin F. Wright, ed., *The Federalist* (New York: Barnes and Noble Books, 1996), p. 133.

8. National Archives, "From Thomas Jefferson to Edward Carrington, 16 January 1787," http://founders.archives.gov/documents/Jefferson/01-11-02-0047 (accessed January 2, 2014).

9. John Dewey, *The Public and Its Problems* (Athens, OH: Swallow Press, 1954), p. 138.

10. William Wirt Henry, *Patrick Henry: Life, Correspondence and Speeches* (New York: Charles Scribner's Sons, 1891), p. 496 (emphasis is mine).

11. *A Few Good Men*, directed by Rob Reiner (Castle Rock Entertainment and Columbia Pictures Corporation, 1992).

12. *Time*, "The Nation: Ellsberg: The Battle over the Right to Know," modified July 05, 1971, http://content.time.com/time/magazine/article/0,9171,905293,00.html (accessed January 2, 2014).

13. *New York Times*, "Saying 'No' to Our Right to Know," modified August 30, 2013, http://www.nytimes.com/2013/08/31/world/europe/Saying-No-to-Our-Right-to-Know.html?ref=bradleyemanning&_r=0 (accessed January 2, 2014).

14. *Chicago Tribune*, "Transcript: *Tribune* Interview with Mayor Rahm Emanuel," modified February 12, 2012, http://articles.chicagotribune.com/2012-02-12/news/ct-met-transcript-emanuel-speed-camera-records-2-20120212_1_transparency-pledge-mayor-rahm-emanuel-interview (accessed January 2, 2014).

15. *New Republic*, "Against Transparency," http://www.newrepublic.com/article/books-and-arts/against-transparency (accessed January 2, 2014).

16. Archon Fung, Mary Graham, and David Weil, *Full Disclosure: The Perils and Promise of Transparency* (Cambridge: Cambridge University Press, 2007).

CHAPTER 2: A HISTORY OF TRANSPARENCY IN AMERICAN POLITICS

1. Robert Douthat Meade, *Patrick Henry, Practical Revolutionary* (Philadelphia: J. B. Lippincott, 1969), p. 28.

2. William Wirt, *Sketches of the Life and Character of Patrick Henry* (Philadelphia: James Webster, 1817), p. 123.

3. William Wirt Henry, *Patrick Henry: Life, Correspondence and Speeches* (Charles Scribner's Sons, 1891), 2:346–47.

4. Ibid., p. 347.

5. Ibid., 3:495–97 (emphasis is mine).

6. Charters of Freedom, "Declaration of Independence," http://www.archives.gov/exhibits/charters/declaration_transcript.html (accessed January 6, 2014).

7. Monticello, "Number of Letters Jefferson Wrote," http://www.monticello.org/site/research-and-collections/number-letters-jefferson-wrote (accessed January 6, 2014).

8. Founders Online, "About the Papers of Thomas Jefferson," http://founders.archives.gov/about/Jefferson (accessed January 6, 2014).

9. Founders Online, "From Thomas Jefferson to Edward Carrington, 16 January 1787," http://founders.archives.gov/?q=Correspondent%3A%22Carrington%2C%20Edward%22%20Correspondent%3A%22Jefferson%2C%20Thomas%22&s=1111311111&r=13 (accessed January 6, 2014).

10. Ibid.

11. Ibid.

12. Ibid.

13. Ibid.

14. James Madison, *Letters and Other Writings of James Madison, Fourth President of the United States*, vol. 3, *1816–1828* (Philadelphia: J. B. Lippincott, 1867), p. 277.

15. Ibid., p. 279.

16. Ibid., p. 276.

17. Benjamin F. Wright, ed., *The Federalist, the Famous Papers on the Principles of American Government* (New York: Barnes & Noble Books, 1996), p. 348.

18. Woodrow Wilson, "Committee or Cabinet Government," *Overland Monthly* 3, no. 2 (1884): 22.

19. Ibid., pp. 26–27 (emphasis is mine).

20. Woodrow Wilson, "Responsible Government under the Constitution," *Atlantic Monthly* 57, no. 342 (April 1886): 542–53 (emphasis is mine).

21. Woodrow Wilson, "Character of Democracy in the United States," *Atlantic Monthly* 64, no. 385 (November 1889): 577–88 (emphasis is mine).

22. Sunlight Foundation, "Brandeis and the History of Transparency," http://sunlightfoundation.com/blog/2009/05/26/brandeis-and-the-history-of-transparency/ (accessed January 6, 2014).

23. Ibid.

24. Ibid.

25. Louis D. Brandeis School of Law, "The Right to Privacy by Samuel Warren and Louis D. Brandeis," http://www.law.louisville.edu/library/collections/brandeis/node/225 (accessed January 6, 2014).

26. Melvin I. Urofsky and David W. Levy, eds., *Letters of Louis Brandeis*, vol. 1, *1870–1907: Urban Reformer* (Albany: State University of New York Press, 1971), p. 100 (emphasis is mine).

27. Louis Brandeis, *Other People's Money and How the Bankers Use It* (New York: Frederick A. Stokes, 1914), p. 92.

28. *New York Times*, "Say Money Trust Is Now Disclosed," http://query.nytimes.com/mem/archive-free/pdf?_r=2&res=9F00E2DB163FE633A25751C1A9679C946296D6CF (accessed January 6, 2014).

29. Ibid.; Brandeis, *Other People's Money and How the Bankers Use It*, p. 92.

30. Brandeis, *Other People's Money and How the Bankers Use It*, p. 101.

31. John Dewey, *The Public and Its Problems* (Athens, OH: Swallow Press, 1927), pp. 176–77.

32. Ibid., pp. 177–79.

33. Ibid., pp. 166–67.

34. Ibid., p. 184.

35. PBS *American Experience*, "The Duties of American Citizenship, 1883," http://www.pbs.org/wgbh/americanexperience/features/primary-resources/tr-citizen/ (accessed January 6, 2014).

36. Benjamin Barber, *Strong Democracy: Participatory Politics for a New Age*, 20th anniversary ed. (Berkeley: University of California Press, 2003), pp. 153–55.

37. Ibid., pp. 153–54.

38. Ibid., p. 154.

39. Ibid., pp. 154–55.

40. "Open Government Initiative," http://www.whitehouse.gov/open (accessed January 6, 2014).

41. "Open Government Directive," http://www.whitehouse.gov/open/documents/open-government-directive (accessed January 6, 2014).

42. InformationWeek, "White House Loses Open Government Leader," http://www.informationweek.com/government/leadership/white-house-loses-open-government-leader/229000485 (accessed January 6, 2014).

43. Daniel Lathrop and Laurel Ruma, eds., *Open Government: Collaboration, Transparency, and Participation in Practice* (Sebastopol, CA: O'Reilly Media, 2010), p. 51.

44. Ibid., p. 53.

45. Ibid., pp. 55–56.

46. Williams College, "Habermas's Theory of Communicative Action and the Theory of Social Capital," http://web.williams.edu/Economics/papers/Habermas.pdf (accessed January 6, 2014).

47. Lathrop and Ruma, *Open Government*, p. 60.

48. Ibid., pp. 62, 63.

49. Ibid., p. 68.

CHAPTER 3: HOW TRANSPARENCY AROUSES CIVIC ENGAGEMENT

1. Donald Gordon, *Piss 'Em All Off: And Other Practices of the Effective Citizen* (Los Angeles: Keylog Books, 2010), p. 9.

2. Edwin O. Guthman and C. Richard Allen, eds., *RFK: Collected Speeches* (New York: Viking Press, 1993), p. 388.

3. Sunlight Foundation, "Brandeis and the History of Transparency," http://sunlightfoundation.com/blog/2009/05/26/brandeis-and-the-history-of-transparency/ (accessed January 8, 2014).

4. Walter Lippmann, *The Phantom Public* (New Brunswick, NJ: Transaction Publishers, 2009), pp. 139–40.

5. John Dewey, *The Public and Its Problems* (Athens, OH: Swallow Press, 1954), p. 142.

6. "America the Uneducated," *Bloomberg Businessweek*, November 21, 2005, www.businessweek.com/magazine/content/05_47/b3960108.htm (accessed January 8, 2014).

7. "Center for Effective Government," http://www.foreffectivegov.org/ (accessed January 8, 2014).

8. Gary Bass and Sam Moulton, in *Open Government: Collaboration, Transparency, and Participation in Practice*, ed. Daniel Lathrop and Laurel Ruma (Sebastopol, CA: O'Reilly Media, 2010), pp. 290–91.

9. Ibid., p. 293.

10. Ibid., p. 291.

11. Ibid., p. 294.

12. Ibid., p. 291.

13. Ibid., pp. 296–97.

14. National Security Archive, "FOIA Legislative History," http://www2.gwu.edu/~nsarchiv/nsa/foialeghistory/legistfoia.htm (accessed January 8, 2014).

15. Archon Fung, Mary Graham, and David Weil, *Full Disclosure: The Perils and Promise of Transparency* (New York: Cambridge University Press, 2007), p. 27.

16. William Clinton, "Statement of the President—October 2, 1996," http://www2.gwu.edu/~nsarchiv/nsa/foia/presidentstmt.pdf (accessed January 8, 2014).

17. Fung, Graham, and Weil, *Full Disclosure*, p. 221.

18. Dr. Mike Evans, "The Evolution of the Web—From Web 1.0 to Web 4.0," http://www.cscan.org/presentations/08-11-06-MikeEvans-Web.pdf (accessed January 8, 2014).

19. Nicholas Carr, "Is Google Making Us Stupid?" *Atlantic*, modified July 1, 2008, http://www.theatlantic.com/magazine/archive/2008/07/is-google-making-us-stupid/306868/ (accessed January 8, 2014).

20. Lloyds TSB, "'Five-Minute-Memory' Costs Brits £1.6 Billion," November 27, 2008, http://www.insurance.lloydstsb.com/personal/general/mediacentre/home hazards_pr.asp (accessed January 8, 2014).

21. Lawrence Lessig, "Against Transparency," *New Republic*, modified

October 9, 2009, http://www.newrepublic.com/article/books-and-arts/against
-transparency (accessed January 8, 2014).

22. City of Chicago, "What We Do—City Budget," http://www.cityofchicago
.org/city/en/depts/obm/provdrs/city_budg.html (accessed January 8, 2014).

23. City of Chicago, "Data Portal Budget—2013 Budget Recommendations—
Appropriations," https://data.cityofchicago.org/Administration-Finance/Budget-2013
-Budget-Recommendations-Appropriations/d6tb-pwze (accessed January 8, 2014).

24. Lessig, "Against Transparency."

25. Arthur Unger, "From Our Files: An Interview with Walter Cronkite,"
Christian Science Monitor, modified July 20, 2009, http://www.csmonitor.com/USA/
Society/2009/0720/p25s01-ussc.html (accessed January 8, 2014).

26. Gordon, *Piss 'Em All Off*, p. 12.

27. Ibid., p. 13.

28. Pew Research Center, "Views of Government: Key Data Points," modified
October22,2013,http://www.pewresearch.org/key-data-points/views-of-government
-key-data-points/ (accessed January 8, 2014).

29. Public Policy Polling, "Congress Somewhere below Cockroaches, Traffic
Jams, and Nickelback in Americans' Esteem," modified January 8, 2013, http://www
.publicpolicypolling.com/main/2013/01/congress-somewhere-below-cockroaches
-traffic-jams-and-nickleback-in-americans-esteem.html (accessed January 8, 2014).

30. Gareth Porter, "How Intelligence Was Twisted to Support an Attack on
Syria," *Truthout*, modified September 3, 2013, http://truth-out.org/news/item/
18559-how-intelligence-was-twisted-to-support-an-attack-on-syria (accessed January 8, 2014).

31. *Chicago Tribune*, "Transcript: *Tribune* Interview with Mayor Rahm
Emanuel," modified February 12, 2012, http://articles.chicagotribune.com/2012
-02-12/news/ct-met-transcript-emanuel-speed-camera-records-2-20120212_1
_transparency-pledge-mayor-rahm-emanuel-interview (accessed January 8, 2014).

32. Gordon, *Piss 'Em All Off*, pp. 33–34.

33. Ibid., p. 35.

34. *Fifth Estate*, "About Us," http://www.fifthestate.org/about/ (accessed
January 8, 2014).

35. IMDb, "*The Fifth Estate*," http://www.imdb.com/title/tt1837703/ (accessed
January 8, 2014).

36. Julianne Schultz, *Reviving the Fourth Estate: Democracy, Accountability
and the Media* (Cambridge: Cambridge University Press, 1998), p. 49.

37. City of Chicago, "Department of Innovation and Technology," http://www
.cityofchicago.org/city/en/depts/doit.html (accessed January 8, 2014).

38. Open City, "About," http://opencityapps.org/ (accessed January 8, 2014).

39. Open City, "Open Gov Hack Night," http://opengovhacknight.eventbrite .com/ (accessed January 8, 2014).

40. Chicago Councilmatic, http://chicagocouncilmatic.org/ (accessed January 8, 2014).

41. City of Chicago, "Chicago Data Portal," http://www.cityofchicago.org/ city/en/depts/doit/provdrs/security_and_datamanagement/svcs/chicago_data_portal .html (accessed January 8, 2014).

42. Center for Neighborhood Technology, http://www.cnt.org/ (accessed January 8, 2014).

43. Center for Neighborhood Technology, "Urban Sustainability Apps Competition," http://cntapps.splashthat.com/ (accessed January 8, 2014).

44. Civic Lab, "About Us," http://www.civiclab.us/about/ (accessed January 8, 2014).

45. Code for America, "About Us," http://www.codeforamerica.org/about/ (accessed January 8, 2014).

46. Code for America, "Peer Network," http://peernetwork.in/ (accessed January 8, 2014).

47. Code for America Brigade, "18 Applications You Can Deploy Now," http:// brigade.codeforamerica.org/applications (accessed January 8, 2014).

48. Joachim Prinz, "Civil Rights," http://www.joachimprinz.com/civilrights .htm (accessed January 8, 2014).

49. Hillsdale College, "Pericles' Funeral Oration," https://online.hillsdale.edu/ document.doc?id=355 (accessed January 8, 2014).

50. Ibid.

51. John Stuart Mill, "Inaugural Address Delivered to the University of St. Andrews 1867," Online Library of Liberty, http://oll.libertyfund.org/?option=com _staticxt&staticfile=show.php%3Ftitle=255&chapter=21681&layout=html&Itemid =27 (accessed January 8, 2014).

52. Civic Lab, "Take a Class," http://www.civiclab.us/class/ (accessed January 8, 2014).

53. Better Government Association, "Programs," http://www.bettergov.org/ watchdog_training/programs.aspx (accessed January 8, 2014).

54. Jerry Ensminger, "Health Care Now for Military Families Poisoned at Camp Lejeune," *Change.org*, modified August 2012, http://www.change.org/ petitions/health-care-now-for-military-families-poisoned-at-camp-lejeune (accessed January 8, 2014).

55. Stop the Lakefront Tower, "Alderman Joe Moore: Deny the Requested Zoning Changes for the Lakefront Car Tower," *Change.org*, https://www.change .org/petitions/alderman-joe-moore-deny-the-requested-zoning-changes-for-the -lakefront-car-tower (accessed January 8, 2014).

56. Facebook, "Rogers Park Positive Loitering," https://www.facebook.com/groups/rppositiveloitering/ (accessed January 8, 2014).

57. Great Lakes Watershed, "Watershed Organizations," http://www.great lakeswatershed.org/watershed-organizations.html (accessed January 8, 2014).

58. Alexis de Tocqueville, *Democracy in America*, ed. Richard D. Heffner (New York: New American Library, 1956), p. 201.

59. Benjamin Barber, *Strong Democracy: Participatory Politics for a New Age*, 20th anniversary ed. (Berkeley: University of California Press, 2003), p. 25.

60. Benjamin Barber, "Service, Citizenship and Democracy: Civic Duty as an Entailment of Civil Right," in *A Passion for Democracy: American Essays* (Princeton, NJ: Princeton University Press, 1998), p. 188.

CHAPTER 4: AN ANALYSIS OF BEST PRACTICES IN MEASURING TRANSPARENCY

1. Thomas Paine, *The American Crisis* (New York: Cosimo Books, 2008), p. 24.

2. John Dewey, *The Later Works of John Dewey*, vol. 17, *1925–1953*, ed. Jo Ann Boydston (Carbondale: Southern Illinois University Press, April 28, 2008), p. 86.

3. John F. Kennedy (inaugural address, Washington, DC, January 20, 1961).

Maryland

1. "Governor O'Malley Launches StateStat Website," Southern Maryland Online, January 4, 2008, www.somd.com (accessed January 29, 2013).

2. Justin Fenton, "O'Malley Installing StateStat," Maryland News, *Baltimore Sun*, February 12, 2007.

3. "The Government Dashboard," special report in conjunction with Public CIO, the Center for Digital Government, March 2012, http://www.optuminsight.com/~/media/Ingenix/Resources/Articles/Gov_DashboardReport_article_04_12.pdf (accessed January 29, 2013), p. 9.

4. Robert D. Behn, "The Seven Big Errors of PerformanceStat," *Policy Briefs*, John F. Kennedy School of Government, Harvard University, February 2008, http://www.hks.harvard.edu/thebehnreport/Behn,%207PerformanceStatErrors.pdf (accessed January 29, 2013).

5. Tina Rosenberg, "Armed with Data, Fighting More Than Crime," *Opinionator* (blog), *New York Times Online*, May 2, 2012, http://opinionator.blogs.nytimes.com/2012/05/02/armed-with-data-fighting-more-than-crime/?_r=0 (accessed January 29, 2013).

6. Participating Agencies include Agriculture, Business and Economic Devel-

opment, Environment, General Services, Health and Mental Hygiene, Housing and Community Development, Human Resources, Juvenile Services, Labor, Licensing and Regulation, Natural Resources, Planning, Maryland State Police, Public Safety and Correctional Services, Transportation.

7. "Introduction to the Governor's Delivery Unit," Maryland StateStat, https:// data.maryland.gov/goals (accessed January 29, 2013).

8. "Health—Childhood Hunger," Maryland StateStat, http://www.statestat .maryland.gov/gdu/12hungerdeliveryplan.pdf (accessed January 29, 2013).

9. Bill Dorotinsky and Joanna Watkins, "Maryland's StateStat: A State-Level Performance Management System," *GET Brief: Ten Observations on StateStat, Global Expert Team, Public Sector Performance*, December 2009.

10. "Bringing Numbers to Life: An Analysis of Maryland's StateStat Initiative," *Advocates for Children & Youth Issue Brief* 5, no. 13 (February 2008).

11. "Reports, Graphs and Meeting Summaries," Maryland StateStat, http:// www.statestat.maryland.gov/reports.html (accessed January 29, 2013).

12. "Customer Spotlight," Socrata, www.socrata.com/customer-spotlight/ (accessed January 29, 2013).

13. "Map Inventory," Maryland Map Center, Maryland StateStat, https://data .maryland.gov/browse?limitTo=maps&utf8=%E2%9C%93 (accessed January 29, 2013).

14. "Maryland Capital State Budget Map," Maryland Map Center, Maryland StateStat, http://www.statestat.maryland.gov/budgetmap.asp (accessed January 28, 2013).

15. "The Executive Committee," MD iMap Administration, http://imap .maryland.gov/Pages/default.aspx (accessed January 29, 2013).

16. The Twitter handle for Maryland StateStat is @StateStat.

17. "StateMaryland" (YouTube profile of the State of Maryland), joined January 7, 2009, www.youtube.com/statemaryland (accessed January 8, 2014).

18. Katherine Barret and Richard Greene, "Interview with Beth Blauer, director of Maryland's StateStat," IBM Center for the Business of Government, March 16, 2010.

19. Nicholas J. Hoover, "Data, Analysis Drive Maryland Government," Information Week Government, March 15, 2010, www.informationweek.com/ government (accessed January 29, 2013), p. 1.

20. Ibid., p. 2.

21. "Trade-Off Time: How Four States Continue to Deliver," *Issue Brief, the Pew Center on the States*, February 2009, p. 5.

22. Hoover, "Data, Analysis Drive Maryland Government," p. 2.

23. "Government Dashboard," p. 9.

24. "Trade-Off Time," p. 5.

25. Hoover, "Data, Analysis Drive Maryland Government," p. 2.

Ontario, Canada

1. Ontario, Canada, Ministry of Infrastructure, https://www.infrastructure app.mei.gov.on.ca/en/ (accessed January 11, 2012).

2. Ontario Ministry of Infrastructure, "By the Numbers," https://www .infrastructureapp.mei.gov.on.ca/en/bythenumbers.asp#infrastructure-investments -09 (accessed January 18, 2012).

3. Open Government Initiative, "Open Data," http://www.open.gc.ca/open -ouvert/data-donnees-eng.asp (accessed January 15, 2012).

4. Open Government Initiative, http://www.open.gc.ca/index-eng.asp (accessed January 15, 2012).

5. Ibid., p. 3.

6. Ibid.

7. Open Government Initiative, "Open Information," http://www.open.gc.ca/ open-ouvert/information-eng.asp (accessed January 15, 2012).

8. Open Government Initiative, "Open Dialogue," http://www.open.gc.ca/ open-ouvert/dialogue-eng.asp (accessed January 15, 2012).

9. Ibid., p. 2.

10. *Time*, "The 2009 Time 100: The Twitter Guys," April 30, 2009, http:// www.time.com/time/specials/packages/article/0,28804,1894410_1893837_189415 6,00.html (accessed February 8, 2012).

11. Suzanne Choney, "Harvard Dropout Zuckerberg to Visit Campus," MSN.com, November 4, 2011, http://technolog.msnbc.msn.com/_news/2011/ 11/04/8637838-harvard-dropout-zuckerberg-to-visit-campushttp://technolog.msnbc .msn.com/_news/2011/11/04/8637838-harvard-dropout-zuckerberg-to-visit-campus (accessed February 8, 2012).

12. Open Government Initiative, "Open Dialogue," p. 3.

13. "A Brief History of Microsoft Excel–Timeline Visualization," Chandoo .org, January 13, 2010, http://chandoo.org/wp/2010/01/13/history-of-excel -timeline/ (accessed February 8, 2012).

14. "A Brief History of Adobe Systems Inc.," Investintech.com, http://www .investintech.com/resources/articles/adobehistory/ (accessed February 8, 2012).

15. "Canada–Ontario Partnership Supports New Wastewater Treatment Facility in Kirkland Lake," Ontario Newsroom, February 2, 2010, http://news .ontario.ca/moi/en/2010/02/canada---ontario-partnership-supports-new-wastewater -treatment-facility-in-kirkland-lake.html (accessed February 8, 2012).

16. Canada Department of Justice, "Freedom of Information Act 1985," http://laws-lois.justice.gc.ca/eng/acts/A%2D1/ (accessed February 11, 2012).

17. "Canada's Population, 2006," *Daily*, Statistics Canada (accessed February 13, 2012).

18. Indiana University, "University of Information Technology Services: What Is a GUI?" http://kb.iu.edu/data/afhv.html (accessed February 10, 2012).

19. Ontario Ministry of Infrastructure, http://www.moi.gov.on.ca/en/index.asp (accessed January 11, 2012).

20. "Government of Ontario News," feed://news.ontario.ca/moi/en/rss/news.rss (accessed January 14, 2012).

21. Ibid., p. 2.

22. Ibid.

23. "@ONinfra," Ont Infrastructure (Twitter account page for the Ontario Ministry of Infrastructure), http://twitter.com/ONinfra (accessed January 9, 2014).

24. John Dewey, *The Ethics of Democracy*, University of Michigan Philosophical Papers, 2nd ser., no. 1 (Ann Arbor, MI: Andrews, 1888).

25. Service Ontario, http://www.ontario.ca/en/services_for_residents/STEL01_105212. (accessed January 11, 2012).

26. Ibid.

27. "Update on Development of Canada's Action Plan on Open Government," Open Government, January 31, 2012, http://www.open.gc.ca/open-ouvert/upd-ela-eng.asp (accessed February 8, 2012).

Boston

1. "2011 Public Officials of the Year," Governing.com, http://www.governing.com/poy/nigel-jacob-chris-osgood.html (accessed January 16, 2013).

2. New Urban Mechanics, http://www.newurbanmechanics.org/about-2// (accessed January 14, 2013).

3. Ibid.

4. Ibid.

5. Nigel Jacob, interviewed by the author, January 28, 2013.

6. Ibid.

7. Ibid.

8. Participatory Chinatown, http://www.participatorychinatown.org/ (accessed January 18, 2013).

9. Ibid.

10. Jessica Bartlett, "Game Aims to Draw in North Quincy," *Boston Globe*, November 14, 2010, http://www.asiancdc.org/files/uploadsfile/Participatory%20Chinatown,%20Boston%20Globe.pdf (accessed January 18, 2013).

11. Ibid., p. 2.

12. Ibid.

13. Hana Schank, "Boston Goes Digital: What We Can Learn from a City That Is Getting It Right," http://www.fastcoexist.com/1679644/boston-does-digital-what-we-can-learn-from-a-city-that-is-getting-it-right (accessed January 18, 2013).

14. Ibid.

15. Ibid.

16. Ibid.

17. Steve Annear, "Up to 70,000 Students Expected to Move Back This Week, But Who Will Be First to Get Their Truck Stuck on Storrow Drive?" *BostInno*, August 28, 2012, http://bostinno.com/2012/08/28/storrow-drive-pool/ (accessed January 28, 2013).

18. Asian Development Community Corporation, http://www.asiancdc.org/pressrelease/macarthur-foundation-awards-170k-bring-virtual-participatory-urban-planning-boston-chin (accessed January 18, 2013).

19. Jeremy Adam Smith, "Participatory Chinatown," May 4, 2010, http://www.shareable.net/blog/participatory-chinatown (accessed January 18, 2013).

20. Ibid.

21. Ibid.

22. Ibid.

23. Metropolitan Area Planning Council, http://www.mapc.org/node/883 (accessed January 18, 2013).

24. 8th Annual Games for Change Festival, http://www.gamesforchange.org/festival2011/awards/direct-impact/participatory-chinatown/ (accessed January 18, 2013).

25. Jacob Smith, "Participation by Design: Community PlanIt in Boston Public Schools," March 23, 2012, http://blog.placematters.org/2012/03/23/participation-by-design-community-planit-in-boston-public-schools/ (accessed January 18, 2013).

26. Andrew Phelps, "Community PlanIt Turns Civic Engagement into a Game—and the Prize Is Better Discourse," Nieman Journalism Lab, September 15, 2011, http://www.niemanlab.org/2011/09/community-planit-turns-civic-engagement-into-a-game-and-the-prize-is-better-discourse/ (accessed January 19, 2013).

27. Community PlanIt, http://www.communityplanit.org/ (accessed January 19, 2013).

28. Nick Judd, "What Is New Urban Mechanics and Why Does Philadelphia Want Some?" Techpresident.com, October 3, 2012, http://techpresident.com/news/22945/what-new-urban-mechanics-and-why-does-philadelphia-want-some (accessed January 20, 2013).

29. Archon Fung, Mary Graham, and David Weil, *Full Disclosure: The Perils*

and Promise of Transparency (New York: Cambridge University Press, 2007), pp. 166–69.

30. Ibid., p. 31.

31. Ibid.

32. Chris Vein, "Helping Our Nation's Cities through Open Government and Innovation," Open Government Initiative, June 20, 2012, http://www.whitehouse.gov/blog/2012/06/20/helping-our-nation-s-cities-through-open-government-and-innovation (accessed January 14, 2013).

33. New Urban Mechanics, *In The News*, http://www.newurbanmechanics.org/about-2/in-the-news/ (accessed January 14, 2013).

San Francisco

1. Joe Eskenazi, "Phil Ting Launches Slick New 'Reset S.F.' Site—But Not to Bolster Mayoral Run. Right?" *SF Weekly*, August 19, 2010, http://blogs.sfweekly.com/thesnitch/2010/08/phil_ting_reset_sf_politics.php (accessed January 3, 2012).

2. John Winsor, "Crowdsourcing: What It Means for Innovation," *Bloomberg Businessweek*, June 15, 2009, http://www.businessweek.com/innovate/content/jun2009/id20090615_946326.htm (accessed January 25, 2012).

3. Jeff Howe, "Wired 14.06: The Rise of Crowdsourcing," *Wired.com*, June 14, 2006, http://www.wired.com/wired/archive/14.06/crowds.html (accessed January 25, 2012).

4. California Common Sense, www.cacs.org (accessed January 2012).

5. "Reset San Francisco Founder Phil Ting Unveils Transparency Portal," YouTube video, 1:49, posted by "ResetSanFrancisco" (profile of California Common Sense), September 16, 2011, http://www.youtube.com/watch?v=-lCJuo7jIZM (accessed January 25, 2012).

6. Reset San Francisco, http://www.resetsanfrancisco.org/ (accessed January 25, 2012)

Portland

1. Rick Turoczy, "Portland Mayor Sam Adams Wants Portland to Be a 'Hub for Open Source,'" *Silicon Florist* (blog), June 18, 2009, http://siliconflorist.com/2009/06/18/portland-mayor-sam-adams-portland-oregon-hub-open-source/ (accessed January 16, 2012).

2. "CivicApps: About," http://civicapps.org/about/sponsors (accessed January 15, 2012).

3. Ibid.

4. "Resolution No. 36735: Regional Technology Community Mobilization and Expansion Resolution," *Portland Auditor's Office*, September 30, 2009, http://efiles .portlandoregon.gov/webdrawer/rec/3675248/view/ (accessed January 16, 2012).

5. "CivicApps: About."

6. "CivicApps: Datasets," http://civicapps.org/datasets? (accessed January 15, 2012).

7. "CivicApps: Ideas," http://www.civicapps.org/ideas (accessed January 15, 2012).

8. "CivicApps: Apps," http://civicapps.org/apps (accessed January 17, 2012).

9. "CivicApps: Datasets."

10. "City of Portland Launches CivicApps Design Contest," *Targeted News Service*, March 17, 2010, http://www.ideaconnection.com/open-innovation -success/CivicApps-for-Greater-Portland-00283.html (accessed January 16, 2012); Paul Arnold, "CivicApps for Greater Portland," *IdeaConnection*, May 15, 2011.

11. "Ordinance No. 183955," Portland Auditor's Office, June 30, 2010, http:// efiles.portlandoregon.gov/webdrawer/rec/3919801/view/ (accessed January 16, 2012).

12. "CivicApps: Ideas."

13. "CivicApps: Official Rules," http://civicapps.org/about/official-rules (accessed January 16, 2012).

14. "CivicApps: Related Events," http://www.civicapps.org/about/related -events (accessed January 15, 2012).

15. "CivicApps: Events," Calagator, http://calagator.org/events/search?utf8 =?&query=civicapps (accessed January 16, 2012).

16. "Come Hack with Us on the City Council Agenda App!" CivicApps, http:// www.civicapps.org/news/come-hack-us-city-council-agenda-app (accessed January 16, 2012); "Help Revolutionize Education at the CivicApps Mobile Apps Hackathon!" May 15, 2011, *CaseOrganic* (blog), http://caseorganic.com/blog/2011/05/looking -for-something-to-do-after-barcamp-portland-come-to-the-civicapps-hackathon -for-education/ (accessed January 16, 2012).

17. "CivicApps: Council Agenda," http://www.civicapps.org/news/come-hack -us-city-council-agenda-app (accessed January 15, 2012).

18. "Resolution No. 36735."

19. "CivicApps: Official Rules."

20. "The Open Source Definition," Open Source Initiative, http://www .opensource.org/docs/osd (accessed January 16, 2012).

21. Joshua M. Franzel, "Urban Government Innovation: Identifying Current Innovations and Factors That Contribute to Their Adoption," *Review of Policy Research* 25, no. 3 (2008): 253–77.

22. "Ordinance No. 183955."

23. "CivicApps: Fire," http://www.civicapps.org/apps/washington-county -fireems-twitter (accessed January 20, 2012).

24. "CivicApps: Reporter," http://www.civicapps.org/apps/pdx-reporter (accessed January 15, 2012).

25. Ibid.

26. "CivicApps: SuperCat," http://www.civicapps.org/apps/super-cat-informs -about-outages (accessed January 20, 2012).

27. "CivicApps: Accessibility," http://www.civicapps.org/apps/ada-pdx -portland-accessibility-maps (accessed January 15, 2012).

28. "CivicApps: Disaster," http://www.civicapps.org/apps/cross-platform-group -messaging-and-location-beaconing-disaster-relief (accessed January 20, 2012).

29. "CivicApps: Show Hands," http://www.civicapps.org/apps/show-hands (accessed January 20, 2012).

30. "CivicApps: Funds," http://www.civicapps.org/ideas/project-funds-finder (accessed January 20, 2012).

31. "CivicApps: Civic Connect," http://www.civicapps.org/ideas/civic-connect (accessed January 20, 2012).

32. "CivicApps: Cashflow," http://www.civicapps.org/ideas/city-cashflow (accessed January 20, 2012).

33. Ron Knox, "App Dancing," *Portland News-Willamette Week*, August 11, 2010, http://www.wweek.com/portland/article-12331-app_dancing.html (accessed January 24, 2012).

34. Ibid.

35. Ted Sickinger, "Oregon Public Employees Want Legislature to Block Release of Names by PERS," *Oregonian*, OregonLive.com, January 17, 2012, http://www .oregonlive.com/business/index.ssf/2012/01/oregon_public_employees_want_l.html (accessed January 24, 2012).

36. Ibid.

CHAPTER 5: CRITICAL FACTORS IN MEASURING TRANSPARENCY

1. Joseph E. Stiglitz, "Information and the Change in the Paradigm in Economics," http://www.nobelprize.org/nobel_prizes/economic-sciences/laureates/2001/ stiglitz-lecture.pdf (accessed January 14, 2014).

2. Ana Bellver and Daniel Kaufmann, "'Transparenting Transparency': Initial Empirics and Policy Applications" (preliminary draft for discussion and comments), September 2005, http://siteresources.worldbank.org/INTWBIGOVANTCOR/

Resources/Transparenting_Transparency171005.pdf (accessed January 14, 2014).

3. Jerry Brito, "Transparency through Technology: Evaluating Federal Open Government Efforts," March 9, 2011, http://mercatus.org/sites/default/files/publication/transparency-through-technology-evaluating-federal-open-government-efforts.pdf (accessed January 14, 2014).

4. Cass Sunstein, "The Power of Open Government," http://www.brookings.edu/events/2010/03/10-open-government (accessed January 14, 2014).

5. Sunshine Review, "Transparency Checklist: Methodology," http://ballotpedia.org/Transparency_Checklist (accessed November 30, 2012).

6. US PIRG, "Report: Transparent and Accountable Budgets," http://www.uspirg.org/reports/usp/transparencygov-20-0 (accessed November 30, 2012).

7. James E. Alt, David Dreyer Lassen, and Shanna Rose, "The Causes of Fiscal Transparency: Evidence from the American States" (paper presented at the Sixth Jacques Polak Annual Research Conference, hosted by the International Monetary Fund, Washington, DC, November 3–4, 2005), http://www.imf.org/external/np/res/seminars/2005/arc/pdf/alt.pdf (accessed January 14, 2014), p. 3.

8. George Kopits and Jon Craig, "Transparency in Government Operations" (International Monetary Fund Occasional Paper 158, Washington, DC, January 1998), http://www.imf.org/external/pubs/ft/op/158/op158.pdf (accessed January 14, 2014), p. 1.

9. Alt, Lassen, and Rose, "Causes of Fiscal Transparency," pp. 3–4.

10. Ibid., p. 3.

11. Ibid.

12. Ibid.

CHAPTER 6: THE TRANSPARENCY INDEX

1. United States General Accounting Office, "Information Management: Update on Freedom of Information Act Implementation Status" (report to the Ranking Minority Member Committee on the Judiciary, US Senate, February 2004), http://www.gao.gov/new.items/d04257.pdf (accessed January 14, 2014).

2. Developing Governmental Accountability to the People, "Campaign Contributions by Industry: Real Estate," http://www.chicagodgap.org/real_estate (accessed January 14, 2014).

3. "Transparency through Technology: Evaluating Federal Open Government Efforts," YouTube video, 1:19:25, from a testimony before the House Committee on Oversight and Government Reform Subcommittee on Technology, Information Policy, Intergovernmental Relations, and Procurement Reform, posted by "oversight-

andreform," March 11, 2011, http://www.youtube.com/watch?v=QOzyDYOtJRE (accessed January 14, 2014).

4. Jerry Brito, "Hack, Mash & Peer: Crowdsourcing Government Transparency," October 21, 2007, http://papers.ssrn.com/sol3/papers.cfm?abstract_id =1023485 (accessed January 14, 2014).

5. "Jerry Brito: Senior Research Fellow," Mercatus Center, George Mason University, http://mercatus.org/jerry-brito (accessed January 14, 2014).

6. *Merriam Webster*, s.v. "crowdsourcing," http://www.merriam-webster .com/dictionary/crowdsourcing (accessed January 14, 2014).

7. Jeff Howe, "The Rise of Crowdsourcing," *Wired* 14, no. 6, June 2006, http:// www.wired.com/wired/archive/14.06/crowds.html (accessed January 14, 2014).

8. Crowdsourcing.org, "About Us," http://www.crowdsourcing.org/about (accessed January 14, 2014).

9. Jerry Brito, "Transparency through Technology: Evaluating Federal Open Government Efforts," March 9, 2011, http://mercatus.org/sites/default/files/ publication/transparency-through-technology-evaluating-federal-open-government -efforts.pdf (accessed January 14, 2014).

10. Brito, "Hack, Mash & Peer."

11. SETI@home, "What Is SETI@home?" http://setiathome.ssl.berkeley.edu/ (accessed January 14, 2014).

Index